THE BRITISH CONSTITUTION: CONTINUITY AND CHANGE

Vernon Bogdanor once told *The Guardian* that he made 'a living of something that doesn't exist'. He also quipped that the British Constitution can be summed up in eight words: 'Whatever the Queen in Parliament decides is law.' That may still be the case, yet in many ways the once elusive British Constitution has now become much more grounded, much more tangible and much more based on written sources than was previously the case. It now exists in a way in which it previously did not.

However, though the changes may seem revolutionary, much of the underlying structure remains unchanged; there are limits to the changes. Where does all this leave the Constitution? Here constitutional experts, political scientists and legal practitioners present up-to-date and in-depth commentaries on their respective areas of expertise. While also a *Festschrift* in honour of Vernon Bogdanor, this book is above all a comprehensive compendium on the present state of the British Constitution.

The British Constitution: Continuity and Change
A Festschrift for Vernon Bogdanor

Edited by
Matt Qvortrup

·H A R T·
PUBLISHING
OXFORD AND PORTLAND, OREGON
2015

Published in the United Kingdom by Hart Publishing Ltd
16C Worcester Place, Oxford, OX1 2JW
Telephone: +44 (0)1865 517530
Fax: +44 (0)1865 510710
E-mail: mail@hartpub.co.uk
Website: http://www.hartpub.co.uk

Published in North America (US and Canada) by
Hart Publishing
c/o International Specialized Book Services
920 NE 58th Avenue, Suite 300
Portland, OR 97213-3786
USA
Tel: +1 503 287 3093 or toll-free: (1) 800 944 6190
Fax: +1 503 280 8832
E-mail: orders@isbs.com
Website: http://www.isbs.com

British Library Cataloguing in Publication Data
Data Available

ISBN: 978-1-84946-988-3

Typeset by Hope Services, Abingdon
Printed and bound in Great Britain by
Lightning Source UK Ltd

Contents

Preface to Paperback Edition   vii
Author Biographies   xi

Introduction: The British Constitution – Continuity and Change   1
Matt Qvortrup

1   The Changing Constitution in Context   7
David Butler

2   Constitutional Reform Since 1997: The Historians' Perspective   17
Mike Finn and Anthony Seldon

3   The Constitution and the Public – How Voters Forgot the Constitution   39
Peter Riddell

4   'Let Me Take You to a Foreign Land': The Political and the Legal
Constitution   55
Matt Qvortrup

5   The Politics-Free Dimension to the UK Constitution   69
Dawn Oliver

6   Constitutional Conventions   93
David Feldman

7   Continuity and Change in Constitutional Conventions   121
Joseph Jaconelli

8   'The Three Hundred and Seven Year Itch': Scotland and the 2014
Independence Referendum   141
Stephen Tierney

9   Constitutional Change and Parliamentary Sovereignty – the Impossible
Dialectic   153
Richard Gordon QC

10   Queen Elizabeth II and the Evolution of the Monarchy   165
Robert Blackburn

11   Constitutional Justice and Constitutional Politics in France   179
Denis Baranger

Epilogue   193
Index   195

Preface

There has been a lot of water under the proverbial constitutional bridges since the first edition of this book was published: the Scottish referendum in September 2014, the general election in May 2015 and the subsequent decision to hold a referendum on British membership of the European Union (by the latest in 2017).

These developments were of great magnitude. The Scottish referendum could have led to the break-up of the United Kingdom. In the end the referendum ended in a narrow victory for the Unionist side – though a pyrrhic one at that; the SNP won all but two of the Scottish constituencies in the 2015 general election. Not since the Irish Nationalist, Charles Stewart Parnell, in the 1880s has a separatist party done so well at the polls. But as in the late Victorian age, the electoral success for those in favour of independence translated into little concrete constitutional changes. To be sure, after the referendum in September 2014, Prime Minister David Cameron promised what amounted to a whole new constitutional settlement. In the end very little changed. The Scottish government received a few new powers – which, perhaps predictably, fell short of what the *Smith Commission* had recommended and was miles from what the Scottish National Party had hoped for.

Some would argue, perhaps, that the Scottish referendum was soon forgotten and did not leave a mark. In terms of legislation and constitutional changes, this is correct Yet the vote showed that the British public (or at least those living in Scotland) could be engaged and live up to the cherished ideals of democratically-enlightened citizens.

A few months before the referendum, I was in Perth in central Scotland. I was ostensibly there as an 'expert' sharing a platform with two seasoned politicos. The audience were polite as they listened to the presentations by, respectively, *Better Together* and *Yes Scotland*. This civility persisted, but during the following debate it soon became clear that the audience was as well informed – if not better informed – than the politicians, and – much as I hate to admit it – my humble self. They asked searching questions about the finer points of 'currency-union', immigration law and a host of other matters.

Of course, the sample of 50 or so Scots from Perth is not a scientific or representative sample of the population. Nevertheless, the audience was surprisingly well informed, enlightened and showed a remarkable degree of interest in the debate. It seems that they were living proof of political theorist Benjamin Barber's observation, 'Only direct participation, activity that is explicitly public, is a completely successful form of civic education for democracy. The politically edifying influence of participation has been noted a thousand times since first Rousseau and then Mill and Tocqueville suggested that democracy is best taught by practic-ing it'.[1]

Looking back at the Scottish referendum it is, of course, easy to fall into the trap of political nostalgia. I believe we have reason to be in a moderately celebratory mood. The fact that the UK government allowed the Scots to have a say in the first place shows a high level of democratic magnanimity. In most countries, the cen-tral government does not allow a referendum on separatism. David Cameron deserves credit for having allowed the referendum to take place at all. But the greatest praise goes to the Scottish voters. That over 85 per cent participated in the referendum is a sign of political maturity and an indication that the Scottish peo-ple (or should I say the voters in Scotland?) desire an involvement in politics that many political scientists had hitherto regarded as unlikely.

The Scottish referendum, it should be admitted, was not just a battle royal between civic spirited democrats. There was shouting, disinformation and dirty tricks. A referendum is not a panacea; not an answer to all democratic or social ills. But such is politics. For all its problems, this referendum showed that the British system of politics can work.

John Stuart Mill noted that 'the meaning of representative government is, that the whole people, or some numerous portion of them, exercise through deputies periodically elected by themselves, the ultimate controlling power'.[2] Mill stressed the public education which every citizen of Athens received from his democratic institutions, and contrasted these engaged citizens favourably with 'those who have done nothing in their lives but drive a quill, or sell goods over the counter'. The private citizen, noted Mill:

> [I]s called upon, while so engaged, to weigh interests not his own; to be guidedÈ, in case of conflicting claims, by another rule than his private partialities; to apply, at every turn, principles of maxims which have for their reason of existence the common good.[3]

He went on to say that from these 'considerations it is evident that the only gov-ernment which [could] fully satisfy all the exigencies of a social state, is one in which the whole people participate'.[4] The Scottish referendum arguably proved Mill right.

After the election, focus turned to the EU referendum. The outcome of that referendum is likely to be more spirited than the Scottish one.

Arguably, the general election should have resulted in soul searching. It is, democratically speaking, problematic that a party that wins a majority in the House of Commons only polled a meagre 36.9 per cent! And, it is even more troublesome, from the point of view of fairness, that UKIP only won seat though Nigel Farrage's party polled a respectable 12.9 per cent. This discrepancy, and this

---

[1] Barber, B, *Strong Democracy: Participatory Politics for a New Age*, (1984, Berkeley, University of California Press) 235–36.

[2] Mill, JS, 'Considerations on Representative Government' *On Liberty and Other Essays*, John Gray (Editor) (1991, Oxford, Oxford University Press) 269.

[3] Mill, JS, *ibid*, 255

[4] Mill, JS, *ibid*, 255–56

level of disproportionality, should have lead to discussions about how to make the system fairer. But no one – and certainly none of the larger parties – suggested another referendum on electoral reform. The defeat of the Alternative Vote in the 2011 referendum, it seems, has buried the issue for the time being.

So, overall, very little has changed since this book was published in 2013. The reader of this book will find that the contributions still reflect the constitutional realities in the United Kingdom. The British Constitution – for better and for worse – is still the same. And Vernon Bogdanor is still making timely and critical contributions to the debate! Long may the latter continue!

Professor Matt Qvortrup
Coventry, September 2015.

Author Biographies

Denis Baranger is Professor of Public Law at the Université Panthéon-Assas (Paris II) and a fellow of the *Institut Universitaire de France*. He studied public administration at Sciences-Po Paris, and law at Paris II and the University of Cambridge (LLM). He teaches constitutional law, jurisprudence and history of political thought. He has held visiting positions at the University of Melbourne and the University of Oxford. He is deputy director of the Institut Michel Villey and co-editor of the online journal of constitutional law <www.juspoliticum.com>. His recent publications include: *Ecrire la constitution non-écrite. Une introduction au droit politique britannique* (Paris, PUF, coll Leviathan, 2008); and *Constitutionalism and the Role of Parliaments* (with Anthony Bradley and Katja Ziegler) (Oxford, Hart Publishing, 2007).

Robert Blackburn, PhD, LLD, is Professor of Constitutional Law at King's College London. He is one of the UK's leading authorities on constitutional and political affairs, and frequently serves as an adviser to government and parliamentary inquiries dealing with questions of law reform, both in the UK and abroad. His many books include studies of Parliament, the monarchy, elections and the voting system, human rights and political reform, and he is the editor of the volume in *Halsbury's Laws of England* on 'Constitutional and Administrative Law'. In addition to his work for the Law School, he is director of both the Institute of Contemporary British History and Centre for Political and Constitutional Studies at King's College.

Sir David Butler is Emeritus Fellow at Nuffield College, Oxford. One of the world's most-cited psephologists, David Butler is the author of many publications, including the Nuffield Election Studies 1945–2007. His *Political Change in Britain: Forces Shaping Electoral Choice* (London, Macmillan, 1969), written with US political scientist Donald Stokes, is regarded as a pioneering analysis of its kind. Elected a Fellow of the British Academy 1994, Sir David was knighted in the 2011 New Year Honours for services to political science.

David Feldman is Rouse Ball Professor of English Law, University of Cambridge, and a Fellow of Downing College, Cambridge. From 2002 until 2010 he was a Judge of the Constitutional Court of Bosnia and Herzegovina (Vice-President 2006–09). He was Legal Adviser to the Parliamentary Joint Select Committee on Human Rights 2000–04, and has advised several other parliamentary committees. He was President of the Society of Legal Scholars in 2010–11. His publications are mainly in the fields of police powers, administrative law, constitutional law and theory, comparative public law, civil liberties, human rights, the relationship between national and international law, and judicial remedies.

Mike Finn is Head of Politics at Wellington College and was formerly chief speechwriter to the Leader of the Liberal Democrats. He taught history and politics at Oxford, Cambridge and Birmingham, and was Kennedy Scholar at Harvard University in 2002–03. In 2001 he was the recipient of the Palgrave/*THES* Humanities and Social Sciences writing prize.

Richard Gordon QC is Visiting Professor at UCL and at Honorary Visiting Professor at Hong Kong University. He is a member of the Advisory Board of the Constitution Society, author of *Repairing British Politics – A Blueprint for Constitutional Change* (Oxford, Hart Publishing, 2010) and co-author of *Select Committee Powers – Clarity or Confusion?* (London, The Constitution Society, 2012).

Joseph Jaconelli is a Professor of Law at the University of Manchester, where he specialises in (amongst other subjects) constitutional law and the law of trusts. Recent publications include *Open Justice: A Critique of the Public Trial* (Oxford, Oxford University Press, 2002); 'Do Constitutional Conventions Bind?' (2005) 64(1) *Cambridge Law Journal* 149; 'The "Bowles Act" – Cornerstone of the Fiscal Constitution' (2010) 69(3) *Cambridge Law Journal* 582; and 'Tax Legislation, Forestalling, and Economic Information' [2013] *Public Law* forthcoming. In 2006 he was awarded the degree of LLD by the University of Cambridge for published work.

Dawn Oliver, FBA, LLD, QC, is Emeritus Professor of Constitutional Law at University College London. She has published widely on constitutional reform, law and politics, and comparative constitutional law. Her book *Constitutional Reform in the UK* was published by Oxford University Press in 2003; she has edited and contributed to books on *Human Rights and the Private Sphere: A Comparative Study* (Routledge Cavendish, 2007), *Justice, Legality and the Rule of Law: Lessons from the Pitcairn Prosecutions* (Oxford University Press, 2009), *How Constitutions Change* (Hart Publishing, 2011) and *Parliament and the Law* (Hart Publishing, 2013); with Professor Sir Jeffrey Jowell QC, she has co-edited seven editions of *The Changing Constitution* (Oxford University Press).

Matt Qvortrup earned his doctorate at Brasenose College, University of Oxford. Winner of the Oxford University Law Prize and the PSA Prize for best political science paper published in 2012, he has been described by the BBC as 'the World's leading expert on referendums'. In addition to his academic career, Dr Qvortrup was member of President Obama's Special Envoy Team in Africa 2009–10.

Peter Riddell is Director of the Institute for Government. He was previously a political journalist on both the *Financial Times* and *The Times*, and has written seven books on British politics. He is a Fellow of the Royal Historical Society, a recipient of the president's medal from the British Academy and has two honorary doctorates. He chaired the Hansard Society for five years.

Anthony Seldon is the 13th Master of Wellington College and the author of over 25 works on British political history. He is an authority on British prime ministers and Cabinet government, having written acclaimed studies of John Major, Tony Blair and Gordon Brown. In the 1980s, with Peter Hennessy, he founded the Institute for Contemporary British History.

Stephen Tierney is Professor of Constitutional Theory at the University of Edinburgh and Director of the Edinburgh Centre for Constitutional Law. His works include *Constitutional Law and National Pluralism* (Oxford University Press 2004) and *Constitutional Referendums: The Theory and Practice of Republican Deliberation* (Oxford University Press 2012). He serves as adviser to the Scottish Parliament Referendum Bill Committee in 2013.

Vernon Bogdanor understands like few others the connections between history, politics and institutions - and that is what makes him such an authority on the British system of government.

The Rt Hon David Cameron MP, Prime Minister

I think Vernon's guiding principle at Brasenose was to treat all his students as if they might one day be Prime Minister. At the time, I thought this was a bit over the top, but then a boy studying PPE at Brasenose two years beneath me became Prime Minister.

Toby Young, The Spectator

Introduction

The British Constitution – Continuity and Change

MATT QVORTRUP

There is no period so remote as the recent past.

Alan Bennett, *The History Boys* (2004)

T HE BRITISH CONSTITUTION 'once an elusive institution has now become much more grounded, much more tangible and much more based on written sources than was previously the case. It now 'exists' in a way that it previously did not. This is in no small part due to the reforms undertaken by the successive Governments since the mid-1990s. Unlike in other countries where constitutional changes have been undertaken after lengthy deliberations in Constituent Assemblies[1], the British Constitutional changes were the result of piecemeal changes and often without much consultation, let alone attempts to reach an overall consensus.

In this book – written as a *Festschrift* to Vernon Bogdanor – 10 topics will be covered in 11 chapters by 12 experts from law, history and political science.

The contributions do not follow an overall theme. Instead, rather like Akira Kurosawa's famous movie *Rashomon*, they present different comments on the same event – here, the recent constitutional changes. None of the perspectives is epistemologically superior to the others but they complement each other to give a more detailed overall view.

In chapters one, two and three, respectively, Sir David Butler, Mike Finn and Anthony Seldon, and Peter Riddell present three perspectives on the overall development of the Constitution from historical and political viewpoints. These are followed by four case studies on different aspects of the Constitution. In the first two of these, Matt Qvortrup and Dawn Oliver consider, respectively, the courts

---

[1] T Ginsburg (Editor) *Comparative Constitutional Design* (Cambridge: Cambridge University Press, 2012).

(chapter four) and the apolitical constitution (eg QUANGOs, tribunals, etc – chapter five). Those two chapters are followed by two contrasting – and complementing – essays on constitutional conventions by, respectively, David Feldman (chapter six) and Joseph Jaconelli (chapter seven).

One of the most important changes to impact on the Constitution in recent years is devolution. In chapter eight, Stephen Tierney analyses past developments in this area. Another fundamental aspect of the Constitution is the doctrine of parliamentary sovereignty. The degree to which – and whether – this doctrine still stands is analysed by Richard Gordon in chapter nine.

Despite all its changes, Britain is still – and is likely to remain – a constitutional monarchy. But very little has been written about the monarchy – apart from Vernon Bogdanor's much-cited work in the 1990s[2]. In chapter ten, Robert Blackburn analyses the role of the monarchy.

Sometimes it can be difficult to see the wood for the trees. Those who labour away in the middle of the maelstrom can sometime lose their sense of perspective. To understand the British Constitution it may sometimes be necessary to contrast it with another model. The French sociologist Alexis de Tocqueville once noted that he 'did not write one page of [*Democracy in America*] without thinking of [France] and without having her, so to speak, before [his] eyes'.[3] In a similar way, Tocqueville's present-day compatriot, Denis Baranger, presents an analysis in chapter eleven of the French Constitutional Council as a contrast to the arrangements in Britain, which is also written with Britain 'before his eyes'.

Before embarking on a journey into this fascinating topic, an overview and some background will be useful.

American lawyer Bruce Ackerman has famously noted that changes in the fundamental political and legal framework take place during 'constitutional moments'. As he writes:

> Although constitutional politics is the highest kind of politics, it should be permitted to dominate the nation's life only during rare periods of heightened political consciousness. During the long periods between these constitutional moments, a second form of activity – I shall call it normal politics – prevails. Here, factions try to manipulate the constitutional forms of political life to pursue their own narrow interests.[4]

In Britain, it is almost the other way round. The British Constitution has been subject to more or less constant change from 1997 onwards, but the reforms have not 'dominated the nation's life'. And although the issues have concerned the 'highest kind of politics', factions have not refrained from 'manipulating' even the fundamental constitutional changes 'to pursue their own narrow interests'.

At no time since 1911, and probably not even then, has the age-old, (mostly) unwritten British Constitution undergone such profound revision. The Human

---

[2] V Bogdanor, *The Monarchy and the Constitution* (Oxford: Oxford University Press 1995)
[3] Alexis de Tocqueville to Louis de Kergolay, 18 October 1847, in A de Tocqueville, *Selected Letters on Politics and Society* (ed Roger Boesche) (Berkeley, University of California Press, 1985), 191.
[4] B Ackerman, 'The Storrs Lectures: Discovering the Constitution' (1984) 93 *Yale Law Journal* 1022.

Rights Act 1998, devolution to Scotland, Wales and Northern Ireland (1997–98), the modest reform of the House of Lords, the establishment of the Supreme Court, not to mention constant alterations in Britain's relationship with the European Union, are but some of the changes we have witnessed in the past two decades. Add to these the various modifications of the electoral systems (we now have List Proportional Representation for the European Parliament, the Single Transferable Vote for local government in Scotland and for the Belfast Assembly, the Supplementary Vote in London, and Additional Members Systems in Scotland, Wales and for the London Assembly), the increasing use of referendums, changes to the rules governing elections in the form of the Political Parties, Elections and Referendums Act 2000, and various amendments to committees in the House of Commons, and it is unarguable that Britain's constitutional architecture has now changed profoundly, but has done so without a 'constitutional moment'; without a general sense that the system fundamentally has changed. As the political journalist John Rentoul has observed, 'had it been sold as a connected programme of reform, it might have been hailed as a democratic revolution, the greatest constitutional upheaval since votes for women; instead, the nation shrugged and moved on'.[5]

But how has the Constitution changed more fundamentally? Traditional orthodoxy stretching back to AV Dicey and Walter Bagehot held that the British Constitution was the antithesis of the American Constitution with its checks and balances. Bagehot dismissed the American version of countervailing powers in *The English Constitution*, by pointing out that 'the English constitution, in a word, is framed on the principle of choosing a single sovereign authority . . . the American, upon the principle of having many sovereign authorities'.[6] And, Dicey, in *Introduction to the Study of the Law of the Constitution*, cemented the fundamental doctrine of parliamentary sovereignty by quoting Blackwell's dictum, that what 'Parliament doth, no authority upon earth can undo'.[7]

But it is arguably the case that there have been convergences towards 'the American model' in recent years. The British Constitution has recognised more checks and balances. The changing role of the Lord Chancellor is a case in point. Until the Constitutional Reform Act 2005, the Lord Chancellor was a legislator (a member of the House of Lords), a member of the Executive (a Cabinet minister) and the head of the judiciary (the highest judge in the highest court). The situation was seemingly identical to that described in Montesquieu's *The Spirit of the Laws*, in which the Frenchman warned that there would be 'no liberty if the judiciary power is not separated from the legislative and executive'.[8] It would, of course, be unfair and wholly inaccurate to accuse recent Lord Chancellors of 'violence and

---

[5] J Rentoul, *Tony Blair: Prime Minister* (London, Warner Books, 2001) 459.

[6] W Bagehot, *The English Constitution*, 2nd edn (Oxford, Oxford University Press, 1873) 75.

[7] Blackstone *Commentaries*, quoted in AV Dicey, *An Introduction to the Study of the Law of the Constitution*, 8th edn (Indianapolis, Ind, Liberty Press, 1915) 5.

[8] Montesquieu, quoted in MJC Vile, *Constitutionalism and the Separation of Powers*, 2nd edn (Indianapolis, Ind, Liberrty Fund, 1998) 99.

oppression'[9] (Montesquieu's contention), but the fact that a Cabinet minister as recently as 2005 sat as a judge in the highest court of the land,[10] is – in comparative perspective – unparalled and an indication that reform of this part of the Constitution was long overdue. Certainly, since *R v Hinds* it has been 'taken for granted' that 'the basic principle of the separation of powers' is a doctrine of the British Constitution.[11] But it was only with the Constitutional Reform Act 2005 that this was formally recognised in statute, and it was only after this change that the Lord Chancellor stopped combining the roles of judge and Cabinet minister.

The other fundamental principle, the doctrine of parliamentary sovereignty, though still the 'bedrock of the British Constitution',[12] has also been watered down, challenged and even questioned. True, the principle of parliamentary sovereignty had already been challenged as a result of British entry into the EEC in 1973, as the *Factortame* cases showed,[13] yet *Factortame* did not question the principle of parliamentary sovereignty in domestic legislation. Nevertheless, this too has changed. While still the general principle of our Constitution, it would have been improbable a generation ago that House of Lords/Supreme Court could reach the conclusion that it 'is not unthinkable that circumstances could arise where the courts may have to qualify a principle established on a different hypothesis of constitutionalism'

Still, *plus ça change, plus c'est la même chose*. The changes may seem revolutionary, but much of the underlying structure remains unaffected. At a time when the press especially is talking about an emboldened judiciary and the much-reviled 'rights culture', it is worth noting that there are limits to the changes. For example, even the much-debated Human Rights Act 1998 is subject to repeal – though this is a fact often lost in the tabloids. 'The Human Rights Act,' as Lord Nicholls pointedly explained, "reserves amendment of primary legislation to parliament . . . the Act seeks to preserve parliamentary sovereignty".[14]

But just in case we had come to believe that we had adopted the hallmark of constitutionalism – namely, a system of checks and balances and limits on the exercise of power – the Legislative and Regulatory Reform Act 2006 was passed. This enables ministers to make secondary legislation that – in theory – can amend, repeal or replace primary legislation. Though the Government partially backed down, it was clear that it did so only because of considerable political pressure, and it still made what some have characterised as only rather cosmetic changes to the original Bill.[15] Those who favour a more balanced Constitution have not won the war.

[9] Montesquieu, *ibid.*

[10] Lord Irvine of Lairg presided over the House of Lords and Privy Council, and performed the role of Chief Justice. M Beloff, 'Law and the Judiciary' in A Seldon (ed), *Blair's Britain 1997–2007* (Cambridge, Cambridge University Press, 2007) 295.

[11] *R v Hinds* [1979] Crim LR 111 . . . 39, per Lord Diplock.

[12] *R (Jackson and Other) v Attorney General* [2005] UKHL 56, at 9, per Lord Bingham

[13] Eg *Factortame Ltd v Secretary of State for Transport (No 1)* [1989] 2 All ER 692 and *Factortame Ltd v Secretary of State for Transport (No 2)* [1991] 2 All ER 697.

[14] *Re S (Minors) (Care Order: Implementation of Care Plan)* [2002] UKHL 10, [2002] 2 AC 291 [39], per Lord Nicholls

[15] 'How we move ever closer to becoming a totalitarian state', *Guardian*, 5 March 2006.

Where does all this leave the British Constitution? Is it new? Has it changed in a revolutionary way, or is it just an example of piecemeal changes? Will the recent changes been seen as fundamental in 20 or even in 10 years' time? The answers to these questions will be discussed in the chapters that follow.

1

The Changing Constitution in Context

DAVID BUTLER

ALL CONSTITUTIONS EVOLVE – but an unwritten constitution evolves obscurely. The rules of the game of British government have changed subtly, year by year. It is up to political scientists to monitor these changes, constantly reassessing whether seemingly established rules still apply. Vernon Bogdanor's notable achievement in putting together *The British Constitution in the Twentieth Century* emphasised this theme in well-annotated detail.[1] What follows is an attempt to illustrate in a different way the transitory basis of our governmental arrangements and to set them in their changing social context.

But first, what is a constitution? The word can denote anything from a single written document to a whole collection of conventions, laws, judgments and writings that set out the rules under which politics and government should be conducted. Almost all democracies enjoy a single written document, but these 'tablets of stone' vary enormously in their scope and detail. The American Constitution had only seven Articles when it was drafted in 1789. The Constitution of Fifth French Republic of 1958 has now reached 95 Articles. The Indian Constitution, drawn up in 1949–52, currently contains 395 Articles. In Britain we are guided, for the most part, by ideas handed down about 'what usually happens'.

Britain has what Arend Lijphart calls a 'majoritarian' constitution. Indeed, the 'Westminster Model', as he calls it, is the archetypical example of this type of constitution.[2] Geoffrey Marshall, after offering four conflicting understandings of what constitutes a constitution, settles on this formulation: 'The combination of legal and non-legal (or conventional) rules that provide the framework of government and regulate the behaviour of the main political actors.'[3] However, he points out that no country has a fully codified constitution – or would think of producing

---

[1] A further summary of his views is the be found in V Bogdanor, 'Our New Constitution' (2004) 120 *LQR* 242.

[2] A Lijphart, *Patterns of Democracy: Government Forms and Performance in Thirty-Six Countries* (London, Yale University Press, 2012) 9.

[3] G Marshall, 'The Constitution: Its Theory and Interpretation' in V Bogdanor (ed), *The British Constitution in the Twentieth Century* (Oxford, Oxford University Press, 2003) 31.

one. 'Since the real constitution is indeterminate as to its boundaries, the task is beyond human capacity.'[4]

Using Marshall's definition, let me set out, in one portmanteau sentence, what, half a century ago, any middle-of-the-road teacher of politics might have put to his students as the essence of the United Kingdom Constitution:

> Britain is (1) governed under an (2) unwritten constitution that is (3) unitary, and (4) centralised, by a (5) Cabinet that is (6) individually responsible and (7) collectively responsible to a (8) sovereign Parliament, dominated by (9) two disciplined parties, chosen (10) first-past-the-post by (11) a stable electorate.

Each of the 11 propositions implicit in that sentence has come under challenge during the last half-century:

(1) *Britain is governed?* But how far are we governed? The sense that there is an authority in Westminster capable of controlling the economy and shaping the nation's future has diminished with the advance of globalisation and the entry into Europe. A widespread scepticism has developed about the ability of governments to govern and about the ability of politicians to make a difference to everyday life.

(2) *An unwritten constitution?* A century ago Austen Chamberlain could say 'unconstitutional is just a term used in politics when the other fellow does something you don't like'.[5] Over the last three centuries, Montesquieu, Blackstone, Bagehot and now Bogdanor have talked about 'the Constitution', but despite Magna Carta, the Bill of Rights and the Great Reform Acts, there never was a document which politicians or judges could consult in order to determine what was constitutionally proper in a time of crisis. There has never been a serious demand for a comprehensive written constitution.

However, since 1972 the United Kingdom has subscribed to the Treaty of Rome and its successors. In 1998, the Scotland Act, the Government of Wales Act and the Human Rights Act set further limits to the things that the Government at Westminster can do. The Constitution Reform Act of 2005 carried things a bit further. Many of the rules of the game are still unwritten, but much is now set down in *de facto* unrepealable law which the judges in London, Luxembourg or Strasbourg can and do interpret.

(3) *Unitary?* Fifty years ago it was possible to agree with Bagehot that Montesquieu and Blackstone were fundamentally wrong, and that there was no 'separation of powers' in Britain. The executive and the legislature were merged, buckled together through a Cabinet dependent on parliamentary approval. In contrast to the United States, parliamentary actions could not be overridden by a judiciary which was concerned only with the application of established civil and criminal law. Today there is more conflict between executive and legislature.

---

[4] *Ibid.*
[5] As quoted by Stanley Baldwin, HC Deb 8 February 1932 vol 261, col 530 (1932).

Party rebellions in the Commons have significantly increased.[6] The Upper House presents much more of a problem to the Government.

But the separation of the judiciary has become even more important. Government policies have been increasingly challenged under European Union law and still more under the European Convention on Human Rights which, since the Human Rights Act 1998, has produced significant cases for British judges to consider. Even domestically, the activism of judges has increased; the number of judicial review cases expanded 25-fold between 1980 and 2010.[7] The transformation of the role of Lord Chancellor and the decision to set up a Supreme Court separate from the House of Lords has far-reaching implications, still to become fully apparent; the transfer of judicial appointments form the Lord Chancellor to the Lord Chief Justice adds to the 'separation of powers'. The growth in the influence of the judiciary means that today's student of British government needs to be versed in law to an extent unimaginable in the 1950s.

(4) *Centralised?* The overwhelming bulk of public business used to be conducted in London. In the last 30 years it has moved increasingly to Brussels as well as to Edinburgh and Cardiff (and indeed to the Greater London Council). There has also been a great deal of administrative devolution to provincial centres. For a while the possibility of elected English regional authorities joined the political agenda. The formal dominance of Westminster and Whitehall has significantly diminished.[8]

(5) *Cabinet?* The Cabinet meets for many fewer hours than it did 40 years ago.[9] Far fewer papers are subject to full discussion with all ministers present; the number fell from 326 in 1950 to 119 in 1978–79, Callaghan's last year; in 2003 the figure was 10 (plus eight 'presentations').[10] Government decisions now tend to be announced in the name of the Prime Minister rather than the Cabinet, often with senior ministers having had no opportunity to see or comment on them. Margaret Thatcher and Tony Blair, by their own unilateral changes in practice, demoted the Cabinet. Cabinet membership still gives a politician status, but the idea that government decisions all emanate from serious collective discussion around the Cabinet table is now seen as absurd.

(6) *Individually responsible?* There used to be a doctrine that 'for every action of a servant of the Crown a minister is answerable to Parliament' and that 'ministers take both the praise and the blame for policies and administration while civil servants remain anonymous'.[11] The doctrine still stands, but it has been

---

[6] *P Cowley, The Rebels: How Blair Mislaid His Majority* (London: Politico's, 2005).

[7] Applications for leave to apply for judicial review: 1979, 410; 2003, 5,949; 2010, 11,200 (Ministry of Justice Judicial and Court Statistics for individual years).

[8] V Bogdanor, *Devolution in the United Kingdom* (rev edn) (Oxford, Oxford University Press, 2001).

[9] Annual average number of Cabinet meetings: 1950–54, 90; 1971–75, 61; 1996–2000, 37. *Sources*: 1950–54, 1971–75 and 1996–2000, P Hennessy, *Cabinet* (Oxford, Basil Blackwell, 1986).

[10] Papers discussed in full Cabinet: 1950, 326; 1978–79, 119; 1980, 74; 2003, 10 (plus 8 presentations). *Sources*: 1950, 1978–79, 1980 and 2003, Hennessy, above n 9.

[11] D Woodhouse, 'Ministerial responsibility' in Bogdanor (ed), above n 3, 281.

weakened by officials appearing more in public and testifying before Select Committees, as well as by Civil Service tasks being hived off to agencies and regulators.[12] It has also been weakened by ministers passing the buck to officials, with contorted arguments about the division between policy and administration.[13] Public servants worry about their decline in status and ask for a Civil Service Act to clarify it.

(7) *Collectively responsible?* The old doctrine survives that 'any minister who disagrees with government policy must resign – or at least keep silent,' for the old reason 'we must all hang together lest we hang separately'. But leaks about ministers' disagreements and reservations have vastly increased, and the fact that so much less is now debated in full Cabinet means that the doctrine has been seriously eroded, even though recent decades have still seen principled resignations over collective responsibility (eg Heseltine 1986, Lawson 1989, Howe 1990, Cook 2003).[14]

(8) *A sovereign Parliament?* The absolute sovereignty of Parliament, idealised by Blackstone and Dicey and Jennings, has been much reduced. Since Britain's adherence to the Treaty of Rome in 1972, authority has passed increasingly to European institutions. The European Convention of Human Rights, ratified in 1950, has, especially after the Human Rights Act 1998, increasingly guided British courts. Authority over many matters has been moved to independent agencies and commissions only answerable to Parliament in indirect ways. Since 1998, the Scottish Parliament has resumed many of the powers that it transferred to London in 1707. Referendums do in practice move power from the legislature to the people.[15] The absolute sovereignty of Parliament looks more and more mythical.[16]

(9) *Two disciplined parties?* Every general election but two since 1945 has produced a clear majority for a single party. In 1955, 97 per cent of the popular vote was divided between Conservative and Labour, and all but seven of the 630 Members of Parliament were attached to one of those parties. In 2010 the two big parties shared only 69 per cent of the vote, while the number of MPs representing other groupings had risen to 85 out of 650. In nine of the 17 post-1945 Parliaments, that figure would have been enough to deny the Government a clear majority. The increasing possibility of a hung Parliament was fully realised in 2010. It produced a new burst of speculation about the rules of the game in British politics.

---

[12] In the 10 years following the *Ibbs Next Steps Report* (London, H.M.S.O, 1988), almost 200 independent agencies were established.

[13] The most celebrated example comes from the conflict in 1995 between the Home Secretary, Michael Howard, and the Director of the Prison Service, Derek Lewis. For a concise account, see Diana Woodhouse's version in Bogdanor (ed), above n 3, 326–27.

[14] Oonagh Gay and Thomas Powell, 'The Collective Responsibility of Ministers: an Outline of the Issues' (15 November 2004) House of Commons Library Research Paper 04/82, and 'Individual ministerial responsibility-issues and examples' (5 April 2004) House of Commons Library Research Paper 04/31.

[15] M Qvortrup, *Direct Democracy* (Manchester, Manchester University Press, 2013).

[16] See ch 9 of this volume by Richard Gordon.

(10) *First-past-the-post?* The electoral system for the House of Commons remains unchanged – but since 1974 it has become the subject of active discussion. The Labour Party entered government in 1997 committed to holding a referendum on a change of the system. The referendum was not held by Labour and the pioneering Jenkins Report[17] was not taken seriously. Nonetheless the government installed the Additional Member System for the new devolved assemblies in Scotland and Wales as well as versions of list proportional representation for London and for the European Parliament. The Single Transferable Vote is now used in Northern Ireland and in Scottish local elections. Its application to UK parliamentary elections was soundly defeated in a 2011 referendum. The first-past-the-post electoral system for Westminster (which now works in an increasingly capricious way) can be less and less trusted to produce clear single party governments.

The image of British elections has also changed. Turnout has fallen spectacularly. The winning party's share of the vote, and therefore its mandate, touched a new low: Labour's 35 per cent in 2005 would, a generation earlier, have earned not victory but abject defeat. Anxieties over fraud and money have reached a level never approached in the twentieth century. The electoral system still produces legitimate governments, but it stands in less high repute; the Electoral Commission, established as a monitoring body in 2001, has made this plain.

(11) *A stable electorate?* Party loyalties used to be much stronger than they are today. In the 1960s, 80 per cent of people said that they felt 'very strongly' or 'fairly strongly' committed to one of the three parties. By 2005 that figure had fallen to 52 per cent. Party membership dropped from four million in 1950 to 700,000 in 2005, and to just over 400,000 in 2010.

Between 1945 and 1959, only one by-election in 20 saw the defeat of the incumbent party; between 1974 and 1997, the figure jumped to one in three. Opinion polls also showed much more violent fluctuations. In these circumstances, it becomes increasingly necessary to expect the unexpected.

These 11 points do not encompass the whole story. There have also been a number of explicit changes affecting the conduct of politics and government. Here is a list, far from exhaustive, of Acts of Parliament that have affected constitutional arrangements:

1949 *Parliament Act.* This curtailed the delaying powers of the House of Lords to one year.

1955 *Television Act.* This introduced competition to television and led to a much livelier coverage of politics.

1958 *Life Peerages Act.* This revivified the House of Lords with an influx of Labour and Independent life peers.

---

[17] Secretary of State for the Home Department, *The Report of the Independent Commission on the Voting System* (Cm 4090, 1998) ch4.

1962 *Immigration Act.* This partially closed the door to the influx of Commonwealth immigrants that had started in 1953.

1963 *Peerage Act.* This allowed the renunciation of peerages and allowed Lord Home to become Prime Minister.

1969 *Representation of the People Act.* This lowered the voting age to 18.

1972 *European Communities Act.* This made Britain part of what is now the European Union.

1975 *Referendum Act.* This authorised the first nationwide referendum in the United Kingdom.

1986 *Single European Act.* This increased British involvement with the European economy and abolished the veto over EU legislation by individual States.

1998 *Bank of England Act.* This regularised the 1997 transfer of authority over interest rates from the Treasury to the Bank of England.

1998 *Scotland Act.* This re-established the Scottish Parliament.

1998 *Government of Wales Act.* This established the Welsh Assembly.

1998 *Northern Ireland Act.* This opened the possibility of a transformed status for Northern Ireland.

1998 *Human Rights Act.* This enshrined the European Convention on Human Rights in United Kingdom law.

1999 *House of Lords Act.* This greatly reduced the hereditary element in the House of Lords.

1999 *European Parliamentary Elections Act.* This introduced proportional representation into a UK-wide election for the first time.

1999 *Greater London Act.* This provided for an elected Mayor and new powers for a Greater London Council.

2000 *Political Parties, Elections and Referendums Act.* This established the Electoral Commission with oversight over party finances.

2005 *Constitutional Reform Act.* This gave effect to the 2003 changes to the position of Lord Chancellor; it set up a Supreme Court and a Judicial Appointments Board.

2011 *Fixed Term Parliament.* This provides for Parliament lasting 5 years except in specified circumstances.

Although these Acts, each in their incremental way, modified the British Constitution, as it was understood 50 years ago, most of the essentials survived. How are we to understand both modification and survival?

A constitution works within a social context. If the rules of the game under which British politics operate have altered, so too, even more imperceptibly, has British society evolved – and in ways that transform politics. Table 1 below sets out in an arbitrary fashion some of the most spectacular changes in the framework of life over the last half century. Each of the comparisons in the table reflects a development which has had a political impact. Every one has altered the demands or needs of the electorate, or has produced a modification of government processes.

Table 1 Indicators of Change 1950–2010

	1950/1	2011
Total UK population	51m.	61.8m.
Population over 65	11%	19.4%
Expectation of life	67 years	79.8 years
Non white population	0.4%	16%
One-person households	11%	29%
Children born out of wedlock	5%	46%
Owner-occupied households	29%	69%
Television households	1%	99%
Car-owning households	12%	77%
Telephone-owning households	12%	99%
Computer-owning households	Nil	76%
Internet-connected households	Nil	73%
Share owning households	7%	28%
Airline journeys	2m.	218m.
GDP (at 2004 prices)	£304,221m.	£1.39bn.
Value of 1950 £	£1	£25.50
Top Income Tax Rate	90%	50%
At school after leaving age	31%	76%
17-19s entering higher education	6%	47%
Self-described working class	47%	31%
Women in workforce	31%	65%
Manual jobs	64%	28%
Mining and heavy industry jobs	39%	10%
Unemployed	1.5%	8.1%
Armed forces regulars	688,000	173,900
Coal production	216m. tons	11.4m. tons
Criminal convictions (*E & W*)	17,100	351,600
Prison population	20,000	83,200
Major party members (*combined*)	4m.	476,000
Voting turnout	84%	65%
Permanent Select Committees	5	19
MPs pay	£1,000	£65,738
MPs expenses	Nil	£125,715

Table 1 (*Cont.*)

	1950/1	2011
Women MPs	24	143
Non-white MPs	Nil	27
Life peers (*exc Law Lords*)	Nil	673
Lords daily allowance	Nil	£300
Independent C'wealth Members	8	54

Note: Most of these figures are drawn from the *Annual Abstract of Statistics or Social Trends.*

The most striking changes lie in the figures for residence and for occupation. The move from a country where only 29 per cent lived in owner-occupied property to one where 66 per cent do so has transformed the political agenda. The move from a country where nearly two-thirds of the workforce were in manual employment to one where manual workers amount to barely one-third (especially with the number in heavy industry and mining having decreased by nearly 75 per cent) has meant that the Labour Party can no longer win elections as essentially the party of council tenants and trade unions. The appeal of 'the party of the working class' is much diminished when only 31 per cent of the electorate positively describe themselves as 'working class'.

These trends have to be seen together with other major developments: the quadrupling of GDP; the coming of television; the end of Empire; the jump from almost none to 16 per cent non-white population; the transformation of the House of Lords. Every party – but especially Labour – has had to revolutionise its approach to the electorate. The agenda of government has changed, and so have the rules under which it is played.

In an affluent and undeferential society, well-stocked with consumer goods, all major parties have learned to focus their appeal on the voters of middle Britain; they have to concentrate on popular anxieties about health and education and taxation; they have to offer reassurance on crime and immigration; they have to accept the necessity of political change to cope with technological change. In adapting to the situation, all parties have taken advantage of new tools of communication. Polls and focus groups yield much the same message to all sides. Spin-doctoring and advertising skills offer new but similar ways of putting out converging messages. It is hard to demonstrate the direct link between these changes in the framework of political life and the changes in the framework of politics. But it is there.

Circumstances alter attitudes. The end of Empire made Britain turn towards Europe. The growth of affluence helped to end deference. The spread of education extended the politically-informed class, and, together with a more free-wheeling media, it fostered anincreasingly sceptical approach to the institutions and activities of government. It made acceptance of a purely hereditary second chamber more and more impossible. It also fostered Scottish and Welsh nationalism, and the establishment of alternative centres of government in Edinburgh and Cardiff. It encouraged an increased turning to legal remedies with recourse to judicial review and the Convention on Human Rights.

If we look again at the 11 constitutional points with which this chapter started, we can see how they all link back to an evolving social base. The enlargement of the politically-educated class and the liberation of the media have changed the dialogue, and helped to break down conventional objections to change:

(1) *Governed?* Scepticism about how far we are governed from Westminster may be attributed not only to the obvious facts of global politics and trade, but also to the way that government decisions are portrayed on television and in the press. Declining respect for politicians as a class has weakened faith in government.

(2) *An unwritten constitution?* The unwritten nature of the Constitution was subverted not only by devolution upwards through the Treaty of Rome and by devolution downwards to Edinburgh and Cardiff, but also by increasingly sophisticated demands for due process. Migration and travel made people more willing to look at best practice elsewhere. Devolution requires formal definition, and the anxieties of an increasingly litigious population have produced pressure for formal judgments and codification.

(3) *Unitary?* The same forces have fostered the separation of powers. The changed intellectual climate has encouraged Parliament, and particularly the House of Lords, to challenge the Government. It has also encouraged the judges to go farther in their interpretation of Acts of Parliament and the Human Rights Convention. Travel and migration have increased awareness about what goes on in the rest of the world.

(4) *Centralised?* The moods that pushed the United Kingdom into Europe as well as into devolution were reflected in many ways. People were led to explore the ambiguities in the new rules of the game. It also became fashionable for politicians and administrators to pay lip service to local solutions. Questioning fosters change.

(5) *Cabinet?* Scepticism about Bagehot's version of the primacy of the Cabinet has developed not only because of the free-wheeling and individualistic innovations of Margaret Thatcher and Tony Blair, but also because of the growing complexity of modern government. The network of Cabinet Committees (the existence and membership of which have been made public only in the last two decades) has largely taken over from the full Cabinet. The leisurely conventions of the nineteenth-century device, immortalised by Bagehot, had to be modernised by Lloyd George. But his reformed system has in its turn had to yield to the pressures of the twenty-first century.

(6) *Individually responsible?* Individual responsibility has survived better than most parts of the conventional wisdom. But the proliferation in the 1990s of agencies and independent commissioners and regulators, largely removed from ministerial control, has changed the extent of answerability. At the same

time, ever-bolder journalists have felt free to probe in greater detail into what actually happens between ministers at the top and the civil servants at the coalface.

(7)   *Collectively responsible?* Collective responsibility became more and more of a charade as the agenda and the hours of Cabinet discussion became increasingly attenuated. The circulation of Cabinet papers has greatly diminished. The leaks, often deliberate, from Cabinet ministers and their army of political advisers have steadily diluted the idea that government decisions are genuinely collective.

(8)   *A sovereign Parliament?* The sovereignty of Parliament has been challenged not only by the establishment of other bodies in Europe, Scotland and Wales in obvious ways, but also by popular willingness to go to law and to find legal holes in the increasing volume of often ill-drafted Acts.

(9)   *Two disciplined parties?* As party loyalty and involvement has declined, the door has opened both to new parties and to alienation from politics. The Whips have found increasing difficulty in keeping MPs in line. The traditional caution which stands in the way of constitutional innovation has diminished.

(10)   *First-past-the-post?* The electoral system operated honestly and (granted its self-evident exaggeration of majorities) fairly throughout the twentieth century. It produced excessive victories first for one side and then for the other, while smaller parties were squeezed out; but, on the whole, it excited little controversy. However, the multiplication of parties and the diminished share of the vote for the victorious party, together with the growing one-sided bias in the working of the system, has added to public scepticism.

(11)   *A stable electorate?* Voters perceiving less and less difference between the parties therefore worry less about the risk to their own well-being whichever side wins; they become less easily aroused about changes in the rules of the game.

At every point the constitutional assumptions of the 1950s have been challenged by the changing moods and circumstances of Britain as the twentieth century drew to a close. The process continues. Since 2010, the novelty of a 'hung' Parliament has produced extensive modifications in constitutional and parliamentary practice. Parliamentary conventions, Civil Service rules and electoral arrangements have come into question.

This chapter has stressed change, often unnoticed change. Yet there is also continuity. The end is not nigh. Much of Britain's long-established parliamentary, judicial and administrative culture survives. The past usually remains a good guide to the future.

But change goes on. There can be no doubt that exact observation and thinking about constitutional rules is going to be needed by official committees, by think-tanks and by individual scholars. A new edition of Vernon Bogdanor's invaluable work, *The British Constitution*, is already overdue.

2

Constitutional Reform Since 1997: The Historians' Perspective

MIKE FINN AND ANTHONY SELDON

A government setting out to modernise Britain cannot be conservative about Britain's institutions. We cannot face the challenges of the twenty-first century with a hangover of habits, attitudes and privileges that reflect views of parliamentary representation as it was in the nineteenth. We need to institute a modern view of the relationship between the citizen and the state.

Peter Mandelson and Roger Liddle, The Blair Revolution (1996)[1]

What's all this constitutional reform shite?

Ian Davidson MP (1 June 2009)[2]

Had it been sold as a connected programme of reform, it might have been hailed as a democratic revolution, the greatest constitutional upheaval since votes for women; instead, the nation shrugged and moved on.

John Rentoul, Tony Blair: Prime Minister (2001)[3]

I. THE CONSTITUTION AND HISTORY

CONSTITUTIONAL REFORM IN the United Kingdom must necessarily be approached, by both practitioners and analysts, with a sense of history. As Vernon Bogdanor (following AV Dicey) has shown, the British Constitution is 'historic' by nature; 'original and spontaneous, a product of historical development rather than deliberate design'.[4] An historical sense is vital to understand the dimensions and dynamics of a constitutional settlement which is

---

[1] P Mandelson and R Liddle, *The Blair Revolution: Can New Labour Deliver?* (London, Faber & Faber, 1996) 192.
[2] Cited in C Mullin, *Decline and Fall: Diaries, 2005–2010* (London, Profile, 2010) 336.
[3] J Rentoul, *Tony Blair: Prime Minister* (London, Warner Books, 2001) 459.
[4] V Bogdanor, *The New British Constitution* (Oxford, Hart Publishing, 2009) 12.

innately contingent – the product of an accumulation of myriad events and political calculations across the course of centuries rather than any revolutionary 'year
zero'.[5] Historians also tend to view constitutional reform in a different light and
through different modes of analysis than legal scholars or political scientists, even
as they trespass on the territories of both.

As such, this chapter examines how the constitutional reforms enacted under the
Labour Governments of 1997–2010 might be viewed in historical perspective. It is
necessary also to make brief comments about the initial programme and initiatives
of the Conservative–Liberal Democrat coalition which succeeded it, as constitutional reform is an area which remains in flux, and the coalition's priorities have
implications for the impact of Labour's reforms in the long term. On the arrival of
the coalition, the Deputy Prime Minister Nick Clegg announced the 'biggest shake-
up of our democracy since 1832,' with an agenda including a referendum on the
voting system for Westminster, fixed-term parliaments and the promise of further
reform of the House of Lords.[6] On that note, it is perhaps opportune to reflect on
the potential for hubris that constitutional reform offers policymakers intent to
leave their mark on history. Ultimately Clegg's campaign for the alternative vote
came to naught, whilst at time of writing his endeavours on Lords reform are mired
in coalition politics and at the mercy of Tory backbenchers.

The Scylla of hubris notwithstanding, it is worthwhile daring the Charybdis of
hyperbole: The changes which have taken place in the British constitutional settlement since 1997 have been profound, and unprecedented. It is difficult to
'rank' constitutional reforms in order of historical significance: Was greater devolution[7] to Scotland, Northern Ireland, Wales and London of the same order of
magnitude as the 'leap in the dark' of 1867?[8] Was the passage of the Human Rights
Act a shift in British liberties to rival Magna Carta (although, as Sir Louis Blom-
Cooper wittily noted, even Magna Carta only meant 'one baron, one vote')?[9] Such
questions miss the essential characteristic of what took place after 1997 – what
was significant about constitutional reform after 1997 was the volume of change

   [5] *Ibid*, 11.
   [6] Cited in V Bogdanor, *The Coalition and the Constitution* (Oxford, Hart Publishing, 2010) xii.
   [7] 'Greater' is a significant qualification. As others have noted, there has always been significant
autonomy from the centre in the constituent nations of Britain, with Scotland in particular retaining a
distinctive identity in legal and educational terms. With respect to Scotland, Neil McGarvey notes: 'The
pre-devolution legacy should not be under-appreciated. The 1999 settlement merely added a Parliament
to the executive, administrative and policy-making powers already devolved to the Scottish Office'. Neil
McGarvey, 'Devolution in Scotland: Change and continuity' in J Bradbury (ed), *Devolution, Regionalism
and Regional Development: The UK experience* (London, Routledge, 2008) 26.
   [8] See the following for a variety of perspectives, old and new, on the significance of 1867: C Hall,
K McClelland and J Rendall, *Defining the Victorian Nation: Class, Race, Gender and the Reform Act of
1867* (Cambridge, Cambridge University Press, 2000); J Lawrence, 'Class and gender in the making of
urban Toryism, 1880–1914', *English Historical Review* 108:428 (1993), 629; G Himmelfarb, 'The politics
of democracy: The English Reform Act of 1867' (1966) 6:1 *Journal of British Studies* 97; M Cowling,
1867: Disraeli, Gladstone and Revolution: The passing of the Second Reform Bill (Cambridge, Cambridge
University Press, 2005).
   [9] Sir Louis Blom-Cooper, quoted in Sir Antony Clarke, 'Constitutional justice: Lessons from Magna
Carta', lecture delivered at Royal Holloway, University of London, 16 June 2008 [accessed at http://www.
judiciary.gov.uk/Resources/JCO/Documents/Speeches/mor_magna_carta_lecture_june_08.pdf].

in a short space of time, rather than its quality. In the course of just over 14 years Britain gained fixed-term parliaments, the ancient office of Lord Chancellor was remoulded almost out of existence, the fusion of powers was weakened with the creation of an independent Supreme Court, the automatic right of hereditary peers to sit in the House of Lords was removed, devolution was granted to the nations of the United Kingdom (save, apart from regional devolution, for England), and the human rights of the British were set down in accordance with the principles of the European Convention and integrated into British law for the first time as statute.[10] This is far from an exhaustive list.

All these reforms had unintended, though not always unforeseen, consequences. The famed West Lothian Question had been imagined by Tam Dalyell on the floor of the House of Commons in 1977, yet remains at the heart of the Scottish devolution settlement as it has come to pass.[11] The Human Rights Act has caused conflict between the executive and the judiciary, and given its status as statute law, eternally vulnerable to the vicissitudes of parliamentary sovereignty, is hardly the entrenched Bill of Rights many had hoped for. Lastly, the removal of the hereditaries was supposed to usher in a new era of a more accountable and 'technocratic' House of Lords, but was instead followed seven years later by the cash-for-honours scandal relating to alleged abuses of life peerages.[12] Commentators have differed in their assessments of the impact of these reforms: Vernon Bogdanor has remarked that the changes in the settlement amount to a 'new British constitution'[13]; others have spoken of its 'rape'.[14] Lord Norton meanwhile has reflected that

> Tony Blair presided over major changes in the nation's constitutional arrangements. They did not go as far as initially envisaged in 1997 and they had a number of unintended consequences . . . They changed the contours of the British Constitution, but without any clear view of the type of Constitution that was being created for the United Kingdom.[15]

For some, the lack of a 'grand plan'[16] has had the consequence of a constitutional mess. With this in mind, it is salutary to examine how previous constitutional reforms have been viewed by historians. It is perhaps ironic that both Whig

---

[10] Though it is important to note, following Bogdanor, that this was not tantamount to the 'incorporation' of the European Convention into British law, as Parliament reserved the right to ignore the decisions of the courts (although in practice it has not done so). V Bogdanor, 'Constitutional reform' in A Seldon (ed), *The Blair Effect* (London, Little, Brown, 2001) 146.

[11] P Bowers, 'The West Lothian Question', Parliamentary Standard Note SN/PC/2586 (House of Commons Library), 18 January 2012, 4; T Dalyell, 'Devolution: The end of Britain', in K Sutherland (ed), *The Rape of the Constitution?* (London, Imprint Academic, 2000) 259.

[12] The specific complaint was made under the Honours (Prevention of Abuses Act) 1925 by Angus MacNeil, an SNP MP. Blair himself discusses cash-for-honours in his memoirs in T Blair, *A Journey* (London, Hutchinson, 2010) 605–09, whilst Andrew Rawnsley gives a significantly more interrogative account in A Rawnsley, *The End of the Party: The Rise and Fall of New Labour* (London, Allen Lane, 2010) 357–74.

[13] Bogdanor, above n 4.

[14] As in Sutherland (ed), above n 11.

[15] P Norton, 'The Constitution' in A Seldon (ed), *Blair's Britain, 1997–2007* (Cambridge, Cambridge University Press, 2007) 122.

[16] Bogdanor, above n 10, 150.

and Marxist historians viewed the constitutional reforms of the nineteenth century as responses to the possibility of revolution. Macaulay, both a practising Whig politician and an historian in the Whig tradition, placed revolution centre-stage in the parliamentary debates on the Great Reform Act itself:

> Every argument which would induce me to oppose universal suffrage induces me to support the plan which is now before us. I am opposed to universal suffrage, because I think that it would produce a destructive revolution. I support this plan, because I am sure that it is our best security against a revolution. The noble paymaster of the forces hinted, delicately indeed and remotely, at this subject. He spoke of the danger of disappointing the expectations of the nation . . .[17]

In the classic Whig view, the pent-up demand for greater political power was alleviated through a gradual enfranchisement of 'deserving' groups which had emerged during the Industrial Revolution and the concomitant remaking of British society. More recent authors, such as Dror Wahrman, have laid greater stress on the difficulties the political establishment faced on determining who the middle classes *were*, a problem which recurred in the build-up to the 1867 Act but which was acute before 1832 in light of fears of Jacobinism in Britain from the 1790s.[18] For EP Thompson[19] and the Marxist historians who followed him, constitutional reform (and, famously, Methodism) was a mechanism of social control which prevented the development of authentic class consciousness (Gareth Stedman Jones refined this model to include patriotism in his memorable study of working-class culture[20]). Eric Hobsbawm, meanwhile, lamented the abduction of the 'labour aristocracy', the vanguard who would have inspired the revolution if only the dastardly aristocrats and bourgeoisie had allowed history to take its supposedly-preordained course.[21]

The Marxist view, perhaps inevitably, tended towards the conspiracy theory of history; the Marxists correctly afforded primacy to politics as the ultimate factor in determining the shape of the constitutional settlement (if it was ever really 'settled'), but were misguided in their views of the problems reformers sought to solve. That in 1832 the aristocracy was concerned about the threat of popular dissent is undeniable, but the Great Reform Act was about more than this. Equally, to think in counterfactual terms, if popular dissent alone was the explanatory motive force for constitutional change then Chartism should not have failed in 1848 and the most recent reforms would never have taken place. In terms of explanatory forces, this chapter takes note of Maurice Cowling's famous injunction about the nature of high politics in the context of the 1867 Reform Act:

---

[17] Thomas Babington Macaulay, in the debate on the Reform Bill, HC Deb, 2 March 1831, vol 2, cols 1190–1220.

[18] D Wahrman, *Imagining the Middle Class: The political representation of class in Britain, c 1780–1840* (Cambridge, Cambridge University Press, 2005).

[19] EP Thompson, *The Making of the English Working Class* (Harmondsworth, Penguin, 1963).

[20] G Stedman Jones, 'Working class culture and working class politics in London, 1870–1900: Notes on the remaking of a working class', *Journal of Social History*, vol 7, no 4 (Summer 1974) 460.

[21] E Hobsbawm, 'The forward march of Labour halted?', *Marxism Today*, September 1978, 279.

The deployments of principle with which nostalgic publicists credit the parliaments of the 1860s will be seen not as examples of 'the classical parliamentary system', where 'the debates were public, the issues were known and the personal struggle for power could take place on the floor of the House or on the hustings' but as assertions of individual and party opinion and personal and party power in a battle – as private as it was public – not just to establish the best constitution but to decide who should establish it . . . The passage of the Reform Act of 1867 was effected in a context of public agitation: *it cannot be explained as a simple consequence.* Parliament in the sixties was not *afraid* of public agitation: nor was its action *determined* by it.[22]

What Cowling understood is that politics is fundamentally about *power*, and who wields it. As Tony Blair would later put it, 'the only purpose of being in politics is to make things happen'.[23] What mattered more than principle was 'parliamentary ambition'. This is the chief concern of practising politicians, as opposed to those of academic scholars who would impart to them more 'principled' motivations. This is not to say that ideology and principle do not have their part to play, merely to note that the contingent nature of the British Constitution owes as much, if not more, to the 'manoeuvres' of party-political animals as to values, traditions (real or invented) and precedent. By restoring the primacy of politics, the chaotic nature of the constitutional reform agenda under Blair and his successors becomes both more explicable and easier to locate in a tradition of constitutional evolution which has always had 'narrowly' political concerns to the fore.

Bearing this in mind, in order to offer a preliminary historical assessment of constitutional reform after 1997, it is necessary to consider the following questions. First, did constitutional reform after 1997 succeed in redistributing power and re-engaging the public with the political process, thus changing the relationship between State and citizen, as Mandelson argued for in 1996? Secondly, did constitutional reform in this period improve the quality of government? Lastly, was constitutional reform in this period coherent? There are also more basic historical questions of continuity, change and causality – did constitutional reform in this period shape events, or was it merely an expression of ephemeral political desires? It does not betray too much of what follows to note that the answer to that last question is pregnant with implications for the answers to the others.

---

[22] Cowling, above n 8, 3 (first emphasis added, later emphases Cowling's). There has been a recent revival in the implications of Cowling's work for the writing of political history, as evidenced in R Crowcroft, SJD Green and R Whiting (eds), *The Philosophy, Politics and Religion of British Democracy: Maurice Cowling and Conservatism* (London, IB Tauris, 2010); R Crowcroft, 'Maurice Cowling and the writing of British political history' (2008) 22:2 *Contemporary British History* 279; DM Craig, '"High politics" and the "new political history"' (2010) 53:2 *Historical Journal* 453. Mike Finn would like to note his thanks to Hannah Todd of Peterhouse, Cambridge, for several discussions on the work of Cowling.

[23] Blair, quoted in A Rawnsley, *Servants of the People: The Inside Story of New Labour*, 2nd edn (London, Penguin, 2001) 4.

II. THE POLITICS OF CONSTITUTIONAL REFORM:
DEVOLUTION AND THE LORDS

Constitutional reform played a significant role in the 1997 Labour manifesto purely because of political necessity. The paranoia of those at the top of the Labour leadership – memorably chronicled by Andrew Rawnsley – and the fear of another 'near-miss' akin to that of 1992, this time resulting in a hung Parliament rather than outright defeat, were key spurs to cooperation with the Liberal Democrats.[24] It was this, in addition to a rhetorical desire to fulfil John Smith's legacy on devolution,[25] which fuelled, in Andrew Gamble's words, 'the most far-reaching programme of constitutional reform since 1832'.[26] Though political dynamics were critical, the desire to deliver on Smith's devolution pledges was a real motive force. Smith had served as devolution minister in the Callaghan Governments during the later 1970s, and was, in Iain McLean's view, one of the few Labour figures who 'truly believed in devolution, in and for itself'.[27] His leadership of the Labour Party from 1992–94 dovetailed with the proceedings of the Scottish Constitutional Convention, which he had supported.[28] It was Smith who declared devolution 'the settled will of the Scottish people,' and who referred to it consistently as 'unfinished business'.[29] After his death, his widow Elizabeth would continue to campaign for devolution as her husband's constitutional legacy. This enabled the issue to be seen as a Labour one, and allowed Blair to portray the implementation of the new devolution agenda as a continuity between his leadership and the Smith years.[30]

Liberal objectives were fundamentally dissimilar to those of the Labour Party, though with the advent of Blairism they found – initially – more congenial stablemates there than had been the case for decades. Through Roy Jenkins, who served as Blair's mentor for a period, there was a direct route to the soon-to-be Prime Minister,[31] and Derry Irvine, Blair's Lord Chancellor, echoed Liberal priorities with regard to constitutional reform.[32] Blair would appoint Jenkins to chair a commission on electoral reform for Westminster once Labour was in power.[33]

As Blair saw it, constitutional reform was an area where a political compromise could be hatched which would have no impact on the Labour Party's core social

---

[24]   *Ibid*, 1.

[25]   Dalyell, above n 11, 257–58.

[26]   A Gamble, 'Remaking the constitution', in P Dunleavy et al (eds), *Developments in British Politics 7* (London, PalgraveMacmillan, 2003), 18 For the Smith legacy in constitutional reform, see A Seldon, *Blair* (London, Free Press, 2005) 207–09.

[27]   I McLean, 'The national question' in Seldon (ed), above n 15, 488.

[28]   N McGarvey, above n 7, 25–26.

[29]   *Ibid*, 25.

[30]   As in his speech at Millbank on 12 May 1999: *BBC News*, 'Blair's tribute to John Smith', Wednesday, 12 May 1999, <http://news.bbc.co.uk/1/hi/uk_politics/341901.stm>, accessed on 19 July 2012.

[31]   Seldon, above n 26, 265–77.

[32]   *Ibid*, 207.

[33]   *Ibid*, 274.

agenda, and which could effectively be spun as part of his plans for the modernisation of Britain. In this Blair was a Labour leader in the tradition of Harold Wilson or Hugh Gaitskell, forever lamenting the backwardness of his own country through tilting at ideological windmills, often of little real consequence.[34] For Blair himself, constitutional reform was and remained a low priority, save for when key votes arose in the House of Commons or when it allowed him to play the role of statesman, as with the Belfast Agreement of 1998. Gamble notes that Blair 'rarely mentioned constitutional reforms . . . and [up to 2003] has never devoted a whole speech to the subject. The major speech on the Constitution planned for the first term was shelved.'[35]

From the Liberal perspective, this was no bad thing, as it allowed them to make the intellectual running on any proposed changes. Blair – initially – worked well with Ashdown, both personally and through the mechanism of the Joint Consultative Committee the two had constructed. The Liberal Party, even before the foundation of the Liberal Democrats in 1988, had long been supporters of a federal United Kingdom. There were self-serving reasons for this; the Liberals, after their annihilation in 1929, retained some influence in the Celtic fringe and sought to consolidate it against the ambitions of Westminster – and where possible, use it as a springboard for future success at general elections. The prospect of devolution was pregnant with possibilities for them, not least that were alternative electoral systems employed, the Liberals might enjoy a measure of real power. This was ultimately the case, as the Liberal Democrats played a key role in the first Scottish Governments and the administrations in the Welsh Assembly.[36] It was also felt that the success of alternative electoral systems in the devolved assemblies might provide support for a future campaign advocating the adoption of some form of proportional representation at Westminster, the 'game-changer' that would, in theory, restore the Liberal Democrats' ability to compete as a truly national political force for the first time in 70 years. This was aside from the fact that for much of the first year of Blair's tenure in office, Ashdown allowed himself to be deluded into thinking that the new Prime Minister would follow through on his pledge to bring Liberal Democrats into government.[37]

Devolution also had roots in Labour politics, though – aside from the ghost of Smith – these were more tenuous. To an extent, the spectre of devolution haunted Labour – it had after all been the issue which indirectly triggered the fall of the Callaghan Government in 1979.[38] Devolution also seemed inimical to any kind of democratic socialism, as Bogdanor notes, one Labour MP in the 1970s remarking

---

[34] As in T Blair, *New Britain: My Vision of a Young Country* (London, Fourth Estate, 1996).

[35] Gamble, above n 26, 18.

[36] M Laffin, 'Coalition Formation and Centre-Periphery Relations in a National Political Party: The Liberal Democrats in a Devolved Britain', ESRC Devolution and Constitutional Change Working Paper (2005).

[37] Rawnsley, above n 23, 192–99. That it was a serious possibility is reinforced by Alastair Campbell's diary entry for 5 October 1997: 'He was now moving towards an April reshuffle in which he would like to bring two Liberals into the Cabinet'. A Campbell, *The Blair Years* (London, Hutchinson, 2007) 249.

[38] C Pilkington, *Devolution in Britain Today* (Manchester, Manchester University Press, 2002) 64.

that 'if comprehensive education is right in Glasgow, it is right in the south of England'.[39] It was testament to Blair's own views on New Labour's policy agenda that he did not consider this any sort of problem. But for others, socialism, whether of the social democratic or democratic socialist bent, did not admit national divides: 'concessions to nationalism would threaten Labour's economic and also its social philosophy'.[40] In the minds of some on the Labour benches, there was always the danger that devolution would be little more than an apologia for continuing inequalities across British society. The proposals for devolution in the 1970s had been a simple political response to the rise of the Scottish National Party, and were designed to attenuate that threat in Labour's heartlands.[41]

The 1997 Labour manifesto promised referendums on devolved assemblies in Scotland and Wales, with the ultimate objective of 'strengthening the Union':

> Subsidiarity is as sound a principle in Britain as it is in Europe. Our proposal is for devolution not federation. A sovereign Westminster Parliament will devolve power to Scotland and Wales. The Union will be strengthened and the threat of separatism removed.[42]

In contrast to the protracted devolution debates of the 1970s, devolution legislation establishing the representative assemblies went through the Commons quickly and straightforwardly, aided by Blair's 179 majority, following the positive outcomes to the promised referendums.[43] Dalyell remarked ruefully that the colossal scale of Blair's landslide victory effectively rendered Commons scrutiny pointless (a charge that would be repeated by others with respect to other legislation later in Blair's tenure): for MPs in such a situation, 'there was little or nothing they could do'.[44] The manifesto also pledged to restore city-wide government in London.[45] The assemblies eventually established, in Scotland, Wales, Northern Ireland and London, all featured some element of proportional representation. In Scotland, Wales and London, the electoral system chosen was the Additional Member System (AMS), which sought to satisfy the competing demands of retaining a constituency link and the need for a more equitable distribution of representation. One group of members is elected for constituencies, others through regional top-up lists. The influence of the Liberal Democrats here was particularly telling. In November 1995, Ashdown noted in his diary a conversation with Blair on a flight from Israel, returning from Yitzhak Rabin's funeral, which is worth quoting at some length:

> There was no way he could get devolution legislation through the Lords without reducing the number of MPs after devolution. And since Scotland was overwhelmingly

---

[39] Bogdanor, above n 10, 153.

[40] V Bogdanor, *Devolution in the United Kingdom* (Oxford, OPUS, 1999) 170.

[41] Pilkington, above n 38, 59–64.

[42] Labour Party Manifesto 1997, in I Dale (ed), *Labour Party General Election Manifestos, 1900–1997* (London, Routledge, 2000) 375ff.

[43] Dalyell, above n 11, 259.

[44] *Ibid.*

[45] Labour Party Manifesto 1997, above n 42, 376.

Labour this would in future reduce Labour's ability to get a majority. But again, PR and a relationship with us would solve the problem.

He then asked me, rather pointedly, 'What system [for elections] do you want?'

I told him that there were only two systems that were acceptable. The system that George Robertson and Jim Wallace had agreed upon in the Scottish convention (Alternative Vote Plus). We were not at all keen on this. It might be OK for Scotland, but for the UK, Single Transferable Vote (STV) was best. He agreed with me that if we had Proportional Representation, the Tories would break up . . .[46]

Ultimately AMS was preferred, but there was never any question that some proportional element would be included; in May 1995, at a meeting at Derry Irvine's house, Robin Cook confirmed to Ashdown in the presence of Blair that 'Labour's position was that there would be PR for Europe, PR for regional government, PR for the Scottish and Welsh assemblies'. Significantly, Blair noted that he was 'unpersuaded' on the question of PR for Westminster.[47] In Northern Ireland, the fully-proportional Single Transferable Vote (STV) was opted for, on the pragmatic grounds that this would enforce coalition between the parties, and thus foster rapprochement and power-sharing between the unionist and nationalist communities.

The first elections in 1999 returned a Labour–Liberal Democrat coalition in Scotland, with devolution architect Donald Dewar as First Minister. In Wales, again a Labour–Liberal Democrat coalition was the result – although the strong showing of Plaid Cymru, the second party (and excluded from government) alarmed some unionists. Elections continued in a pattern of coalition until a significant breakthrough in 2007, when the Scottish National Party formed a minority Government in Holyrood, with a pledge to bring forward a referendum on Scottish independence. Four years later, they achieved the rare feat of a majority Government under AMS. It was in this climate that serious concern began to be felt by the new coalition Government at Westminster that Scotland might secede. This in turn led to a political contest between Alex Salmond and David Cameron, with the lowest stakes for the former being the offer of 'devo-max', still greater power for the devolved executive in Scotland.

The experience of Scotland is significant in any historical verdict on constitutional change. For the opening eight years of its existence, proceedings in the Scottish Parliament echoed those of Westminster. This was a matter of both style and substance. At the time of its foundation, it was the 'frequently expressed . . . hope that [the Scottish Parliament] would be a new type of institution, with a new approach to the way that the business of government is carried on'.[48] The Scottish legislature nonetheless drew inspiration from the House of Commons in several respects – ministerial questions, committee work and aspects of the legislative

[46] Paddy Ashdown, diary entry for 6 November 1995 in P Ashdown, *The Ashdown Diaries, vol I, 1988–1999* (London, Allen Lane, 2001) 353.

[47] *Ibid*, diary entry for 3 May 1995, 312–13.

[48] J McFadden and M Lazarowicz, *The Scottish Parliament* (London and Edinburgh, LexisNexis, 2002) 38.

process, if not the seating plan.[49] More significant in the short term was the reality of Labour-led government; conflicts with the metropolis were few and far between during the first two Scottish Governments – for the simple reason that Labour First Ministers and Labour Prime Ministers were unlikely to come to blows.[50] Scrutiny of the executive was no better in Holyrood than Westminster until the advent of minority government – McGarvey remarking bluntly that 'despite a much slimmer parliamentary majority the McConnell administration suffered fewer defeats than the Blair administration!'[51] During the period of minority government, it was possible for an alliance of opposition parties to get their way – as with the establishment of the Calman Commission in 2007, which would, ironically, ultimately provide a blueprint for 'devo-max' for an SNP majority administration to negotiate over – the 2011 SNP majority saw the restoration of the *status quo ante*.

The Scottish people, meanwhile, seemed unmoved. Although part of the New Labour agenda to modernise politics, and though the referendum on devolution had attracted a turnout of 60 per cent, no Scottish parliamentary election subsequently managed this level of participation, reaching a low of 49.4 per cent in the second election in 2003.[52] The situation in Wales was worse, with the turnout for the referendum barely breaking 50 per cent and the proportion in favour only just managing the same feat. This lack of legitimacy was further reflected – or perhaps fostered in the first place – by the lack of actual power granted to the Welsh Assembly – no tax-varying powers were ever mooted here. The crisis of legitimacy in Wales only became worse with the denouement of 2003, when only 38 per cent of voters bothered to cast their ballots.[53] For many in Wales, and in Scotland, it appeared as though they believed – as the parties' own leaderships did – that the real action remained in Westminster. In Alan Trench's words,

> devolved elections are indeed seen as 'second-order' elections by the electorate in general. They may elect a government, but not *the* Government. That in turn suggests that the electorate do not see enough as being at stake in the devolved elections (whether in terms of the importance of the institutions elected or the likelihood of the election result leading to change in composition of the government) to justify people turning out to vote. This conclusion supports a broader one drawn by Curtice . . . that devolution has not succeeded – or not yet succeeded – in reconnecting voters with government.[54]

The retention of the Sewel motion – whereby Scottish affairs can be referred to Westminster legislation at the instigation of Holyrood – and the constitutional device that the United Kingdom Parliament remains sovereign in Scotland and Wales make that perception a legal fact.

---

[49]   *Ibid.*

[50]   McGarvey, above n 7, 30-33.

[51]   *Ibid*, 31.

[52]   The Electoral Commission, *Scottish Elections 2003* (London, Election Commission, 2003) 5.

[53]   The Electoral Commission, *The National Assembly for Wales Elections 2007* (London, Electoral Commission, 2007). Historical figure for 2003 is given *ibid* at 4.

[54]   A Trench, 'Introduction: Has devolution made a difference?', in A Trench (ed), *The State of the Nations 2004* (London, Imprint Academic, 2004) 3 (original emphasis).

In terms of the future, the potential breakup of the Union has now become a real, if unlikely, possibility. Much will depend on the arguments to come before the independence referendum is put before the Scottish people in the latter stages of the current Scottish parliamentary session. False moves from the Westminster Government and independence becomes more than a theoretical possibility. The practical political impact of genuine differences in public spending and public services – not least care provision and tuition fees arrangements in Scotland – have fostered resentment in England, and created another divisive force in the politics of the United Kingdom. In this sense, constitutional reform in the shape of devolution has had spectacular unintended consequences, though not wholly unforeseen ones.[55]

Northern Ireland, after a series of hiatuses, finally delivered a consistently-functioning power-sharing executive from 2007, with Peter Robinson of the Democratic Unionist Party as First Minister and Martin McGuinness of Sinn Fein as his deputy. The principal unionist party which delivered the Good Friday Agreement, the Ulster Unionists – then led by David Trimble, who received the Nobel Peace Prize for his endeavours – was severely damaged by the post-devolution settlement, now retaining only 15 seats in the Assembly and none at Westminster. Trimble himself defected to the Conservative Party, for whom he now sits in the House of Lords. Northern Ireland is often seen as at the margins of constitutional reform in the United Kingdom for a number of reasons, not least because in the area of devolution it was ahead of the rest in some respects, having had a devolved assembly from the 1920s until the Troubles forced Stormont's suspension in 1972. Its original devolved parliament – notoriously a 'Protestant parliament for a Protestant people' – and the makeup of its successor reinforce the idea that Northern Ireland is a *sui generis* case, outside the mainstream of constitutional reform in the rest of the United Kingdom. Whilst this is surely true, and generalised assessments of constitutional reform must regard it thus, it is worth noting that the use of constitutional machinery to engineer a peace settlement in the Province may yet go down to posterity as the greatest achievement of the Blair era, building as it did on the ground laid by John Major's Government.[56] London meanwhile was intended to be the precursor to greater regional government, a project which stalled on the rejection of the proposed assembly for the North East in the referendum of 2004.[57]

Another principal achievement of Blair's first term was House of Lords reform. This was also a prospect which appealed to Liberals, partly due to the inbuilt Conservative majority amongst the hereditaries but also as 'backdoor' reform to the Westminster electoral system, partly through their agenda of greater federalism:

On the few occasions federalism has been considered seriously by governments or by Royal Commissions, it has been dismissed. The 1973 Kilbrandon Commission on the Constitution, for instance, dismissed federalism as a viable model. Before, and since, the

---

[55] Dalyell, above n 11.

[56] A Seldon, *Major: A political life* (London, Weidenfeld & Nicolson, 1997) 425–30.

[57] *BBC News*, 'North East votes "no" to assembly', 5 November 2004, <http://news.bbc.co.uk/1/hi/uk_politics/3984387.stm>, accessed on 9 July 2012.

Kilbrandon Commission, the Liberal Democrat Party has been the most pro-federalist political party in Britain. Liberal Democrat policies have continually advocated implementing . . . measures . . . such as turning the House of Lords into an 'elected second chamber capable of representing the nations and regions of the UK.'[58]

This proposal was to resurface later. Federalism more broadly would be reaffirmed by the Steel Commission as Liberal Democrat policy in 2006, following the breakdown in Labour–Liberal Democrat cooperation under Charles Kennedy.[59] Labour for their part had explicitly rejected federalism or 'federation' in the 1997 manifesto, but Liberal Democrat proposals for the Lords consistently emphasised a regional element and proportional representation.[60]

The scheme eventually embarked upon by Labour in the shape of the House of Lords Act 1999 was considerably less ambitious. Following a series of negotiations with relevant parties in the Lords, including Viscount Cranborne (ultimately dismissed by William Hague for going beyond his brief), the Conservative leader in that House, the Labour Government proposed 'stage one' reform – the removal of the right to sit in the House of Lords for all but 92 hereditary peers.[61] This did not introduce a system of election, but essentially reduced the chamber to the patronage of the Prime Minister and the recommendations of opposition leaders through the life peerages system. Though the House of Lords Appointments Commission was established in 2000, with the scope to nominate 'people's peers', this did not alter the perceptions that the Lords was still a retirement home for superannuated politicians or a paid vacation for prominent party donors. It was the objection of the Appointments Commission to the then Prime Minister's nomination of three Labour donors to peerages which triggered the cash-for-honours scandal in 2006.

There is a legitimate question as to whether 'stage one' reform made the Lords more effective in its work. Through Blair's second term it remained the principal source of opposition to his agenda, especially when contrasted with the supine House of Commons. Notwithstanding Philip Cowley's work on rebellions in the 2001–05 Parliament, it remains the case that Blair did not lose a single Commons vote during that period.[62] At the same time, it was the House of Lords (and the judiciary, of which more later) which offered the most significant opposition, especially in relation to civil liberties issues – increasingly to the fore following both the passage of the Human Rights Act in 1998 and the advent of international terrorism after 11 September 2001.[63] As Cowley notes, there was a spectacular change in attitude on the part of the Lords following 'stage one' reform:

---

[58] R Deacon and A Sandry, *Devolution in the United Kingdom* (Edinburgh, Edinburgh University Press, 2007) 200.

[59] The Steel Commission, *Moving to Federalism: A new settlement for Scotland* (London, Liberal Democrats, 2006).

[60] S Hughes, 'Democracy: Towards a new constitutional settlement' in J Astle, D Laws, P Marshall and A Murray (eds), *Britain After Blair: A Liberal Agenda* (London, Profile, 2007) 277.

[61] Rawnsley, above n 23, 201–03.

[62] P Cowley, *The Rebels: How Blair mislaid his majority* (London, Politico's, 2005).

[63] Most notably in the debates over the Prevention of Terrorism Act 2005, where the Lords engaged in all-night sittings in an attempt to wrest more judicial oversight for the Government's proposed scheme of control orders.

The pre-reform House of Lords – conscious that its legitimacy was limited by the presence of so many hereditary peers – frequently practiced [*sic*] a self-denying ordinance pulling back from many confrontations with the government. But with the hereditaries largely gone, those peers that remain see themselves as more legitimate and have become more assertive than before. If the government hoped it had created a poodle of an upper chamber, then it was much mistaken. The full consequences of reform became clear during the second Blair term . . . the 2001–5 Parliament saw the government defeated on 245 separate occasions.[64]

A number of plans put forward for 'stage two' reform, notably the recommendations of the Wakeham Commission, came to naught.[65] After the 2001 election, Robin Cook – freshly demoted from the Foreign Office – found himself handed the poisoned chalice of further Lords reform, and pursued the agenda with little success, culminating in a series of Parliamentary defeats – which Cook implied had been partly inspired by Blair himself – in 2003.[66] To return to Cowling, 'stage two' occupied little concern in Blair's mind simply because it did not benefit him to worry about it – 'stage one' had removed the Conservative majority and left him with greater freedom of action than previously. To endorse an elected house would culminate in a challenge to his own supremacy in the Commons, and that was self-defeating. On Lords reform – as on so many other issues – the British Constitution remains, as Simon Hughes has lamented, in 'limbo, somewhere between the old system and something new'.[67]

III. RIGHTS AND LIBERTIES

Few aspects of the Blair Government's legacy on constitutional reform have excited as much controversy as the Human Rights Act 1998. Much has been made of Blair's electoral commitment to 'bring rights home', to end the constant stream of cases migrating from the British judicial system to the purview of the European Court of Human Rights in Strasbourg.[68] The Human Rights Act sought to establish certain aspects of the European Convention on Human Rights in British law, whilst also providing judicial mechanisms for declaring statute law incompatible with it, and providing ministers with a fast-track system to take appropriate remedial action.[69] This would have the dual benefits of ending the legal logjam to

[64]   P Cowley and M Stuart, 'Parliament' in Seldon and Kavanagh (eds), above n 9, 38.
[65]   Royal Commission on the Reform of the House of Lords, *A House for the Future*, Cmnd 4534 (London, HMSO, 2000). Rentoul described Wakeham as an 'intellectually shabby attempt to provide what the Prime Minister wanted': Rentoul, above n 3, 453.
[66]   R Cook, *The Point of Departure* (London, Simon & Schuster, 2005) 278–79.
[67]   Hughes, above n 60, 271.
[68]   S Chakrabarti, H Kennedy, F Klug, M McWilliams and A Miller, *Common Sense: Reflections on the Human Rights Act* (London, Liberty, 2010). It should be noted that this was not the sole cause – Klug goes so far as to argue this is over-emphasised and that political agitation outside Parliament was the primary factor in the development of the Act (*ibid*, 10).
[69]   H Barnett, *Britain Unwrapped: Government and constitution explained* (Harmondsworth, Penguin, 2002) 304–50.

Europe, and providing something approximating to a British Bill of Rights, a cause célèbre of many on the British left.[70]

The key problem which prompted resistance was, as Rodney Brazier has noted, the issue of entrenchment[71]. An entrenched Bill of Rights, akin to that of the United States, is incompatible with the fundamental principle of the British Constitution – parliamentary sovereignty. This principle – that 'what the Queen in Parliament enacts is law'[72] – and that no other body can possess such sovereignty in the UK, does not brook excessive intervention by judges. Although judges can and do make law through the common-law tradition, they have not historically been expected to have the power to challenge statute law directly. Whereas US Supreme Court justices may strike acts of Congress down with immediate effect, this was never on the cards in Britain. With this in mind, the protection of rights was both *de facto* and *de jure* weaker in Britain than on the other side of the Atlantic:

> One of the Labour Party's reasons for its former policy of spurning . . . the adoption of a new Bill of Rights . . . was that no such document could be entrenched against amendment or repeal . . . Every first-year law student knows what Dicey said about Parliamentary sovereignty: that Parliament can make or unmake any law whatever. So how would rights in a new declaration of rights be any better protected against the rapacity of elective dictatorship, given that fresh legislation could encroach on the rights declared in it? The Government could easily get Parliament to amend, or entirely repeal, any inconvenient provisions with the assistance of the Whips . . .[73]

Brazier ultimately dismisses the problem of entrenchment as a 'red herring', noting a number of mechanisms by which entrenchment could be achieved, but it was a real question in the minds of policymakers.[74] For once, the lack of provision for entrenchment in the Human Rights Act was, as Louis Blom-Cooper notes, by design; Blom-Cooper argues that the mechanism of the declaration of incompatibility, whereby judges could rule UK statute in breach of the European Convention (but not strike it down) was an

> ingenious device to preserve parliamentary sovereignty, and thereby to stop short of establishing a constitutional court with a power to strike down unconstitutional legislation. The move obviates the need for a written constitution or even a Bill of Rights in which sovereignty is wrested from the executive and legislature and resides ultimately in unelected judges.[75]

Despite Blom-Cooper's enthusiasm for the peculiarly British compromises of the Act, it is not at all clear that it has pleased either liberals or conservatives broadly

---

[70]   Klug, in Chakrabarti *et al*, above n 68, 9–14.

[71]   R Brazier, *Constitutional Reform: Reshaping the British Political System* (Oxford, Oxford University Press, 2008) 129–34.

[72]   Bogdanor, above n 4, xii.

[73]   Brazier, above n 71, 129–30.

[74]   *Ibid*, 130–31.

[75]   L Blom-Cooper, 'Government and the judiciary', in A Seldon and D Kavanagh (eds), *The Blair Effect, 2001–5* (Cambridge, Cambridge University Press, 2005) 238.

defined, and it is subject to the threat of repeal. Blom-Cooper's argument that repeal is 'unthinkable (if only because it would mean leaving the Council of Europe)' does not hold water; repealing the Human Rights Act would simply return the UK judiciary to the *status quo ante* where British citizens and others were compelled to pursue cases to Strasbourg for satisfaction.[76] Hilaire Barnett for her part argues that the Act has failed even in terms of its stated objective of 'bringing rights home', arguing instead that it is unduly difficult for the average complainant to bring suit under its provisions:

> The restriction to direct victims of the unlawful act is contentious: it places the whole burden of commencing proceedings, and the potential cost of proceedings, on the shoulders of the individual, and excludes the possibility of actions being brought by an organization representing the interests of a defined section of the population equally affected by the act in question. Coupled with the cost of litigation, the limitations on legal aid, and the need to pursue the action to the level of High Court or above for a declaration of incompatibility to be granted, this exclusion places the individual in a disproportionately disadvantageous position *vis-à-vis* the public authority in question.[77]

This has not been the chief source of controversy; rather, tabloid attention has focused on the extent to which the Human Rights Act has, it is argued, protected the rights of terrorists and terrorist suspects (who in the mind of many journalists, if not the law, are one and the same thing). The Belmarsh case of 2004, where the Law Lords ruled that indefinite detention of foreign terrorist suspects without trial was unlawful, occasioned much criticism that the judiciary was soft on terrorists.[78] The subsequent Afghan hijackers case in 2006, where the courts ruled that returning the hijackers to Afghanistan would breach their human rights, further exacerbated the criticism and led to the Leader of the Opposition, David Cameron, calling for a review of the Human Rights Act, a process which led to the ultimate Conservative commitment to replace it with a British Bill of Rights.[79] That this has been stymied both by coalition politics and the legal ramifications does not alter the fact that human rights are once again up for grabs.

The Human Rights Act was only one symptom of the changed place of the judiciary, who became increasingly assertive during the Blair years and, at times, took on the character of an official opposition – leading to sharp confrontations between the then Home Secretary David Blunkett and the Lord Chief Justice.[80] The rise of judicial review had been a symptom of changing legal practice in the latter part of the twentieth century, and the Blair Government's ultimate decision to opt for a UK Supreme Court – formally to end the fusion of powers between the legislature and the judiciary – was both welcome and unsurprising in legal circles.[81]

---

[76] *Ibid*, 239.

[77] Barnett, above n 69, 340–41.

[78] *A and others v Secretary of State for the Home Department* [2004] UKHL 56.

[79] 'From hijacker to airport cleaner', *Sun*, 16 May 2008, is typical of the coverage which followed the decision. The Conservative policy was stated clearly in *An Invitation to Join the Government of Britain: The Conservative Party General Election Manifesto 2010* (London, Conservative Party, 2010) 79.

[80] Blom-Cooper refers to the exchanges as 'Blunkett's blunderbusses': Blom-Cooper, above n 9, 251ff.

[81] *Ibid*, 241–43.

The Human Rights Act itself has, in Bogdanor's view, become the heart of the new British Constitution he identifies. For Bogdanor, even though it is merely a piece of statute law, it is unlike any other – it has taken on the characteristics and garb of 'fundamental law'.[82] It enshrines the 'ideological force' of 'liberal constitutionalism' at the heart of the British political system.[83] And yet, at the beginning of the twenty-first century, with the gradual erosion of freedom of speech through anti-terror legislation, with restrictions on the right to jury trial and with Governments using any statutory mechanism necessary to escape from the proscriptions of the Act (including discussing its ultimate repeal), many in the British public began to fear that the Human Rights Act represented inadequate protection for their rights, whatever real power it had granted to judges.[84] Much of this illustrated the continuing salience of the concept of parliamentary sovereignty and, in an era of collapsing turnout, the issue of an increasingly illegitimate executive's domination of it.

IV. THE ROAD NOT TRAVELLED

Constitutional reforms, since 1997, together with Britain's membership of the European Union, have served to provide us with a new British constitution . . . The radicalism of the reforms should not be underestimated, nor the challenge they offer to traditional assumptions about the constitution. These assumptions, and in particular the sovereignty of Parliament, have been crucially, and almost certainly, permanently undermined . . .[85]

There is something approaching a consensus now that the constitutional reforms which took place after 1997 have, in Vernon Bogdanor's phrase, amounted to a 'new British constitution'; a consensus exemplified in the sudden outpouring of monographs on the new *status quo*.[86] For reasons which are obvious, historians have had little to say on the issue. Much of the scholarship has been analytical and has shied away from evaluation in terms of success or failure, and rightly so – such evaluation requires a thorough assessment of aims and intentions. Lacking access to the traditional tools of historical scholarship (namely, archival sources), such evaluation is necessarily risky.

Nonetheless, published sources abound for the period after 1997, and these must be the principal resources used by the contemporary historian. To quote (appropriately) Bogdanor, 'it is a modern historian's delusion that what is unpublished is, by definition, more important than what has been published'.[87] Constitutional reform,

---

[82] Bogdanor, above n 4, 276.
[83] *Ibid.*
[84] The rise of what became dubbed as a 'surveillance society' in the aftermath of 9/11 was documented in C Atkins, S Bee and F Button, *Taking Liberties* (London, Revolver Books, 2007).
[85] Bogdanor, above n 4, 271.
[86] Prominent examples include Bogdanor, *The New British Constitution* (above n 4), Brazier, *Constitutional Reform* (above n 71) and A King, *The British Constitution* (Oxford, Oxford University Press, 2007).
[87] V Bogdanor, 'How they stopped the revolution', *Daily Telegraph*, 24 November 2003.

it has been argued here, far from being seen as an unvarnished success on the part of the Blair Governments and their successors, may actually come to be seen by historians as a failure – if it is regarded as a serious programme pursued for principled ends. To this extent, historical judgement is in the eye of the beholder; to approach constitutional reform after 1997 from the perspective of a latter-day Cowling would be to assess it as a narrowly-political success. Constitutional reform worked for Blair, and for successive politicians such as Brown, Cameron and Clegg who wished to espouse progressive values whilst pursuing other policies which would inevitably undermine their status in the eyes of progressives. However, the measure of the substance of constitutional reform is to be found in terms of the criteria used in the opening of this chapter; the distribution of power. Constitutional reform did, in practical terms, redistribute power – but Bogdanor is right to note that it did so only between elites.[88] Though in a legal sense parliamentary sovereignty was not undermined by the new authority (not to be confused with power) granted to the devolved assemblies and the UK Supreme Court, in a practical sense it was. Devolution in the United Kingdom did not halt the forward march of nationalism, except perhaps in Wales (where it was weaker to begin with). This meant that even under a Conservative-led Government after 2010, the UK executive was reluctant to engage in open warfare with the Scottish Government for fear of strengthening, rather than weakening, the position of the SNP. Even against Tory backbenchers' distaste for the courting of Alex Salmond and the much-hyped differences in funding between Scottish public services and those in England, the British Government cannot risk a direct confrontation for fear of consequences for the Union. This was very much an unintended consequence of devolution.

Equally, the arrival of the Human Rights Act and the establishment of the UK Supreme Court amounted to more than simply 'rearranging the furniture'.[89] As has been shown, the 1998 Act emboldened judges and gave them a practical 'weapon' to use against the executive.[90] But the Act, and the debate over a British Bill of Rights, also illustrates the extent to which power has *not* shifted. In 2001, Vernon Bogdanor was able to refer to the potential repeal of the Human Rights Act as only 'theoretical'; today it is a commitment of one of the political parties currently in government.[91] As we have seen, one thing both parties now in government agreed on in the build-up to the 2010 General Election was the need for a British Bill of Rights. What form that would take, and what it would imply for the Human Rights Act, was, however, the subject of intense disagreement.[92] Whilst the Human Rights Act handed the judiciary new mechanisms with which to confront the executive, it did not materially alter the pattern of increasing judicial activism. Judicial review had already been on the increase before the Blair

---

[88] Bogdanor, above n 4, 297.
[89] To paraphrase one of Vernon Bogdanor's characteristic metaphors.
[90] Bogdanor, above n 10.
[91] *Ibid.*
[92] Klug, in Chakrabarti *et al*, above n 68, 14–18.

Government took office, rising from 491 cases in 1980 to nearly 4,000 in 1996.[93] Without doubt, the Supreme Court and the changed mechanisms for the appointment of judges offer the possibility of greater judicial independence in future, and greater transparency in the adjudication of the law. However, it is testament to the continuing vitality of parliamentary sovereignty that confirmation hearings for Supreme Court justices (as they now styled) have been mooted.[94] Governments are not afraid to take on judges, and so the legacy of the Blair years may be an increasing willingness to remake the judiciary as necessary rather than to defer to its independence. It is in this light that trial by jury continues to be restricted[95], and the actions of individual judges are called into question.

Entrenched, emphatic, real constitutional change of substance – in terms of the dispersal of power – could have taken place after 1997. To the extent that it did, jeopardising the future of the Union in the form of devolution to Scotland, the consequences were unintended. The reality was that for successive Prime Ministers, most notably Tony Blair, constitutional reform – whatever its volume – was a low priority. As Anthony Seldon has shown, it was never top of the agenda:

> Blair was no more interested in constitutional reform than in 'management'. Neither set him alight . . . Blair's own attitude was not encouraging. 'He was bored absolutely rigid by it,' said one aide. 'Supremely uninterested in the details' said a senior official.[96]

What, then, is the lasting legacy of constitutional reform? What, then, will be the historians' perspective decades from now? It is our belief that the pursuit of contemporary history – as distinct from journalism – can offer insights in line with the more traditional aspirations of the discipline. Returning to the rhetorical questions which opened this chapter, the distribution of power was not significantly altered by what took place after 1997. As noted above, power was moved around between elites, but it was not shared with the masses. Nor did the quality of government improve; despite the Blair agenda of openness and transparency, abuse of executive power reached epic levels, culminating in illegal warfare, involvement in rendition and the UK Government's complicity in torture overseas. Key to this was a failure to grasp the nettle of the reform of Parliament beyond House of Lords 'stage one'; Robin Cook was willing to take on the issue of House of Commons reform after 2001 but was sidelined by Blair.[97] Parliament remained the executive's lapdog; the whipped votes over the Iraq War in 2003 occasioned significant rebellions but the vote was passed, and, as Christopher Hill notes, the uncritical, careerist way in which much of the House of Commons viewed the decision to put British lives at risk (not to mention Iraqi ones) was

---

[93] BBC, 'The rise and rise of judicial review', 11 March 2008, <http://news.bbc.co.uk/1/hi/programmes/law_in_action/7289243.stm>, accessed at 19 July 2012.

[94] J Grant, 'A law unto themselves', *Prospect* (May 2011).

[95] O Boycott, 'Government considers "cutting defendant rights to jury trial"', *Guardian*, 12 January 2012.

[96] A Seldon, *Blair Unbound* (London, Simon & Schuster, 2007) 202.

[97] P Norton, 'Parliament' in Seldon and Kavanagh (eds), above n 9, 21–22.

cavalier in the extreme.[98] The Iraq debates also pointed up the weaknesses of the committee system; again Hill points out that the Foreign Affairs Select Committee was wholly ineffective in challenging the bogus '45-minute' WMD claims produced in the 'dodgy dossier' of 2002.[99] Committee 'grillings' of witnesses have produced mixed results; David Kelly committed suicide two days after his humiliation on television by the otherwise irrelevant Foreign Affairs Select Committee, whilst more recently the Treasury Select Committee has offered unimpressive interrogations of leading figures implicated in the Libor scandal.

The great untrodden path remained electoral reform for Westminster; however, the defeat of the AV proposal in 2011 (a bastard child which even the Liberal Democrats never really wanted) shut the door on this and ensured the continuation of the eternal bugbear of British parliamentary politics, namely, safe seats. When fused with the whipping system, it is hard not to sympathise with the public's own view that power is as far removed from them as ever. Neither devolution, nor regional government changed this. The arrival of a Mayor of London and the Greater London Assembly restored London-wide government, and gave Londoners a vocal ambassador – first in the form of Ken Livingstone, and later in the guise of Boris Johnson. But 'Red Ken' was essentially returning to the role he had previously played as leader of the GLC before its abolition, and though there were real successes – notably the successful bid for the 2012 Olympic Games, and Livingstone's personal response to the 7/7 tragedy – the fact that regional government did not 'catch on' in a country disillusioned with (in Peter Oborne's phrase) the 'political class' as a whole spoke volumes.[100]

On the final question, that of coherency, the answer is clear. The massive amount of constitutional reform which took place after 1997 was unprecedented, if only in sheer volume. Its content was often more dubious, and it was principally pursued – by successive Prime Ministers – for reasons of short- or medium-term gain. Even if dangerous long-term consequences were predicted (as with devolution), they were ignored. To paraphrase John Maynard Keynes, political careers, like people, are all dead in the long run. As such, the 'new British Constitution' which Bogdanor has identified is by no means stable, and no means permanent. Some of its provisions – though not devolution – may prove to be ephemeral, whilst others (such as the establishment of the UK Supreme Court) reflect real transitions which were already taking place. Perhaps the greatest constitutional reform of all since 1997 is one which is implicit, and which is pregnant with implications for reform as a whole in historical perspective. This is the violation of a constitutional norm – that there are certain principles to the UK Constitution, discerned by Bagehot, Dicey and others – to which politicians in the past at least paid lip-service. Now, the Constitution is viewed by politicians in practice as it always has been in theory – a series of statutes and conventions amenable to

---

[98]   C Hill, 'Putting the world to rights' in Seldon and Kavanagh (eds), above n 9, 399–400.
[99]   *Ibid*, 397–98.
[100]   P Oborne, *The Rise of the Political Class* (London, Simon & Schuster, 2007).

change for narrowly-political ends. The reluctance which attended much of the debates on the Reform Acts of the nineteenth century is nowhere to be seen on the part of the executive. Human Rights Act or no, this is dangerous for the fundamental relationship between State and citizen. More fundamentally, the legacy of the behaviour of the Governments of 1997–2010 (at least) was that of a flagrant disregard for the principle of the rule of law. This was one of Dicey's constitutional foundations, and for all the remaking of a legal system, one with which Prime Ministers have, at times, played fast and loose.

Lastly, though historians affect to loathe counterfactuals, this period is likely to come to be regarded as a missed opportunity.[101] The greatest issue alive in the UK Constitution on a daily basis, that of prime ministerial power, and its proper exercise in the context of a representative democracy, has barely been addressed. As we (and Cowling) have stressed, politics is about power. Over 30 years ago now, Tony Benn called for a 'constitutional premiership'[102]; what we have in fact witnessed has been the transition to a 'personal system'[103] of government, one which withstood the controversies over Iraq and which lends itself to abuse. Gordon Brown, on succeeding to the premiership, considered the possibility of real retrenchment in terms of prime ministerial power.[104] Unsurprisingly, this fell by the wayside; in Andrew Rawnsley's words, 'Brown was, at heart, a constitutional conservative'.[105] Early in his premiership, Brown had decided to step back from the possibility of arguing for a codified constitution.[106] Constitutional reform was another way of seeming progressive and – fundamentally – 'different' from Blair; whilst Blair's reforms had left the Prime Minister untouched, Brown's would address the perceived problems of his predecessor – control-freakery, an obsession with the media, an unwillingness to listen to Cabinet.[107] Naturally, once the proposals had served their purpose of 'differentiation', most of them were quietly forgotten, to the dismay of those who had dared to believe in them.[108] In so far as constitutional reform made progress under Brown, it was of the 'conventional' sort (pun intended) – the *Cabinet Manual* drafted by Gus O'Donnell ahead of a potential hung Parliament offering the 'starting place' as O'Donnell saw it, for the discussion of a codified constitution. Critics such as Anthony Barnett were less charitable, drawing on the recent experience of government behaviour and characterising the *Manual* as a 'high class villain's charter'.[109]

---

[101] Though for one strident defence of them, see N Ferguson, 'Introduction', in N Ferguson (ed), *Virtual History* (London, Picador, 1997).

[102] T Benn, 'A constitutional prime minister' in A King (ed), *The British Prime Minister*, 2nd edn (London, Macmillan, 1985).

[103] A Seldon, 'The cabinet system' in V Bogdanor (ed), *The British Constitution in the Twentieth Century* (Oxford, British Academy, 2003) 130.

[104] Rawnsley, above n 12, 547–48.

[105] *Ibid*, 548.

[106] A Seldon and G Lodge, *Brown at 10* (London, Biteback, 2010) 18.

[107] *Ibid*, 17–18.

[108] Rawnsley, above n 12, 548.

[109] A Barnett, '"We the people" deserve something better than a high-class villain's charter', *Guardian*, 14 December 2010.

The advent of David Cameron and Nick Clegg as leaders of a coalition naturally had implications for the office of the Prime Minister – though early legislation such as fixed-term parliaments (although pledged by Liberal Democrats for some time) were motivated by the political calculation of strengthening a political executive with a tenuous grasp on parliamentary power. Perhaps inevitably, once secured, attention moved away from that key issue and back to Lords reform, a subject which does not resonate with the public and which has gained additional significance in the Westminster village only because of the crushing defeat of the Liberal Democrats' aspirations for electoral reform in the 2011 AV referendum. Notwithstanding the work of Rod Rhodes,[110] the British Prime Minister remains first without equals, save in the ephemeral circumstances of the present coalition. Despite the continuing scrutiny of this central problem, the British people remain as far from the levers of power as they did before 1997.[111] It will be this missed opportunity, and the fate of Scotland, which will be the chief historical legacies of an era of constitutional reform which was in keeping with the past in one sense above all – the primacy of political calculation in determining the fate of the British political system.

---

[110] RAW Rhodes, *Understanding Governance* (Buckingham, Open University Press, 1997).

[111] Notwithstanding the work of groups such as the Power Commission, whose report, *Power to the People*, was published in 2006.

3

The Constitution and the Public –
How Voters Forgot the Constitution

PETER RIDDELL

PUBLIC DEBATE ON the British Constitution for most of the post-1945 period has been both fragmented and limited – at least in England, and in the worlds of Westminster and Whitehall. Constitutional issues have been regarded by most of the media and many MPs as second order, of little interest to voters and a matter mainly for enthusiasts and for academics. This is curious historically in view of the vigour of earlier debates, while constitutional issues have often been at the forefront of political argument in recent decades: the UK's links with the European Union; relations between central and local government; devolution; the growth of judicial activism and human rights; the balance between the executive and the legislature. However, in most cases, these changes have been discussed in isolation, on their own terms and merits, rather than as part of a broader constitutional picture.

Professor Vernon Bogdanor – along with several of the other contributors to this volume – has been among the rare exceptions who have both thought and talked in broader constitutional terms, linking otherwise separate changes. He has not only produced a formidable array of books on constitutional issues based on his deep grasp of British political history over the past two centuries, but he has been an active participant in public and media debate. Whenever a controversy arises, he has invariably been called upon to pronounce in newspapers, in broadcast studios and in front of parliamentary committees. He has attained the status of a constitutional authority.

In this chapter I address the question of why the broader constitutional debate has, been piecemeal, and has attracted so little public and media attention. As Matt Qvortrup noted in the Introduction to this volume, Vernon Bogdanor has himself provided part of the answer by joking that he has made his living from 'a subject that doesn't exist – the British constitution'. As he would be the first argue, that represents both complacency and a misreading of constitutional developments in the UK, a false belief in British exceptionalism. The very absence of a written/ codified constitution in one document is part of the explanation. We do not talk about a constitution because we believe we do not have one, or at least a written one as all but two other countries do. Or, as was fashionable from the 1940s to the 1960s, the constitution was dismissed as merely about what happens or as executive and parliamentary precedent. The links between constitutional issues have seldom been discussed. Reforms have commonly been seen as contingent and particular.

In historical terms, the denial of the existence of a constitution is nonsense, not least as we approach the 800th anniversary of Magna Carta in 2015. As Professor Linda Colley[1] has pointed out, there has been a long list of texts supporting a British Constitution – the Petition of Right, the Bill of Rights, the Acts of Union with Scotland and Ireland, the three major Reform Acts of the nineteenth century – all of which were discussed specifically in terms of a constitutional settlement. The intense and bitterly divisive debates from the 1880s until 1914 over Irish Home Rule and the power of the House of Lords were conducted in terms of their broader constitutional terms, as the various editions of the increasingly partisan Dicey's *Study of the Law of the Constitution* show. Moreover, as Colley has vividly demonstrated,[2] the British have been prolific constitution writers for other people – notably in the colonies Britain ruled and, then, in alliance with their new leaders, for the subsequent self-governing dominions, first within the Empire and then within what became the Commonwealth. British officials and lawyers have eagerly provided constitutions for other countries not directly linked to the UK and for international organisations.

But that fertile constitutional imagination and energy was somehow forgotten after 1945. As in so many other areas, victory induced a sense of superiority: a widespread belief and assertion that British parliamentary democracy had triumphed not only over totalitarianism, but also over the weaker constitutional systems of the defeated Continental countries. There was no need to change much in the way that Britain was governed. This was the period of judicial acquiescence in executive dominance and a time when even modest proposals for parliamentary reform were easily brushed aside. The UK was a largely unified, as well as a unitary, State, and the voices of Irish, as well as Scottish and Welsh, nationalism were largely silent. Constitutional activists focused their attention elsewhere, helping to write the European Convention on Human Rights (initially intended for defeated and conquered countries rather than the UK) and constitutions for newly-independent former colonies. Wolfram Kaiser argues that the decline of radicalism started earlier[3]:

> After 1918, and especially after 1945, there was a conviction, strengthened by experience, and shared widely among the political elite as well as the electorate, that the state of the British constitution was broadly satisfactory and that it needed only minor

---

[1] Linda Colley, in evidence to the Political and Constitutional Reform Committee of the Commons, Thursday, 12 January 2012, House of Comms paper 1178-iv, questions 154–56, session 2010-120.

[2] *Ibid.*

[3] W Kaiser, 'The Decline and Rise of Radicalism: Political Parties and Reform in the Twentieth Century' in P Catterall, W Kaiser and U Walton-Jordan (eds), *Reforming the Constitution –Debates in Twentieth Century Britain* (London, Frank Cass Publishers, 2001) 57–58.

improvements, if any. The satisfaction with Britain's system of government reflected a decline of constitutional radicalism until the 1950s which mainly resulted from three factors: a preoccupation with questions of economic management and social reform, the progressive marginalization of the Radical tradition within Labour as the new main reform party, and the mental de-Europeanisation of Britain since 1914.

This complacency was reinforced by ingrained attitudes in the two main political parties. The Conservatives saw themselves as defending what they believed were self-evidently successful political institutions which did not need changing, though, in practice, the Conservative administrations of of 1951–64 did introduce constitutional innovations, notably by the creation of life peerages in 1958 and, subsequently, the admission of women as members of the House of Lords. But both measures were seen as ways to revive what was becoming a moribund and poorly-attended second chamber. Labour too was equally conservative in this period, despite earlier, more radical ideas of the guild socialists. That partly reflected an executive-mindedness which developed out of the wartime and post-war Attlee administrations, as epitomised by Douglas Jay's often misquoted and misunderstood phrase that 'the man in Whitehall knows best'. This was not a world of pluralism and democratic accountability. There was little sympathy for strengthening judicial checks and balances, since judges were seen, understandably at the time, both socially and ideologically as defenders of the ruling class. One consequence, noted by Colley,[4] is that, particularly since the Second World War,

> we have lost a lot of the broad knowledge of important constitutional texts. As a result we have a kind of black hole. We have neither a written constitution, which crucially could serve an informational purpose, nor, at civil service level, or among MPs and certainly not among the general public, a strong sense of constitutional history.

Constitutional issues have not played a significant part in any general election campaign since 1945, except always in Northern Ireland and intermittently in Scotland and Wales, but with little spill over into the main battle in England. The successive Nuffield studies produced by Sir David Butler, Dennis Kavanagh and others since 1945 show that constitutional reform never featured amongst the top 10 issues. For instance, in the 'who governs Britain' election of February 1974, the Common Market, as it was then called, the main constitutional issue of the period, was seen as important by between 6 and 11 per cent of those interviewed by ORC during the campaign. This was way behind rising prices and the cost of living (at 55 to 58 per cent). By the time of the October 1974 campaign, when the Wilson Government had developed proposals to renegotiate the terms of Britain's membership, the percentage regarding the issue as important for the election had risen to between 9 and 12 per cent.[5]

---

[4] Colley, above n 1.
[5] D Butler and D Kavanagh, *The British General Election of February 1974* (London, Macmillan, 1974).

As discussed later, the debate shifted during the 1980s, particularly after 1987. According to Butler and Kavanagh's account of the 1992 election,[6]

> apart from reorganizing local government finance and the civil service, the Conservatives showed little interest in reform of government and constitutional matters. That agenda had traditionally been left to the Liberals. But Labour, for so long out of power, also had plans to curb the executive via the introduction of a charter of rights, decentralization of power from Whitehall to the regions, and the creation of an elected second chamber: the party also demonstrated an open mind by establishing a working party on electoral reform.

However, the issue did not make much public impact. It was raised occasionally during the campaign itself, but caught fire only when, on Charter 88's Democracy Day, Neil Kinnock went further than before in seeming to endorse proportional representation (PR). He invited the Liberals to join Raymond Plant's working party on electoral systems. Not only did Kinnock's intervention raise the profile of the PR issue, but it also affected the campaign by opening up the possibility of Lab/Lib cooperation in a hung Parliament. That turned out to work against not only Labour but also the Liberals. It created an opportunity for John Major. As Butler and Kavanagh report[7]:

> At the end of the campaign he gave heavy emphasis to a theme which he had ventilated earlier without attracting much notice, the need to maintain unity of the United Kingdom. Some expressed scepticism about taking up a subject which was seen as a vote loser north of the border and of little interest elsewhere. But there seems to be little doubt that he touched a patriotic chord as he spoke with clarity and conviction on constitutional issues about which Neil Kinnock seemed to equivocate.

Major made this the main theme of his London press conferences on both the final Saturday and Monday of the campaign. He said, 'If I could summon up all the authority of this office, I would put it into this single warning – the United Kingdom is in danger. Wake up, my fellow countrymen! Wake up now before it is too late!' The main effect may have been in affecting Major's public image as a leader, showing him as a man of passion with convictions. That was probably more important than the specific issue of devolution and the unity of the UK, which did not feature among the top issues of importance to voters.

Five years later, Butler and Kavanagh record[8]:

> Devolution and constitutional reform intruded intermittently in the campaign. John Major saw his stress on the unity of the United Kingdom as a key element in his 1992 victory and, together with Michael Forsyth and others, spoke repeatedly of the dangers of a tax raising Scottish Parliament.

Major's warnings about the dangers of the break-up of the UK did obtain front page coverage – '72 hours to save the Union' – in the *Daily Telegraph* and *The*

---

[6] D Butler and D Kavanagh, *The British General Election of 1992* (London, Macmillian, 1992) 19.
[7] *Ibid*, 130.
[8] D Butler and D Kavanagh, *The British General Election of 1997* (London, Macmillan, 1997) 109–10.

Times three days before polling day. But these warnings had little effect given the scale of the Conservatives' defeat throughout Britain and their complete wipe-out in Scotland. Yet, as in previous and later general elections, the campaign in Scotland was different from that in the rest of Britain. In general, constitutional issues were not significant or decisive in most of Britain, and certainly not in England.

The same pattern continued in the period from 1997 onwards, despite the scale of the Blair Government's constitutional programme. This was presented in a largely piecemeal way. Revealingly, opinion polls, such as those conducted regularly by IpsosMORI, show that constitution/devolution made it into double figures only once (in September 2004) as among the issues which 'will be very important to you in helping you to decide which party for vote for at the next general election', and often hovered around 5 or 6 per cent, compared to around a half of those polled mentioning asylum/immigration, education and healthcare. These figures are from a prompted list where interviewees were shown a list of issues. Where the topic was not shown and people were asked to name issues which would be important to them in deciding their vote, constitution/devolution was mentioned by barely 1 per cent of those interviewed.

These poll findings have matched the lack of sustained interest in constitutional issues in the mainstream London media (as opposed to those in Edinburgh, Cardiff and Belfast). News editors, even on smaller circulation quality papers, have regarded constitutional matters as generally arcane and of little interest to readers, except, rarely, when a row blows up. Once the devolution legislation had been passed in the late 1990s, there was a tendency in London-based media organisations to view developments in Scotland, Wales and (later) Northern Ireland (except when there was violence) as of interest just to these nations, and to have no nationwide interest or implications. English politicians took the same view.

The explanation for the low level of public interest lies partly in the fragmented way that constitutional issues have been discussed by politicians and the media since 1945. After a decade or more of quiescence, the debate – among academics and some politicians, though not the public as a whole – began to change in the 1960s as part of a wider soul-searching about Britain's place in the world and decline. Penguin Books published a series of 'What's wrong with . . .?' paperbacks, including one on Parliament written anonymously by two Commons clerks. This period also saw the publication in 1964 of *The Reform of Parliament* by the academic Bernard Crick, and *The Power of Parliament* by the commentator Ronald Butt. The ideas of Crick and some younger academics and clerks were associated with the very modest efforts of Richard Crossman, as Leader of the Commons from 1966 to 1968, to strengthen the Select Committee system. But the changes were limited in the face of resistance from most of Crossman's Cabinet colleagues. The Labour Governments of both the late 1960s and the late 1970s attempted changes to the House of Lords, but these foundered because of opposition from both right and left, and, as so often before and since, because of fears that a reformed second chamber might also be regarded as a more legitimate one and therefore challenge the supremacy of the Commons. This fuelled demands on the left for unicameralism.

The most significant constitutional change of this period was entry into the then European Common Market in January 1973, following more than a dozen years of debate and off/on negotiations. This decision produced strong passions and arguments, and turned out to have profound consequences for ideas of sovereignty, and particularly for the scope and role of the courts. These implications were under-discussed at the time, providing ammunition for later charges by Eurosceptics of misleading arguments and betrayal by the Heath Government. Again, this was seen as in isolation from other constitutional changes.

A wider constitutional debate was initiated by the second Wilson Government when the Royal Commission on the Constitution was launched in April 1969, initially under Lord Crowther and then, after his death in 1972, under Lord Kilbrandon. It was set up in response to growing demands for home rule or full independence for Wales and Scotland following by-election victories by Plaid Cymru and the Scottish Nationalists in 1966 and 1967. The Commission's terms of reference were to examine

> the functions of the present legislature and government in relation to the several countries, nations and regions of the UK; and to consider, having regard to changes in local government organization and in the administrative and other relationships between the various parts of the UK . . . whether any changes are desirable in those functions or otherwise in present constitutional and economic relationships.[9]

The Commission was unable to reach unanimous agreement, with the final Report including a number of options and a memorandum of dissent.[10] The majority of members favoured legislative devolution for both Scotland and Wales (with a reduction in the number of MPs representing the two nations), though not for England as a whole or for any English region. The Report finally came out at the end of October 1973, just as the Heath Government was grappling with the oil price crisis, sharply rising inflation and a renewed dispute with the miners' union. The incoming Labour Government produced limited devolution proposals in September 1974, just before the general election of that year. This was followed by a convoluted legislative process which eventually produced the separate Scotland and Wales Acts of 1978 and the referendums of March 1979. The proposed Welsh Assembly was rejected by a majority of voters, while the Scottish plan failed to gain sufficient support under a requirement that it should have the support of 40 per cent of the Scottish electorate. The West Lothian – or perhaps more accurately the English – question was raised then about the broader implications for representation at Westminster of the differences in powers of MPs from various parts of the UK. But apart from some rumbling from mainly Labour MPs from north-east England, there was little broader discussion for the govern-

---

[9] The Royal Commission on the Constitution (the Kilbrandon Commision) 1969–73, Volume 1, report, Stationary office, Command 5460.
[10] Ibid.

ance of the whole UK. A striking feature was, however, the divisions on the left. Several younger Labour MPs, such as Neil Kinnock from Wales and Robin Cook from Scotland, opposed devolution then on the socialist, and centralist, grounds than only a strong national Government would introduce more redistribution and produce greater equality, with resources being shifted from richer to poorer areas. By contrast, devolving power even to sizeable nations such as Scotland and Wales would risk lower levels of provision, since there would be fewer resources to redistribute.

By the end of the 1970s, more Conservative than Labour MPs appeared to be interested in constitutional issues, though this interest was never shared by Margaret Thatcher, whose radical instincts were concentrated on economic and industrial policy and on the structure of the public sector. She was a traditionalist on the Constitution, and her concerns over what became the European Union really developed only in the final two years of her premiership. Tory support for constitutional reform was partly in response to what was seen as a crisis of ungovernability in the mid-to-late 1970s, as well as to some of the policies of the Labour Government. Lord Hailsham, the past and future Lord Chancellor, famously warned about an 'elective dictatorship' in a lecture in 1976, though his radical prescription was soon forgotten when he returned to office in May 1979. Some Tories at that stage supported electoral reform, and some were sympathetic to Scottish, if not Welsh, devolution. These interests largely disappeared during the Thatcher years.

The contrast in attitudes between Conservatives and Labour in this period was most clearly shown by the debate over the incorporation of the European Convention on Human Rights into British law.[11] The campaign, which developed in the early to mid-1980s, was led in Parliament by Conservative, rather than Labour, lawyers, though Thatcher herself was opposed. The Labour frontbench line then was hostile, on the grounds that the judiciary was predominantly drawn from a narrow, atypical section of the population – instinctively conservative and sympathetic to the Establishment. This reflected a series of what were seen as anti-trade union rulings by judges in the 1970s and 1980s, and in particular the views of the prominent left-wing academic lawyer, Professor JG Griffith of the London School of Economics, who argued that a Bill of Rights is 'by its nature anti-democratic and authoritarian'. These views were being expressed just as a big change was happening in the legal world, with the growth of judicial review challenging the decisions of the executive and with the rise to prominence of a new generation of lawyers and judges more concerned with human and civil rights.

The turning point in the debate over constitutional reform came after the third Thatcher victory in 1987. Conservative support for reform, already on the retreat in view of Thatcher's lack of interest, dwindled to a few Tory peers and lawyers, and a small group of mainly pro-European supporters of electoral reform. The

---

[11] P Riddell, 'Labour's Conversion to Constitutional Reform' in A McDonald (ed), *Reinventing Britain: Constitutional Change Under New Labour* (London, Politico's Publishing, 2007) 33–35.

supporters became increasingly isolated and had little influence over the subsequent 20 years. The key change was in the Labour Party, which moved away from its longstanding majoritarian view towards a greater interest in creating checks and balances on a strong executive – in particular as represented by the Thatcher Administration. Tony Wright, a political scientist and, from 1997 until 2010, an influential MP in this debate, argued[12]:

> In a sense it is Mrs Thatcher who perhaps has the best claim to be regarded as the real architect of constitutional reform in Britain. She provided an object lesson in the nature of power in Britain's flexible constitution, and, at the same time, a crash course of constitutional education for the Labour Party.

That shift provided the foundation for closer cooperation between what became the Liberal Democrats and Labour, ahead of, and in the two and a half years after, the 1997 election – as shown by the Cook–Maclennan agreement on constitutional priorities before the election and the joint Cabinet committee afterwards. The Liberal Party had always favoured constitutional reform, including not only PR but also devolution and incorporation of the European Convention. The split which led to the creation of the Social Democratic Party (SDP) in 1981 deprived Labour of many prominent, mainly lawyer, supporters of reform, such as the later Lords Goodhart, Lester and Maclennan. That partly accounted for Labour's hostility to reform and incorporation of the Convention during the period up to 1987. Later, however, the former SDP lawyers were key allies for the new generation of supporters of reform in Labour.

The shift took two forms, which have continued until now and explain much of the paradoxical character of the constitutional debate in Britain. First, the comprehensive approach, which has treated the Constitution as a whole and has recommended wholesale reform. Secondly, individual campaigns to address specific grievances or proposals, from Scottish devolution, via freedom of information, to the Human Rights Act. The latter, specific campaigns have been more successful.

The comprehensive approach first emerged in the work of the Constitutional Reform Centre from 1985 onwards, and then with the creation of Charter 88 three years later, in both of which Richard Holme, a leading Liberal and then peer, played a prominent part. Charter 88 was launched by a group of 348 mainly left-wing intellectuals and activists. They sought to mobilise support for a declaration covering a wide-ranging series of reform: a Bill of Rights; subjecting executive powers and prerogatives to parliamentary scrutiny; a statutory right to freedom of information; a fair electoral system based on PR; a democratic, non-hereditary second chamber; the independence of a reformed judiciary; legal remedies for abuses of power by the State; guaranteeing an equitable distribution of power between the nations of the United Kingdom and between local, regional and central government; and drawing up a written constitution. The main impact of Charter 88, and parallel bodies, was in making this broader constitutional reform

---

[12] *Ibid*, 37.

agenda part of the common core of beliefs among many on the progressive left. That was not, however, the same as having all its ideas accepted by the Labour leadership, where there remained divided views, notably on electoral reform, as well as on cooperating with the Liberal Democrats who made a priority of constitutional reform and advocated much of the Charter 88 programme. Many in Labour, particularly on the old right and among party managers, retained majoritarian instincts and were hostile to wholesale constitutional reform.

Nonetheless, the Labour statement, *Meet the Challenge: Make the Change*, published in May 1989,[13] committed the party to wide-ranging of reform, featuring devolution, a less precise decentralisation within England, a charter of rights and the creation of an elected second chamber. That formed the basis of Labour's 1992 manifesto platform. John Smith, who took over as Labour leader in July 1992, had an even greater commitment to wholesale reform than Kinnock. This was because he was a Scot, and debates on the issue had been more vigorous north of the border; because, as a minister in the late 1970s, he had handled the abortive devolution legislation; and because he was a lawyer. His two-year leadership was the high point of Labour's commitment to wholesale reform, In a speech in March 1993, he repeated support for the earlier package, including freedom of information legislation and incorporation of the European Convention into British law, but what was striking was his language:

> Our crumbling constitution can no longer be dismissed as a side-show. It is at the heart of what is wrong with our country, People care, and they want change. Indeed, the more we scrutinize the way in which we are governed and the lack of legal rights at our disposal, the more clear it becomes that our present democratic process is both anachronistic and inadequate.[14]

As Shadow Home Secretary, Tony Blair had been involved in the creation of Labour's constitutional reform programme, as reflected in an enthusiastic speech in support at the 1993 Party Conference. But his commitment was never as deep as Smith's, and on becoming leader in July 1994, Blair adopted a more pragmatic and piecemeal approach. This was partly signalled by his appointment of Jack Straw as his successor as Shadow Home Secretary, then responsible for the main constitutional measures. In particular, Straw, MP for the north-western seat of Blackburn, was concerned that English interests should be safeguarded and that the policy should not be determined solely by the Scots.

Blair also believed that English voters in the critical target seats would not be won over by a long list of promises on the Constitution and were much more concerned with the economy and the state of schools and the NHS. He did not, as he once said, want the tail of constitutional reform to wag the dog of New Labour. Blair wanted to avoid legislative commitments which would take up a lot of parliamentary time and which could hold up the enactment of other, to him, more important parts of his domestic programme. He surprised and shocked the

---

[13] *Making the Challenge: Make the Change* (London, Labour Party, 1989).
[14] John Smith, Charter 88 lecture, 'A Citizen's Democracy', March 1993.

Scottish and Welsh Labour Parties by announcing in June 1996, without any prior warning, that referendums would be held in both these countries in advance of introducing detailed legislation. Moreover, in Scotland, there would be a second question on tax-raising powers. Various other changes were made, all with the motive of making passage of the legislation easier, especially if Labour had only a small Commons majority, in the hope of avoiding all the problems that made the late 1970s' devolution legislation so time-consuming and divisive. Blair's worries turned out to be misplaced in view of the scale of Labour's landslide victory. But the holding of referendums ensured not only that the legislation passed through Parliament smoothly, but also that the changes were effectively entrenched, since the plans could not, in practice, be modified without a further referendum.

Blair's pragmatism led to a watering down of other proposals such as House of Lords reform, where the immediate aim became the removal of hereditary peers rather than moving to an elected second chamber. In other areas, Labour's commitment to a referendum on the voting system for the Commons was repeated, but with a prior commission to recommend an alternative to the first-past-the-post system (which became the Jenkins Commission). But references to subjecting the royal prerogative to parliamentary scrutiny were dropped, as was talk of a home-grown Bill of Rights. Instead, the priority would be to incorporate the European Convention into British law. Labour was cautious as well about regional government for England. The language was also recast away from the remaking constitution rhetoric of John Smith to the more limited talk of 'cleaning up politics' in response to the widespread and often ill-defined allegations of 'sleaze'. In the John Smith Memorial Lecture in February 1996, Blair, while respecting the memory of his predecessor, was cautious in his promises. 'We do not propose, as some suggest, a Great Reform Bill which would attempt all this change at once. The ambition and extent of the programme will not be achieved in one Bill but over a period of time.'

The programme implemented by the Blair Government was wide-ranging; it was essentially incremental, with distinct parts having their own separate roots. For instance, the proposals for Scottish devolution which emerged during the 1990s and were enacted in 1998 had specifically Scottish roots – in response to the defeat of the devolution plan in the March 1979 referendum and in reaction to what was widely seen as alien Thatcherite rule. Scotland provided the ballast for Labour during the Party's worst days in the 1980s – both in numbers and in the quality of its MPs – and also led the recovery, accounting for nearly half its overall gains in 1987. The subsequent discussions on devolution in the Scottish Conventional Convention – in which neither the Conservatives nor, after the first meeting, the Scottish Nationalists took part – produced 'a made in Scotland' plan. There was no English input even though it had far-reaching implications for the constitutional structure of the UK. Many English Labour MPs felt they had been bounced by the powerful Scottish lobby at the top of the Party, and acquiesced in, rather than enthused about, the plan. Wales was junior partner in these plans partly because of divisions within the Welsh Labour Party, but also because of greater doubts about the merits of devolution. The Welsh plan in 1997 was for executive rather than legislative devolution. However, like Scotland, it was largely a matter of the Welsh talking to the Welsh, rather than a nationwide discussion also involving the English

The same specific and distinct origins may be seen in the proposals for a domestic Bill of Rights, later enacted as the Human Rights Act, and for freedom of information legislation. During the 1980s and 1990s, a greater willingness by the judiciary to challenge the decisions of the executive led to growing discussion about the role of judges in filling gaps in the law. Some judges even sought to qualify the doctrine of absolute parliamentary sovereignty. This tied in with increasing demands for a domestic Bill of Rights, mainly led by lawyers and groups such as Charter 88 and Liberty. As with devolution, a specific, albeit powerful, group pushed forward its own proposal and gained the support both of a new – and younger – generation of Labour MPs and of influential figures such as Derry Irvine, a close friend of John Smith and the pupil master of Tony Blair.

Support for a Freedom of Information Act, based on precedents in both the USA and Commonwealth countries, was a more long drawn-out process, starting in the mid-1970s. The Thatcher Government was not keen, but change began from the late 1980s onwards, with a revision of the very restrictive Official Secrets Act of 1911. The Major Government went further in making more official information available under the 'Open Government' initiative, but this was an administrative code and stopped short of establishing a legally-enforceable right under statute. Again, the lead was taken by a specific, single issue group, the Campaign for Freedom of Information, which had been set up in 1984 shortly after legislation along these lines in a number of Commonwealth countries.

This pragmatic, piecemeal view of constitutional reform was also reflected in government after May 1997. The programme of change was unprecedented: six Cabinet committees were devoted to reform (out of 30 committees in total) and nine separate constitutional Acts were passed in the first, long parliamentary session of 1997–98. These covered: allowing referendums to be held on devolution in Scotland and Wales (held in September 1997), and on creating a mayor and assembly in London; the setting up of devolved bodies in Edinburgh and Cardiff; two measures on Northern Ireland following the Good Friday Agreement of Spring 1998; the registration of political parties; the creation of regional development agencies; and the enactment of the Human Rights Act 1998 to incorporate the European Convention on Human Rights into British law. Later, in the 1997–2001 Parliament, legislation was passed in 1999 to remove all but 92 hereditary peers from the House of Lords; to change the method of electing the European Parliament to a regional list system of PR; to create a mayor and assembly for London; to alter the way local government is run to strengthen the executive, including directly-elected mayors; to establish a limited right to official information under the Freedom of Information Act; and to set up an Electoral Commission to regulate elections and party funding.

In total, this represented a big change in the operation of the British Constitution – and only one measure, on regional development agencies, was repealed after

Labour lost the 2010 general election. But the striking feature was how discon-
nected these reforms were. They aroused the interest, and occasional passions, of
those most directly affected, the Scots, the Welsh and the Northern Irish in particular, lawyers, the media and, for a time, the churches on the Human Rights Act.
The last measure was carefully drafted to preserve parliamentary sovereignty,
since the courts could not strike down or annul an Act of Parliament, but they
could issue a declaration of incompatibility saying that a law or decision was
incompatible with the Human Rights Act. In virtually every case, the Government
responded by taking remedial action and changed the laws.

However, there was little wider interest in these measures, partly because of the
disconnection. Unlike the Blair Government's public service reforms, there was
no 'big picture'. There was a sense of ticking a box as each reform was enacted, so
that, certainly in Blair's view, it could then be forgotten. As Lord Irvine of Lairg,
Lord Chancellor from 1997 to 2003 and coordinator of the early reforms, stated[15]:

> We made decisions based on empirical evidence, about precisely which aspects of our
> constitution needed earlier attention, and on what basis. We are conscious of the way
> different elements of any constitutional settlement can impact on each other. Of course,
> many parts of the package are not interdependent. They address particular problems,
> which are the product of lengthy and complex pre-histories of their own.

The priority was consistency rather than coherence. As I argued,[16] 'while only passionate constitutional reformers favour a Big Bang approach of wholesale change,
the Blair Government's piecemeal changes have lacked a sense of direction or
strategy'. Overall,

> all these laws have changed the balance between the government and the governed. Yet
> there has been something half-hearted about it, as if Tony Blair and many of his inner
> circle did not really believe in, or even understand, the changes.[17]

The same pattern of significant change but little public attention continued
later in the Blair Government, notably over the proposals to reshape the post of
Lord Chancellor and reorganise the senior judiciary. The first of these far-reaching
changes was announced without consultation, partly because of the opposition
of the then incumbent Lord Irvine, who was then replaced by Lord Falconer of
Thoroton. The basic proposal was not amended and involved changing the role of
the Lord Chancellor from his tripartite position – as Cabinet minister, head of the
judiciary who appointed top judges, and presiding officer of the House of
Lords – into the single position of Cabinet minister in charge of the courts and
probation system in what would become the Department of Constitutional Affairs
(and then, after 2007, the Department of Justice, after the running of prisons was
transferred from the Home Office). In addition, there were proposals to set up a
statutory Judicial Appointments Commission and to turn the Law Lords, techni-

---

[15] Lord Irvine of Lairg, *Human Rights, Constitutional Law and the Development of the English Legal System* (Oxford, Hart Publishing, 2003) 96.

[16] P Riddell, *The Unfulfilled Prime Minister: Tony Blair's quest for a legacy* (London, Politico's, 2005) 168.

[17] *Ibid*, 188.

cally a committee of the Lords, into a free-standing Supreme Court, with its own building on the opposite side of Parliament Square, though with no change in legal powers. Both sets of proposals, notably those in relation to the Lord Chancellor, turned out to be more complicated, and involved unravelling much more earlier legislation, than had been envisaged when the plan was prepared. The method of announcement in July 2003 aroused fury, and led to lengthy negotiation with the senior judiciary and the creation of a special select committee, before the plan, with safeguards for judicial independence, became law shortly before the 2005 general election. Yet the lengthy wrangling aroused little wider interest, again because the issue was presented as very much a matter for judges and lawyers.

The volume of the constitutional reform debate was raised temporarily after Gordon Brown became Prime Minister in June 2007. Brown had always been much more interested in constitutional issues than Blair. This was partly because, as a Scot, such issues had been more central to his political life. Brown gave a number of lectures on Britishness, an attempt to highlight common political values across the United Kingdom at a time of devolution. This debate had also been stirred by the POWER Inquiry, which had been established in 2004, with the backing of the Rowntree charitable and reform trusts, to explore how political participation and involvement might be increased and deepened. Chaired by Helena Kennedy, the Inquiry's Report in February 2006, 'Power to the People',[18] recommended sweeping changes, such as caps on donations for political parties linked to taxpayer funding; a cut in the voting age from 18 to 16; a two-thirds elected second chamber; restrictions on the powers of party whips; electoral reform for Parliament and local councils; and increased citizen participation through various forms of direct democracy. The POWER Report was welcomed by many on the centre-left, though more selectively by the Conservatives, even though at a conference held in May 2006, David Cameron, the new Party leader, argued for a Lords with 'a significant elected element' – a commitment he later watered down. Vernon Bogdanor has strongly supported greater public participation after the horizontal transfers of power during the Blair period. But many political scientists criticised the Report as exaggerating the extent of public support for, and interest in, wholesale reform and increased voter participation.

Within days of taking office, Brown launched 'The Governance of Britain',[19] a Green Paper intended to be 'the first step in national conversation' over 'our constitutional settlement'. The hastily-written document set out a series of proposals for constitutional renewal: limiting the powers of the executive to act without involving Parliament on the deployment of troops abroad; the dissolution and recall of Parliament; ratification of treaties, and the rules governing the Civil Service; making the executive more accountable; developing proposals for a substantially or wholly-elected second chamber; reviewing voting systems; placing a duty on public bodies

[18] *Power to the People*, Final Report of the POWER Inquiry, chaired by Baroness Kennedy of the Shaws (London, 2006).
[19] *The Governance of Britain* (Cm 7170, 2007).

to involve local people in major decisions; and initiating a national debate on a British statement of values. As so often with Brown's initiatives, the follow-up was disappointing. The Conservative peer and constitutional academic Philip Norton argued[20] a year after the Green Paper that 'There remained no clear end point. There was no articulation of the type of constitution that Brown wanted to see for the United Kingdom.' From 2007 until 2009, there were many speeches, a lengthy consideration of a draft bill by a Joint Committee of both Houses of Parliament and then inaction – and practically no public interest.

The Government claimed that the banking crisis and subsequent recession were a greater priority, so the eventual, wide-ranging Bill was not published until two years later, and received its second reading in the Lords only on 24 March, 2010, shortly before the election was announced. This meant that many of the most controversial elements had to be dropped during the 'wash-up', the period between the election announcement and dissolution of Parliament, including proposals for a referendum on the alternative vote, on the suspension and expulsion of peers, and ending by-elections for hereditary peers; as well as on public order and some other smaller matters. That left some important, diverse provisions on providing statutory backing for the Civil Service, on parliamentary regulation and reducing the 30-year rule for the release of official records to 20 years for some records. All this was a far cry from the ambitious language of early July 2007. Meanwhile, talk about a statement of British rights and responsibilities produced an interesting, though limited, debate but no action.

The formation of the Conservative/Liberal Democrat coalition was itself a significant constitutional innovation involving a shift away from the familiar majoritarian style of governing and operating in Parliament. But, at the time of writing, it is naturally unclear whether this is a one-off or the start of a trend in which no single party gains an overall Commons majority. The coalition also embarked on a number of constitutional changes, largely at the instigation of the Liberal Democrats – such as the referendum on moving to the alternative vote, which was heavily defeated in May 2011 – while Conservative backbench opposition to an elected second chamber halted Lords reform in the summer of 2012. Looking back after a long series of failed attempts to change the composition of the Lords, Chris Ballinger concluded[21]:

> The principal reason for the lack of reform is that no government has been united in a commitment – whether or its own volition or of necessity – to secure reform. Reform that placed the membership of the upper House on a popular basis would take away the lack of legitimacy which, at least since the 1920s, has inhibited the Lords in using the considerable powers with which the Parliament Act left them . . . The other reason for the lack of reform across a century is that the series of non-reforms have met the needs of the changing constitution.

---

[20] Lord Norton of Louth in M Rush and P Giddings (eds), *When Gordon took the Helm* (London, Palgrave Macmillan and the Hansard Society, 2008) 29.
[21] C Ballinger, *The House of Lords 1911–2011 – A Century of Non-Reform* (Oxford, Hart Publishing, 2012) 219.

These non-reforms have included the introduction of life peers in 1958, the payment of peers and the removal of most of the hereditaries in 1999.

Various other proposals, such as introducing a power of recall of errant MPs, made little progress. The biggest innovation was the introduction of five-year fixed-term Parliaments, which introduced an element of certainty into the working of the coalition. The UK did, however, face some significant constitutional challenges – in the promised referendums on Scottish independence in September 2014 and over future relations with the European Union, which David Cameron promised in January 2013 would be held after the 2015 general election if the Conservatives won a majority. This reflected growing support from Tory MPs, including some ministers, for a referendum on, and indeed for withdrawal from, the European Union. These two issues did excite public interest, but there was no evidence of great interest in, or enthusiasm for, other constitutional changes.

If you compare the constitutional arrangements in 2013 with those in the mid-1980s when the broader debate revived, the scale of change is striking – not only the closer integration with the European Union (at least for the moment), but also substantial and developing devolution of powers to Scotland, Wales and Northern Ireland; elected mayors in London and some other large English cities and towns; statutory oversight of elections and party funding; the move from a largely hereditary to a predominantly appointed House of Lords; the Human Rights Act; and statutory entitlement to freedom of information (which Tony Blair later regarded as one of his biggest mistakes). Vernon Bogdanor argued[22] that this amounted to

> a new British constitution. This has been little noticed, partly because the various reforms have been legislated piecemeal, and because they have seem without internal coherence. They have been regarded, therefore, as a disparate collection of unrelated measures rather than as a package. In addition, the process is incomplete, and its end-product by no means clear. The reforms have made less impact that they would have done in a country with a codified constitution where they would have been the subject of constitutional amendment, and, no doubt, considerable discussion and debate.

Of course, as Bogdanor acknowledges, much has now been written down in statute; what previously would have been largely tacit and based on convention and precedent is now explicit. But there are still many uncertainties – over the balance between the judiciary and Parliament; over the quasi-federal nature of the United Kingdom; over the role and composition of the second chamber; and over relations with the European Union. Each tends to be debated separately. While there may be a growing constitutional sense in informed debate, it is still piecemeal. We lack an overall framework for constitutional debate. As Bogdanor argued a year into the life of the coalition,[23] 'Far from the British constitution having reached a stable resting place, it remains in flux. Reforming the constitution is most definitely a process, not an event.'

---

[22] V Bogdanor, *The New British Constitution* (Oxford, Hart Publishing, 2009) 271.

[23] V Bogdanor, *The Coalition and the Constitution* (Oxford, Hart Publishing, 2011) xii.

4

'Let Me Take You to a Foreign Land': The Political and the Legal Constitution

MATT QVORTRUP[1]

Mr Podsnap's world was not a very large world, morally; no, nor even geographically: seeing that although his business was sustained upon commerce with other countries, he considered other countries . . . a mistake, and of their manners and customs would conclusively observe, 'Not English!' when PRESTO! with a flourish of the arm and the flush of the face, they were swept away.

Charles Dickens, *Our Mutual Friend*[2]

I N SOME WAYS, the opponents of constitutional reform had a certain affinity with Charles Dickens' fictional caricature Mr Podsnap.[3] In a controversial speech before the Parliamentary Election in 2001, William Hague, the then leader of the Opposition, warned against the consequences of constitutional reform by repeating the phrase 'Let me take you on a journey to a foreign land.' His criticism was that constitutional reform would lead to 'parliament's powers parcelled out in every direction, outwards to Brussels, downwards to devolved assemblies and sideways to our judges through the Human Rights Act'.[4] Britain would be like 'a foreign land'; a place with checks and balances, with regional powers and a strong judiciary.

Without sharing in the slightest the belief system or the aspirations of Mr Hague's speech-writer Daniel Hannan (later a prominent conservative Member of the European Parliament), there was a prescient element of objective truth in the speech, which went beyond the intended polemic intentions of both the orator and his ghost-writer.

[1] The author is grateful to Arend Lijphart, University of California San Diego and to Professor John Ferejohn, NYU, for helpful comments and suggestions. The usual caveat applies.
[2] C Dickens, *Our Mutual Friend* (New York and London, Belford, Clarke & Co, 1884) 58–59.
[3] *Ibid*, 59
[4] 'Hague's Foreign Land Speech', *Guardian*, 4 March 2001.

Constitutionally speaking, Britain is now 'a foreign land'! To the presumed horror of Diceyan purists, the United Kingdom of Great Britain and Northern Ireland now has a semi-written constitution (namely, the Human Rights Act 1998), an apolitical and independent judiciary (after the Constitutional Reform Act 2005) and – as in federal States – a de facto constitutional court that adjudicates in matters pertaining to ultra vires acts of the devolved parliaments and assemblies. Before 1998, these characteristics were the hallmarks of 'foreign lands'. Now they are a part of the British Constitution. This chapter explains how.

I. THE TRADITIONAL CONSTITUTION

Paraphrasing Dicey's dictum that 'the King in Parliament can do anything',[5] Vernon Bogdanor once observed that the British Constitution may be summed up in eight words, 'What the Queen in Parliament enacts is law.'[6] It is testament to the stability, longevity and the small-'c' conservatism of our constitutional arrangements that essentially the same doctrine was taught to students of constitutional theory for more than 100 years. It followed from this view that the courts were, in the words of Ivor Jennings, 'free to act . . . only within a small diameter' and that the 'possibility of interpretation [was] . . . limited by legislation passed'.[7] Of course, the courts could review the 'illegality, irrationality or impropriety' of decisions by public bodies, and did so frequently, but decisions by Parliament were beyond their reach.[8]

The British Constitution used to be a purely political and uncodified framework which, largely through informal mechanisms and conventions of the Constitution, regulated the behaviour of political actors. In the words of Lijphart, the Westminster Model, of which Britain is the archetypical example, was characterised by its 'absence of judicial review' of enactments by Parliament.[9]

II. THE POLITICAL CONSTITUTION

This political Constitution was based on two premises. On the one hand, it was founded upon a number of shared – but not legally enforceable[10] – conventions of the Constitution, such as the *Salisbury Convention* (the Lords will not block a manifesto commitment),[11] the Foreign Secretary and the Prime Minister have to

---

[5] AV Dicey, quoted in A King, *The British Constitution* (Oxford, Oxford University Press, 2007), 34.

[6] V Bogdanor, 'Our New Constitution' (2004) 120 *LQR* 242, 259.

[7] I Jennings, *The Law and the Constitution*, 5th edn (London, University of London Press, 1959) 254.

[8] *Council of Civil Service Unions v Minister for the Civil Service* [1985] AC 374.

[9] A Lijphart, *Patterns of Democracy: Government Forms and Performance in Thirty-Six Countries* (New Haven, CT, Yale University Press, 2012) 19.

[10] *Madzimbamuto v Lardner-Burke* [1969] 1 AC 645.

[11] Joint Committee on Conventions, First Special Report, HL Paper 189, HC 1151, 2005–06, 25 May 2006.

be a member of the House of Commons, etc, and, on the other hand, an institutionalised system of – to use Arend Lijphart's term – majoritarianism.[12]

Theoretically speaking, the former, the conventions, follow what political scientists James March and Johan P Olsen have called 'the logic of appropriateness'[13]; a kind of adherence to the rules of the game even when this might not have been in the parties' interests. True to its idealised traditions of sportsmanship, the British Constitution relied on a certain level of gentlemanly conduct. In Gladstone's words, our Constitution 'presumes more boldly than any other the good sense and good faith of those who work under it'.[14]

In addition to this, the Constitution relied on a ritualised system of adversarial politics. In the words of Arthur Balfour, our whole 'political organisation is arranged in order that we may quarrel'.[15] Through the seemingly inevitable swing of the pendulum of electoral fortunes, this quarrelsome system provided an opportunity for Her Majesty's Loyal Opposition to reverse the excesses of their opponents when they won power. As Samuel H Beer, the great and late American chronicler of our political system, put it, 'the Opposition performs the function of checking, criticizing and ventilating grievances'.[16]

The knowledge that legislative excesses were likely to be reversed often made governments weary of enacting radical legislation. Consequently, in its heyday, the majoritarian system, paradoxically, resulted in consensus outcomes or 'Butskellism'.[17] Under this system, the courts were hardly needed; and perhaps for this reason, they rarely strayed into the political sphere. The courts could but accept the will of the Queen-in-Parliament. A parliamentary statute was 'the highest form of law that is known to this country . . . the law, which prevails over every other form of law, and it is not for the court to say that a parliamentary enactment, the highest law in this country, is illegal,' as a judge had noted.[18]

From a strictly legal point of view this is still technically the case. Notwithstanding the lonely dissenting voice of Lord Steyn in *Jackson v HM Attorney-General*,[19] the sovereignty of Parliament is still – in Lord Bingham's words – the "bedrock of the British Constitution".[20] But from a practical point of view, the political Constitution has become more and more outdated.

The political Constitution had worked tolerably well until the mid-1970s, but Lord Hailsham's charge that the Labour Government (which had been elected by a minority of the voters in 1974) was presiding over an 'elected dictatorship',[21] and the radicalism of the Thatcher Government (of which Lord Hailsham himself

---

[12] A Lijphart, *Democracies: Patterns of Majoritarianism and Consensus Government* (New Haven, CT, Yale University Press, 1984) 1.

[13] J March and JP Olsen, *Rediscovering Institutions* (New York, The Free Press, 1984).

[14] Gladstone quoted in King, above n 5, 27.

[15] Balfour, quoted in S Low, *The Governance of England* (London, T Fisher & Unwin, 1904) 116.

[16] SH Beer, *Modern British Politics* (London, Faber & Faber, 1969) 95.

[17] J Kingdom, *Government and Politics in Britain* (Cambridge, Polity Press, 2003) 301.

[18] *Cheney v Conn* [1968] 1 All ER 779, per Ungoed-Thomas J.

[19] *Jackson v HM Attorney-General* [2005] UKHL 56 [15], Per Lord Steyn.

[20] *R (Jackson and Other) v Attorney-General* [2005] UKHL 56 [9], per Lord Bingham.

[21] Q Hogg, *Elective Dictatorship* (London, BBC, 1976).

was a member), suggested that the cherished principles were no longer an efficient check on the power of the executive. For that reason, it was not inaccurate to conclude, as three prominent American observers have done, that in Britain, 'the judiciary takes on the government only rarely, and on issues that are of relatively minor importance'.[22] However, by the time Ferejohn, Rosenbluth and Shipan concluded this (in 2007), the British courts were 'taking on the government' in some of the most controversial of cases, as we shall see below.

III. THE LEGAL CONSTITUTION

There were idealists who entertained the hope that the constitutional reform programme undertaken in the years immediately after New Labour's election to power in 1997 was the harbinger of a kind of consensus democracy akin to that of the Low Countries and Scandinavia in the post-war period.[23] These hopes and aspirations have not materialised. While elements of consociationalism emerged in Northern Ireland,[24] the bare-knuckle fights between the Scottish National Party and their unionist opponents in Scotland bear little resemblance to the *Verhandlungsdemokratie* ('negotiation democracy') described by European scholars of the consensus school.[25] The constitutional reform programme undertaken by New Labour and later by the Conservative–Liberal Coalition Government has not altered Britain's system of 'adversary politics',[26] the power has not shifted downwards but has been reshuffled between the elite, and none of these has been given a larger role than the unelected judges. This development has not been without controversy.

A. The Role of the Lord Chancellor

The role of the Lord Chancellor has received the least attention, yet from a theoretical and comparative point of view it is arguably the most important. To understand why, it might be useful to go back to some first principles of political theory. In the *Spirit of the Laws*, Montesquieu famously noted:

---

[22] J Ferejohn, F Rosenbluth and C Shipan, 'Comparative Judicial Politics' in C Boix and S Stokes (eds), *The Oxford Handbook of Comparative Politics* (Oxford, Oxford University Press, 2009) 738.

[23] M Rustin, 'Revising Charter 88' (2009) 62(4) *Parliamentary Affairs* 568; and TC Lundberg, 'Electoral system reviews in New Zealand, Britain and Canada: a critical comparison' (2007) 42(4) *Government and Opposition* 471.

[24] J McGarry and B O'Leary, 'Consociational theory, Northern Ireland's conflict, and its agreement 2: What critics of consociation can learn from Northern Ireland' (2006) 41(2) *Government and Opposition* 249.

[25] G Lehmbruch, *Verhandlungsdemokratie. Beiträge zur vergleichenden Regierungslehre* (Wiesbaden, Westdeutscher Verlag, 2003).

[26] SE Finer, '*Adversary Politics and Electoral Reform*' in SE Finer (ed), *Adversary Politics and Electoral Reform* (London, Anthony Wigram, 1975) 3.

When the legislative and executive powers are united in the same person, or in the same body of magistrates, there can be no liberty; because apprehensions may arise, lest the same monarch or senate should enact tyrannical laws, to execute them in a tyrannical manner. Again, there is no liberty, if the judiciary power be not separated from the legislative and executive. Were it joined with the legislative, the life and liberty of the subject would be exposed to arbitrary control; for the judge would be then the legislator. Were it joined to the executive power, the judge might behave with violence and oppression. There would be an end of everything, were the same man or the same body, whether of the nobles or of the people, to exercise those three powers, that of enacting laws, that of executing the public resolutions, and of trying the causes of individuals.[27]

The principle of the separation of powers was always, in theory, a part of the tapestry of the Constitution.[28] But in practice, there was little evidence of this. And the Lord Chancellor was the clearest example of the violation of this principle.

Until the passage of the Constitutional Reform Act 2005, the Lord Chancellor was simultaneously a Cabinet minister, a judge and, *qua* member of the House of Lords, a legislator. Clearly it was not 'the end of everything', but it was – constitutionally speaking – a problem that the 'same man . . . exercise[d] those three powers'. Of course, this arrangement – while it violated Montesquieu's doctrine – would have been less of a problem if the Lord Chancellor in practice was able to wear different 'constitutional wigs'. But, as the case of *Bates v Lord Hailsham*[29] showed, there were situations where it was unclear if the Lord Chancellor was acting as a minister or as a legislator. Nevertheless, what was most extraordinary from a comparative political scientist's point of view was the fact that the Lord Chancellor, at the same time as being a Cabinet minister, was also a judge – indeed, the highest judge in the land. To put matters into perspective, it would be unthinkable that a German *Justitzminister* would have been at the same time a presiding judge in the *Bundesverfassungsrericht*, and it is absurd to think that, say, Chief Justice Earl Warren could at the same time have been a member of Eisenhower's Cabinet and a member of Congress. In Britain, conversely, this fusion of roles existed in Britain until 2005. Again, this would have been less of a problem if the Lord Chancellor had refrained from his right to sit as a judge. But he did not. The Lord Chancellors not only sat as judges, they took an active role and penned the leading judgments in some of the most important cases of the twentieth century, as Lord Hailsham did in *The Siskina*[30] and as Lord MacKay did, to much justified acclaim, in *R v Adomako*.[31]

While not questioning the legal prowess and jurisprudential erudition of the Lord Chancellors in question, it clearly violates the very founding principle of a meritocracy that the system allowed party-political allegiances rather than long, distinguished service on the Bench to determine who should head the judiciary.

[27] C de Montesquieu, *The Spirit of the Laws* (Edinburgh, A Donaldson and Reid, 1762) 165.
[28] *R v Hinds* [1979] Crim LR 111. . . 39, per Lord Diplock.
[29] *Bates v Lord Hailsham* [1972] 1 WLR 1373 267.
[30] *Owners of Cargo Lately Laden on Board the Siskina v Distos Compania Naviera SA* (*The Siskina*) [1979] AC 210, [1977] 3 WLR 818 (HL).
[31] *R v Adomako* [1994] 3 WLR 288.

Again, this would have been less of a problem if the Lord Chancellor had been a largely neutral figure without party political leanings (as was the case with Lord MacKay of Clashfern, who, uniquely, was not a member of the Conservative Party when he was selected by Margaret Thatcher), but it was an obvious problem under very partisan Lord Chancellors like Lord Hailsham (Conservative) and Lord Irvine of Lairg (Labour). Lord Irvine presided over the House of Lords and Privy Council on eight occasions.[32] He was the last Lord Chancellor to do so. His successor, Lord Falconer, never sat as a judge.

The change to the Lord Chancellor's role brought Britain a step closer to being in line with Montesquieu's ideal. But this was by no means the only change. Another was as regards the appointment of judges. In this area, the Constitutional Reform Act 2005 arguably goes beyond what is known from other established constitutions. Comparative experts have pointed out that 'in virtually all common law systems, elected politicians determine which justices get to serve on the courts'.[33] Outside the common law traditions, the same is true in Germany, where the *Bundestag* appoints half of the members of the Constitutional Court and the *Bundesrat* (the Second Chamber) selects the other half.[34] In France, one third of the members of the *Conseil constitutionnel* are selected by the President, another third by the Senate and the last third is appointed by the *Assemblée Nationale*.[35] In Britain, the elected politicians now have practically no role. Sections 26 to 31 of the 2005 Act set out the rules for the appointment of future members of the courts. A selection commission, consisting of the President and Deputy President of the Supreme Court, proposes a name to the Lord Chancellor, who can reject that name only once. In practice the appointment of judges has been removed from the political sphere.

B. The Judiciary in a Semi-Federal System

It is a key part of constitutional politics in a federal State that the judiciary polices the boundaries of competencies allocated to different actors.[36] A similar role has emerged in semi-federal States such as Spain, where *El Tribunal Constitucional de España* has intervened extensively, and frequently has ruled statutes passed by the parliaments in the *autonomías* to be ultra vires. For example, in *Judgment No 103/2008* it held that the Basque Parliament had acted ultra vires, and declared 'the unconstitutionality and subsequent invalidity of the *Basque Parliament Law 9/2008 of 27 June*' (a law on a referendum regarding de facto independence).

---

[32] M Beloff, 'Law and the Judiciary' in A Seldon (ed), *Blair's Britain 1997–2007* (Cambridge, Cambridge University Press, 2007) 295.

[33] Ferejohn *et al*, above n 22, 734.

[34] DP Kommers, 'The Federal Constitutional Court in the German Political System' (1994) 26:4 *Comparative Political Studies* 470.

[35] *Constitution de la République française du 4 octobre*, Art 56.

[36] AG Tarr, 'New Judicial Federalism in Perspective' (1996-1997) 72 *Notre Dame Law Review* 1097.

While in some ways the devolution statutes in Britain were inspired by Spain,[37] there is a difference as the UK does not have written, single-document constitution. But this has not deterred the courts from using the individual devolution statutes as de facto proxy constitutions. In the words of Lord Bingham, in *Robinson v Secretary of State for Northern Ireland*, 'The 1998 Act does not set out all the constitutional provisions applicable to Northern Ireland, but it is in effect a constitution'.[38] This principle was applied in *AXA General Insurance Ltd v The Lord Advocate*, where it was held that 'the Scottish Parliament cannot make or unmake any law it wishes'.[39] These obiter dicta may be of little consequence to the practising lawyer and the practical politician, but to the constitutional theorist and to the comparative political scientist they are significant, as they are yet another proof that Britain, constitutionally speaking, has become a 'foreign land', in which the powers of the sub-units are limited by interventions by the courts. Underscored by the fact that the very first Act passed by the Welsh Assembly was unseccesfully challeneged in the courts for being ultra vires.[40] To quote Anthony King, the cases have 'not merely altered the constitution but have injected a new element of constitutionalism into the British system.'[41]

C. The Human Rights Act: The (Semi) Constitution

Vernon Bogdanor once described the Human Rights Act 1998 as the 'keystone' of an entirely new constitutional order.[42] If by a constitution we mean a statute that limits the exercise of power within the confines of that document then the Human Rights Act has many of the hallmarks of a constitution.

It is beyond the scope of this chapter to provide an exegesis of the 1998 Act. Neither is this the place for the analysis of the general jurisprudence of the Supreme Court in matters pertaining to human rights more generally. The aim here is merely to look at the constitutional implications of the enactment of the Act. But in order to do this, it is necessary to weed out some general misconceptions. One of these is that the Human Rights Act 1998 has somehow brought a foreign element into the Constitution. Nothing, in a sense, could be further from the truth. As the title of the White Paper *Rights Brought Home 1997*[43] suggests, the intention was to incorporate into British law an international convention that was largely drafted by British jurists. Parliament was also adamant that the Act would not interfere with the sovereignty of Parliament.

The main provisions of the Act for our purposes are sections 3(1) and 4(2), which provide, respectively:

[37] B Giordano and E Roller, '"Té para todos"? A comparison of the processes of devolution in Spain and the UK' (2004) 36(12) *Environment and Planning A* 2163.
[38] *Robinson v Secretary of State for Northern Ireland* [2002] UKHL 32 [11], per Lord Bingham.
[39] *AXA General Insurance Ltd v The Lord Advocate* [2011] 3 WLR 871 [46], per Lord Hope.
[40] Attorney General's Reference on Local Government Byelaws (Wales) Bill 2012, 3 WLR 1294.
[41] A King, *The British Constitution* (Oxford University Press, 2007) 149.
[42] V Bogdanor, *The New British Constitution* (Oxford, Hart Publishing, 2009) 62.
[43] *Rights Brought Home: The Human Rights Act* (Cm 3782).

3(1) So far as it is possible to do so, primary legislation and subordinate legislation must be read and given effect in a way which is compatible with the Convention rights.

4(2) If the court is satisfied that the provision is incompatible with a Convention right, it may make a declaration of that incompatibility.

On the face of it, these provisions do not appear to amount to much. In practice, these short paragraphs have done more than anything else to limit the omnipotence of Parliament and are responsible for the greatest change in the British Constitution since the introduction of universal suffrage.

i. The British courts and the theory of legislative activism

Theoretically, it is surprising that the British courts have been so activist and have actually challenged Parliament. In a theoretical article, American political scientists Ferejohn, Rosenbluth and Shipan hypothesised, in a section that deserves to be quoted at length,

> If a court can determine that the rulings of regulatory agencies or other political actors . . . are incompatible with existing law, a legislature has the option, if it has a coherent majority, to pass new legislation that overrides the court's ruling. Spatial models show how the threat of a legislative override can cause the court to implement a policy different from what it would choose if it were completely independent . . . Consider, for example, two actors – a judiciary, denoted by J, and a Parliament, denoted by P – and a status quo point denoted by q, which represents a policy chosen by some other political actor . . . Assume that the judiciary has the option to choose a policy rather than being limited to an up or down vote; that the parliament has the opportunity to respond to the court's decision; and that the parliament will act in this policy area only once another actor, such as the court, disrupts the current equilibrium and makes parliament worse off than it currently is[44] [see figure 1]:

Figure 1

```
_____J_____P_____q____
```

In this scenario, if

> the court were independent and did not need to worry about being overridden, it would simply chose to implement J, its ideal point. But in this example – and in most political systems – the parliament will have the opportunity to respond to the court's action. Thus if the court were to try to implement J, the parliament would respond by selecting P.[45]

The problem with this theoretically sound analysis is that in practice, the House of Lords did the very opposite. Under the Human Rights Act 1998, Parliament *was* free to ignore the courts and the House of Lords was not, according to the letter of the law, able to choose its ideal point. Yet in several cases, including *R v A* and the

---

[44] Ferejohn *et al*, above n 22, 730.
[45] *Ibid*.

'*Belmarsh* case' (see below), the courts did exactly this. Indeed, rather than being influenced by Parliament's preferred preference, the lawmakers moved their policy towards that of the courts.

This is not to say that the spatial model developed by Ferejohn, Rosenbluth and Shipan is without merit in all circumstances. What this analysis shows is merely that the spatial model does not explain the British courts' activism. A couple of examples will show this in practice.

ii. Purposive interpretation

In *R v A*[46] – a case on whether a man charged with rape would be allowed to cross-examine a witness when conducting his own defence – the House of Lords upheld the defendant's rights. The House of Lords in effect rewrote section 41 of the Youth, Justice and Criminal Evidence Act 1999. Lord Steyn said:

> In accordance with the will of Parliament as reflected in section 3 it will sometimes be necessary to adopt an interpretation which linguistically may appear strained. The techniques to be used will not only involve the reading down of express language in a statute but also the implication of provisions.[47]

In doing so, the Lords arguably flouted the ostensible intention of Parliament. The argument that purposive interpretations are acceptable even if they 'linguistically may appear strained', takes the power of the courts to a higher level.

Of course, there is nothing new in legal activism, not even in England. Lord Denning noted approvingly that 'Judges do every day make law, though it is almost heresy to say so'.[48] The difference was that after the enactment of the Human Rights Act 1998, the judges had considerably greater powers, and that they were willing to use them. But even so, the courts acted in a way that was considerably more radical than would be expected by the predictive models developed by theoreticians such as Ferejohn, Rosenbluth and Shipan.

iii. Declarations of incompatibility

It is one thing to interpret statutes purposively, it is quite another to strike down statutes for being in violation of the Constitution. In the Republic of Ireland and in the United States, to take but two examples, the courts can strike down – and on occasion have struck down – legislation passed by respectively the *Oireachtas* and Congress, for violating the Constitution.[49] In the United Kingdom the courts cannot, as we have seen, strike down Acts of Parliament; they merely can make

---

[46] *R v A (No 2)* [2002] 1 AC 45.

[47] *Ibid* [44], per Lord Steyn.

[48] Lord Denning, quoted in R Stevens, *Law and Politics: The House of Lords as a Judicial Body, 1800–1976* (Chapel Hill, NC, University of North Carolina Press, 1978) 490.

[49] A Butler, PW Gregory and DL Vand, 'Not So Distant Mirror: Federalism and the Role of Natural Law in the United States, the Republic of Ireland, and the European Community' (1992–1993) *Journal of Transnational Law* 429.

declarations of incompatibility. What is remarkable is not only that the courts have used this power, but also that Parliament has felt bound to alter legislation that the courts have deemed to be in contravention of the Human Rights Act.

In *A and others v Secretary of State for the Home Department*[50]– also known as the '*Belmarsh* case' – the House of Lords declared that section 23 of the Anti-terrorism, Crime and Security Act 2001 (on indefinite detention of foreign nationals) was incompatible with the European Convention on Human Rights. As a consequence, the House of Lords made a declaration of incompatibility under section 4 of the Human Rights Act 1998. Parliament followed suit and enacted the Prevention of Terrorism Act 2005. In other words, and contrary to what we might expect according to the spatial models developed by Ferejohn, Rosenbluth and Shipan, Parliament moved its preferences closer to that of the courts, not the other way round.

Belmarsh was not the first example of judges using this power. Another often-cited case was *R (on the application of Anderson) v Secretary of State for the Home Department*, in which section 29 of the Crime (Sentences) Act 1997 was ruled to be incompatible with Article 6 of the Convention (right to a fair trial)[51]. The section allowed the Home Secretary to decide how long a term the prisoner had to serve. As a consequence of the issuing of a declaration of incompatibility, the offending provision was repealed by the Criminal Justice Act 2003

Altogether there have been 27 declarations of incompatibility since 2000 when the Act was implemented (see Table 1 below). Contrary to the not always balanced coverage in the press, these have not always been upheld on appeal. For example, in *R (Black) v Secretary of State for Justice*,[52] the House of Lords overturned a declaration of incompatibility made by the Court of Appeal, and in *Nasseri v Secretary of State for the Home Department*[53] their Lordships upheld the Court of Appeal's decision overturning a declaration of incompatibility made by the High Court.

Table 1: Declarations of incompatibility 2000–11

1. *R (on the application of Alconbury Developments Ltd) v Secretary of State for the Environment, Transport and the Regions* [2001] HRLR 2; 13 December 2000, Administrative Court
2. *R (on the application of H) v Mental Health Review Tribunal for the North and East London Region & The Secretary of State for Health* [2001] EWCA Civ 415; 28 March 2001, Court of Appeal
3. *Wilson v First County Trust Ltd (No2)* [2001] EWCA Civ 633; 2 May 2001, Court of Appeal
4. *McR's Application for Judicial Review* [2002] NIQB 58; 15 January 2002, Queen's Bench Division (NI)

[50] *A and others v Secretary of State for the Home Department* [2004] UKHL 56
[51] *R (on the application of A) v Secretary of State for the Home Department* [2003] 1 WLR 330,
[52] *R (Black) v Secretary of State for Justice* [2009] UKHL 1.
[53] *Nasseri v Secretary of State for the Home Department* [2009] UKHL 23.

5. *International Transport Roth GmbH v Secretary of State for the Home Department* [2002] EWCA Civ 158; 22 February 2002, Court of Appeal
6. *Matthews v Ministry of Defence* [2002] EWHC 13 (QB); 22 January 2002, Queen's Bench Division
7. *R (on the application of Anderson) v Secretary of State for the Home Department* [2002] UKHL 46; 25 November 2002, House of Lords
8. *R (on the application of D) v Secretary of State for the Home Department* [2002] EWHC 2805 (Admin); 19 December 2002, Administrative Court
9. *Blood and Tarbuck v Secretary of State for Health* (unreported; 28 February 2003)
10. *R (on the application of Uttley) v Secretary of State for the Home Department* [2003] EWHC 950 (Admin); 8 April 2003, Administrative Court
11. *Bellinger v Bellinger* [2003] UKHL 21; 10 April 2003, House of Lords
12. *R (on the application of M) v Secretary of State for Health* [2003] EWHC 1094 (Admin);16 April 2003, Administrative Court
13. *R (on the application of Wilkinson) v Inland Revenue Commissioners* [2003] EWCA Civ 814; 18 June 2003, Court of Appeal
14. *R (on the application of Hooper and others) v Secretary of State for Work and Pensions* [2003] EWCA Civ 875; 18 June 2003, Court of Appeal
15. *R (on the application of MH) v Secretary of State for Health* [2004] EWCA Civ 1609; 3 December 2004, Court of Appeal
16. *A and others v Secretary of State for the Home Department* [2004] UKHL 56; 16 December 2004, House of Lords
17. *R (on the application of Sylviane Pierrette Morris) v Westminster City Council & First Secretary of State (No 3)* [2005] EWCA Civ 1184; 14 October 2005, Court of Appeal
18. *R (Gabaj) v First Secretary of State* (Administrative Court, 28 March 2006)
19. *R (on the application of Baiai and others) v Secretary of State for the Home Department and another* [2006] EWHC 823 (Admin); 10 April 2006, Administrative Court
20. *Re MB* [2006] EWHC 1000 (Admin); 12 April 2006, Administrative Court
21. *R (on the application of (1) June Wright (2) Khemraj Jummun (3) Mary Quinn (4) Barbara Gambier) v (1) Secretary of State for Health (2) Secretary of State for Education & Skills* [2006] EWHC 2886 (Admin); 16 November 2006, Administrative Court
22. *R (Clift) v Secretary of State for the Home Department; Secretary of State for the Home Department v Hindawi and another* [2006] UKHL 54; 13 December 2006, House of Lords
23. *Smith v Scott* [2007] CSIH 9; 24 January 2007, Registration Appeal Court (Scotland)
24. *Nasseri v Secretary of State for the Home Department* [2007] EWHC 1548 (Admin); 2 July 2007, Administrative Court
25. *R (Wayne Thomas Black) v Secretary of State for Justice* [2008] EWCA Civ 359; 15 April 2008, Court of Appeal
26. *R (on the application of F (by his litigation friend F)) and Thompson (FC) v Secretary of State for the Home Department* [2010] UKSC 17; 21 April Supreme Court
27. *R. (on the application of Royal College of Nursing) v Secretary of State for the Home Department* [2010] EWHC 2761 (Admin), (2011) 117 BMLR 10, (2010) 154(46) SJLB 30; 20 February Queen's Bench Division (Administrative Court)

Note: Declarations 1., 3., 6., 10., 15., 20., 24. and 25. were overturned on appeal: Ministry of Justice 2010.

What determines this activism is debatable. Generally speaking, 'courts reduce their activism when faced with unified opposition from other branches'.[54] This conclusion does not seem to hold for Britain. Indeed, in the areas in which the courts intervened, namely, criminal justice and anti-terrorism legislation, there was practically unanimity between the Government and the Opposition. The courts' action seemingly flies in the face of the established theory. One might speculate that the courts, rather than being animated by strategic and tactical considerations, merely acted as they did because they believed in their position. But such subtleties seem to have been lost on some of the political parties. For example, in 2010, in the manifesto, *Invitation to Join the Government of Britain*, the Conservative Party declared that, if elected, it would 'replace Human Rights Act with a UK Bill of Rights'.[55]

In contrast to Canada, where the in the *Charter of Rights and Freedom 1982* has proved very popular among the citizens (82 per cent approve of the document[56]), the Human Rights Act 1998 has been perceived as a threat to the British legal system. The allegation is that the European Court of Human Rights, through the incorporation of the European Convention on Human Rights, has usurped powers and limited the sovereignty of Parliament. The most recent example of this was the case of votes for prisoners.[57] However, it is important to note that it was the British courts that issued the declarations of incompatibility. In a sense, the consequence of the Human Rights Act is that the British courts have created a kind of 'UK Bill of Rights'. For example, in their rulings on the right to respect for private life under Article 8 the British courts deliberately and rather vocally departed from the decisions of the Strasbourg Court. In *von Hanover v Germany*, the European Court of Human Rights set very strict limits on what the press could report in this case about Princess Caroline of Monaco.[58] When faced with a similar scenario in *Murray v Express Newspapers*,[59] the Court of Appeal held that it could not – and would not – follow *von Hannover* but was bound to follow the precedent of *Campbell v MGN*,[60] which gave the newspapers more leeway to publish private material.

Without in any way entering into a discussion of the balance between the right to respect to private life and freedom of expression, the conclusion that emerges is that the British courts deliberately have developed a British interpretation of the European Convention on Human Rights, and in doing so, they have, arguably, created what almost amounts to a judge-made 'UK Bill of Rights'.

---

[54] Ferejohn *et al*, above n 22, 737.

[55] The Conservative Party, *Invitation to Join the Government of Britain* (London, The Conservative Party, 2010) 79.

[56] P Saunders, 'The Charter at 20', *CBC News Online*, April 2002, retrieved 17 March 2006.

[57] *Hirst v the United Kingdom (No 2)* [2005] ECtHR 681.

[58] *von Hannover v Germany No 2* App no 40660/08 (ECtHR).

[59] *Murray v Express Newspapers* [2008] All ER (D) 70.

[60] *Campbell v Mirror Group Newspapers Ltd* [2004] UKHL 22.

IV. CONCLUSION

After the enactment of the Human Rights Act 1998 and the Constitutional Reform Act 2005, Britain has – constitutionally speaking – become a 'foreign land'. Three things stand out:

(a) the Lord Chancellor no longer sits as a judge;
(b) the Supreme Court has become an active adjudicator in matters concerning the constitutionality of devolution statutes; and
(c) the Human Rights Act 1998 has become a de facto constitution. The fact that 'declarations of incompatibility' have been followed by enactment of primary legislation means that the judges now play a political role akin to that seen in countries like Ireland, Germany, the USA and Canada.

'If legislation results in oppression the judges are powerless to prevent it,' wrote Sir Ivor Jennings in the late 1950s.[61] The constitutional changes enacted since 1997 mean that this is no longer the case. The British courts have become more activist than would have been expected, and their actions go beyond what might have been predicted by theoretical models developed by comparative experts in judicial behaviour, such as Ferejohn, Rosenbluth and Shipan. Whether this will change is an open question, but the fact remains that the British courts – even by international standards – have become very activist, and that this activism flies in the face of established comparative theories of judicial behaviour.

---

[61] I Jennings, *The Law and the Constitution*, 5th edn (London, University of London Press, 1959) 254.

5

The Politics-Free Dimension to the UK Constitution

DAWN OLIVER[1]

I. INTRODUCTION

THE UK CONSTITUTION is still predominantly 'political', as it was when Professor John Griffith delivered his Chorley lecture on 'The Political Constitution' in 1979.[2] Griffith's interpretation of the position was that the UK Constitution and its rules were the outcomes of past and continuing conflicts between groups of individuals making their political claims and seeking to persuade government to accept them.[3] These conflicts were commonly mediated by the political parties.

This view of politics and its place was widespread at the time that Griffith wrote: Crick's *In Defence of Politics*[4] argued:

> In spite of the compromises and half-measures which prompt the impatient idealist to regard politics as a dirty word – indeed because of them – the negotiating processes of politics remain the only tested alternative to government by coercion.

In his lecture Griffith argued that it would be inappropriate for judges to have the power to interfere with the outcomes of these conflicts by striking down statutory provisions or by merits-based judicial review of decisions, because judges were

---

[1] I am grateful to colleagues in the Faculty of Laws UCL for their contributions to discussion of my ideas at a seminar, and to Tom Poole, Adam Tomkins and Richard Rawlings for comments on an earlier draft of this chapter.
[2] J Griffith, 'The Political Constitution' (1979) 42 *MLR* 1. For discussions of the nature of the concept of political constitution, see M Foley, *The Politics of the British Constitution* (1999) 30–37; A Tomkins, 'In defence of the political constitution' (2002) 22 *OJLS* 157 and A Tomkins, *Our Republican Constitution* (Oxford, Hart Publishing, 2005); R Bellamy, *Political Constitutionalism* (Cambridge, Cambridge University Press, 2007); T Poole 'Tilting at Windmills? Truth and illusion in the political constitution' (2007) 70 *MLR* 250; G Gee 'The political constitutionalism of JAG Griffith' (2008) 28 *Legal Studies* 20; G Gee and G Webber, 'What is a political constitution?' (2010) 30 *OJLS* 273.
[3] See Griffith, above n 2, 18.
[4] B Crick, *In Defence of Politics* (Reading, Pelican Books, 1962; 2nd edn, 1982), discussed by D Blunkett, 'Politics as Theory and Politics as Practice' (2012) 83 *Political Quarterly* 645. See also SH Beer, *Modern British Politics* (London, Faber & Faber, 1965).

not elected and were therefore not removable. It was no part of Griffith's argument that politicians were particularly good at politics, or at resolving conflicts or at governing, only that they were dismissible whereas judges were not, and it was due to that distinction that judges should not interfere with politicians' decisions.

Griffith did not concern himself in that lecture with the processes by which conflicts were resolved by politicians and political parties. In practice the resolution of conflicts by politicians is likely to involve confidential discussions and deals with interested sections of their parties and with outside bodies, in which compromises are reached and quid pro quos exchanged. This is what Crick was referring to in writing of 'compromises and half-measures' in the quotation from the cover of his *Defence of Politics*, above. It is not obvious that the outcomes of such bargaining processes will necessarily promote the wider general interest or general welfare, for which the State is commonly supposed to be responsible.[5]

Now, more than 30 years since 'The Political Constitution' was published, most important substantive decisions as to public policy and where the balances between conflicting public interests and between public and private interests lie, still rest with elected politicians or people who are accountable to them. And responsibility for much of the process of conflict resolution still rests with politicians. Despite hints to the contrary, for instance in the *Jackson*[6] and *Axa*[7] cases and in controversial articles by judges in academic journals,[8] the courts have not granted claims for judicial review of primary legislation passed by the UK Parliament, resulting in the disapplication of statutory provisions – save in relation to European Union laws. And, as I shall demonstrate below, judges continue to allow considerable scope for politics and politicking when dealing with challenges to politicians' decisions, especially in relation to planning,[9] foreign relations,[10] and tax and public expenditure issues.[11] Much has not changed since Griffith's article.

Griffith's focus on the resolution of conflicts by politicians left out of account other aspects of 'politics'. Promoting the interests of the governing party without regard to the public interest; party discipline exercised so as to undermine the willingness of MPs and councillors to exercise their functions on their own responsibility; party political point scoring in parliamentary debates and in the media; partisanship; the exercise of unregulated patronage in bestowing benefits for self-interested reasons or as rewards for past favours, or to promote the interests of a political party, for instance in the making of public appointments,

---

[5] See discussion in N Barber, *The Constitutional State* (Oxford, Oxford University Press, 2010) 25–33 and ch 3, with reference to Aristotle, *Politics and the Constitution of Athens*, ed S Everson (Cambridge, Cambridge University Press, 1996).

[6] *Jackson v Attorney General* [2006] AC 262.

[7] *AXA General Insurance Ltd and others v The Lord Advocate* [2011] UKSC 46.

[8] Sir Harry Woolf, 'Droit public – English style [1995] *Public Law* 57; Sir John Laws, 'Law and democracy' [1995] *Public Law* 72.

[9] *Franklin v Minister for Town and Country Planning* [1948] AC 86, discussed in section IV.B. below.

[10] *Council of Civil Service Unions v Minister for the Civil Service* [1985] AC 374.

[11] See *R v Cambridgeshire Health Authority, ex p B* [1995] 1 WLR 898.

awards of government contracts or grants of planning permissions. These are all commonly regarded as 'bad politics' in the UK, and their practice generates widespread distrust.

Over the last 30 years or so – indeed the trend started much earlier – efforts have been made to immunise many areas of public administration and governmental policy-making from 'bad politics', not only by legislation and decisions of the courts, but also as a result of policy changes and changed practices by successive governments. Many of the functions that were formerly performed directly by ministers or in their departments have been privatised (management of the utilities and former nationalised industries are the obvious examples) or transferred either to agencies within departments operating under framework documents, or to independent arm's-length public bodies. Many new such bodies have been created, including the regulators of the privatised utilities. And both the political process broadly understood and processes of specific decision making by politicians and other public officials have become increasingly regulated, by soft law in the form of codes, conventions, guidance, formulae, memorandums and other formal though not 'legal' or justiciable 'rules', and by hard law in the form of legislation, administrative justice arrangements and decisions of the courts in judicial review cases.

A theme running through these developments is the desire to limit party political, subjective, partisan or selfish considerations and processes in politicians' decision making – the aspects of 'politics' with which this chapter is concerned. I regard this process as the development of a non-political dimension to the British Constitution operating in parallel to Griffith's political one. It is the focus of this chapter.

In section II. of this chapter I shall consider the growth of a whole range of arm's-length bodies, including tribunals, to deal with matters which would previously have been the direct responsibility of government or other executive bodies – and would therefore potentially have been influenced by political considerations. In section III. I shall discuss the place and the contents of soft law in politics, including parliamentary practice and many important executive documents, often self-regulating, which seek to remove party politics from aspects of the business of Parliament and to depoliticise aspects of government and public administration. In section IV. I shall discuss the doctrines relating to the place of politics in public decision making that have been developed by the courts. And in section V. I shall reflect upon and draw some conclusions from these matters.

II. ARM'S-LENGTH BODIES[12]

Many decisions of a broadly administrative nature that could have fallen within the responsibilities of government departments or the two Houses[13] – and have

---

[12] See, eg, M Adler (ed), *Administrative Justice in Context* (Oxford, Hart Publishing, 2010).

[13] For instance the transfer of responsibility for the MPs' expenses system to the Independent Parliamentary Standards Authority in 2010.

done so in years past – are nowadays either beyond the reach of politics and of politicians because they have been privatised[14] – a topic on which there is not the space in this chapter to comment – or in the hands of independent arm's-length bodies (ALBs) such as quangos and tribunals.[15] These developments have been in part responses to a range of pressures – for instance, European law requirements for independent regulation and the European Convention on Human Rights' requirement for civil rights to be protected by independent tribunals. But one among these pressures has been concern to legitimate the implementation of policy decisions and decisions affecting individuals by insulating them from 'bad' politics.[16] This would not have been necessary if politicking and party politics had not come to be suspect and mistrusted by many sections of the public, and particularly by those affected by political activities. Thus my focus here is on the politics-related reasons for the creation and retention of quangos and tribunals, and the removal of their functions from government and political control.

A. Quangos, Non-Departmental Public Bodies and ALBs[17]

The existence and independence of quangos not only secure that the functions for which they are responsible are performed professionally and independently of politics in accordance with their mandates, whether statutory or other; they also immunise politicians from public criticism for short-termism or lack of expertise, or for prioritising the interests of their parties or funders over general or independently-determined public interests. The fact that the use of such bodies for these purposes has grown over the years, I suggest, generally reflects not only political but public opinion to the effect that the scope for party politicking in public administration should be restricted so as to encourage public trust and protect the legitimacy of the system as a whole.

However, in recent years a rebalancing of the need for independence and requirements of political accountability has been taking place. This has normally been in response to political and public concerns about the accountability of these often powerful bodies. David Cameron, as Leader of the Opposition in 2009, indicated that two of the three justifications for a quango would be that it is necessary for impartial decisions to be made about the distribution of taxpayers' money, and that it fulfils a need for facts to be transparently determined, independently of

---

[14] Since Griffith's lecture in 1979, most utilities and heavy industries, including coal, steel and motor manufacturing, have been privatised. For discussion of these issues, see C Veljanowski *Selling the State* (London, Weidenfeld and Nicolson,1987).

[15] See Franks Report, *Administrative Tribunals and Enquiries*, Cmnd 218, 1957.

[16] *Ibid.*

[17] For a summary of the position, see *Quangos*, House of Commons Library Standard Note SN/ PC/05609, January 2011; see also Cabinet Office, *Public Bodies*, 2009; M Flinders, evidence to the Public Administration Select Committee (PASC) in its Report *Smaller Government: Shrinking the Quango State*, HC 537 (2010–2011), QGO 02; PASC, *Mapping the Quango State*, HC 367 (2000–2001).

political interference.[18] The Conservative Party manifesto for the 2010 general election stated that 'Any quangos that do not perform a technical function or a function that requires political impartiality, or act independently to establish facts, will be abolished.'[19] This policy, together with a desire to cut costs and to improve accountability to ministers and to Parliament for the functions exercised by such bodies, was given effect in the Public Bodies Act 2011, which empowers ministers to abolish, merge or transfer functions to and from the public bodies listed in the Schedule to the Act.[20] But of course the transfer of ALBs' functions to departments exposes them to political pressures which many of them were formed to prevent. Whether this consideration will be taken into account as ALBs are transferred in remains to be seen. The following examples serve to illustrate the trend towards the depoliticisation of public administration by the establishment of quangos in response to public and political concerns about party politics, and their survival despite the Public Bodies Act.

B. The Committee on Standards in Public Life

The Committee on Standards in Public Life (CSPL) was established as an advisory body in 1994, 'to examine current concerns about standards of conduct of all holders of public office, including arrangements relating to financial and commercial activities, and to make recommendations . . . to ensure the highest standards of propriety in public life'. It was established in the wake of political scandals about MPs taking payments in return for asking parliamentary questions – in other words, for prioritising their own financial interests over the public interests which MPs are commonly required to put first. The disclosure of these activities in the press had incurred public revulsion. The 'Seven Principles of Public Life', formulated by the CSPL in its First Report in 1995,[21] have been adopted and incorporated into codes of conduct by many public bodies, including party-political ones – the Codes of Conduct of the two Houses of Parliament, the Ministerial Code, the Civil Service Code (which are discussed in section III. below) and many others. The principles are elaborated in the CSPL's publications in ways that seek to restrain politicians from engaging in some of the darker arts of politics – such as resolving conflicts by secret deals which would attract condemnation if known to the public:

(a) *Selflessness* requires holders of public office not to act in order to gain financial or other benefits for themselves, their family or their friends, and thus implies that any appointments they are in a position to make should be made on merit

---

[18] Speech by David Cameron, 'Cutting the Cost of Politics', 8 September 2009, quoted in HC Library SN/PC/05609, above n 17.

[19] *An Invitation to Join the Government of Britain* (2010) 81.

[20] For lists of public bodies which have been abolished, see Cabinet Office website, www.gov.uk/government/publications/quango-reform-public-bodies-closed-so-far.

[21] Cm 2850, May 1995.

and not in the exercise of unregulated patronage. This is also reflected in the work of the Office of the Commissioner for Public Appointments (see section II.C. below).

(b) *Integrity* requires holders of public office not to place themselves under any financial or other obligation to outside individuals or organisations – which would no doubt include sponsors or political parties – that might seek to influence them in the performance of their official duties.

(c) *Objectivity* means that in carrying out public business, including making public appointments, awarding contracts or recommending individuals for rewards and benefits, holders of public office should make choices on merit: thus subjectivity and partisanship are restricted.

(d) *Accountability* requires holders of public office to submit themselves to appropriate scrutiny: thus they may not rely simply on the fact that they have authority, but must be prepared to justify their actions in ways acceptable to those they serve.

(e) *Openness* requires holders of public office to be as open as possible and to give reasons for their decisions, and to restrict information only when the wider public interest clearly so demands, thus putting the exercise of some of the dark arts of politics on the wrong side of the line.

(f) *Honesty* requires holders of public office to declare any private interests relating to their public duties and to resolve conflicts in a way that protects the public interest.

(g) *Leadership* requires holders of public office to promote and support these principles by leadership and example.

The CSPL conducts biannual surveys of public perceptions of standards in public life: the results of these surveys indicate the emergence of a shared sense within the population that the 'Seven Principles' ought to be observed, a point to which I shall return in the concluding section of this chapter.[22]

C. The Commissioner for Public Appointments

The Committee on Standards in Public Life recommended specifically the establishment of a Commissioner for Appointments in its First Report, in response to concerns that ministerial appointments to quangos were not always made on merit.[23] The office was established by the Public Appointments Order in Council 2002 and was given responsibility for regulating the processes for the making of

---

[22] See Report of the Open Seminar held by the Committee on Standards in Public Life on 19 January 2012, paras 7–22, presentation by Professor Cees van de Eijk, in which he notes that although different sections of the public have different perceptions of conduct, the expectations of standards in public life are broadly shared by all sections of society: <www.public-standards.gov.uk/Library/> . On perceptions of conduct, see CSPL, *Fourth Biannual Survey of Public Attitudes Towards Conduct in Public Life, 2010*, September 2011, ch 7 (overview).

[23] See CSPL, above n 21, Summary, paras 30, 32, Recommendation 33–44.

public appointments by ministers to public bodies.[24] Previously there was no general regulation of the making of appointments by ministers, and concerns had been expressed that public appointments were made on political grounds or as exercises of ministerial patronage, not based on open competition and merit.[25]

The Commissioner is required to publish a Code of Practice (a new one came into force in April 2012), to require public appointments assessors to chair the panels appointing chairs of public bodies, to investigate complaints about appointment processes within his remit, to monitor and review these processes and to promote effectiveness, diversity and equality of opportunity in public appointments. Although the actual appointments are still made by ministers, the process set by the Commissioner depoliticises them in line with the 'Seven Principles of Public Life', in particular selflessness, openness and objectivity.

D. The Bank of England and the Monetary Policy Committee

The Bank of England, the central bank of the United Kingdom, was founded in 1694 and was nationalised on 1 March 1946. The Bank of England Act 1998 granted the Bank independence in setting interest rates. The background to this measure was the commitment of Chancellor of the Exchequer Gordon Brown to ending the influence of the short-term wishes of politicians in the setting of rates, and thus to end the 'boom and bust' fluctuation of rates.[26] The Bank's monetary policy objective is to deliver price stability – low inflation – and, subject to that, to support the Government's economic objectives, including those for growth and employment. The remit recognises the role of price stability in achieving economic stability more generally, and in providing the right conditions for sustainable growth in output and employment.

E. UK Statistics Authority and the Office for National Statistics[27]

The UK Statistics Authority was established on 1 April 2008 by the Statistics and Registration Service Act 2007 as an independent body operating at arm's length from government, a non-ministerial department directly accountable to Parliament. It is responsible for oversight of the UK's National Statistical Institute (NSI) and of the Office for National Statistics (ONS), which is its executive office and the largest producer of official statistics in the UK.

---

[24] See House of Commons Library Standard Note SN/PC/3368, *The Commissioner for Public Appointments*.

[25] See House of Commons Library Standard Note SN/PC/05609, above n 17, 19–20.

[26] See, eg, BBC report, 6 May 1997, at <www.news.bbc.co.uk>.

[27] This information is taken from the website of the UK Statistics Authority, www.statisticsauthority.gov.uk

The background to the 2007 and previous arrangements for the collection and publication of statistics was concern that government might manipulate statistics for partisan and party-political purposes. The Authority's statutory objective is to promote and safeguard the production and publication of official statistics that serve the public good: by implication politicians cannot be trusted to do so. The Authority is also required to promote and safeguard the quality and comprehensiveness of official statistics, and ensure good practice in relation to them. Thus it seeks to immunise national statistics from political manipulation in the public interest.

F. The Office for Budget Responsibility

The Office for Budget Responsibility (OBR) was established shortly after the May 2010 general election by the Chancellor of the Exchequer, George Osborne. Osborne had been critical of the economic and fiscal forecasts of the previous, Labour Government. The Office was put on a formal statutory footing by the Budget Responsibility and National Audit Act 2011,[28] which seeks to buttress its independence from government. The Act imposes a range of duties on the Treasury with regard to the formulation and implementation of fiscal policy, including through the Charter for Budget Responsibility. The OBR's main duty is to examine and report – objectively – on the sustainability of the public finances. It produces economic and fiscal forecasts, which the Government is to adopt as the 'official' forecasts for the annual Budget. The OBR controls the production of the forecasts and makes the judgements that underpin them, independently of government ministers. Thus the Chancellor of the Exchequer is no longer responsible for these judgments. The OBR also produces long-term fiscal projections and analysis relating to the public sector balance sheet. These functions have all been depoliticised with a view to enhancing the credibility of fiscal policy and projections in the general interest. However, the OBR has been severely criticised for its economic forecasting. It does not follow that these functions would have been better exercised if they had remained within the government department.

G. Tribunals

It was not until the implementation of the reforms proposed by the Franks Committee in 1957 that departments no longer ran 'their' tribunals, and the appointment of tribunal judges was removed from the departments and thus from politics. The Franks Committee[29] considered that tribunals should be properly regarded as machinery for adjudication rather than as part of the machinery

---

[28] See House of Commons Research Paper 11/25, 15 March 2011, for an account of the bill and the support of government and opposition members for the OBR to be fully independent of government.
[29] Cmnd 218, 1957.

of administration as had been the position until then, that they should be governed by (non-political) principles of fairness, openness and impartiality, and that they should therefore be entirely independent of their departments. Although tribunals acquired independence after Franks, it was not until 2009, when the Tribunals, Courts and Enforcement Act 2007 came into force, that they became formally part of the system of justice and entirely independent from politics. The reform was implemented in line with the recommendations of the Leggatt Report of 2001 and to meet the requirement in Article 6 of the European Convention on Human Rights that in the exercise of their civil rights and obligations, everyone is entitled to access to an independent and impartial tribunal.[30]

H. Comments

The foregoing are select examples of ALBs that have been created in part to immunise certain public activities from 'bad politics'. There are many more. They cannot, however, guarantee that the functions in question will be well exercised, only that they will not be subject to undue political interference and manipulation. The points I draw from these examples of the establishment of ALBs to take over or regulate politicians' activities are that they demonstrate how public opinion and opposition politicians can force the depoliticisation of some functions, and that government may feel compelled to give in to such pressures in order to retain trust and legitimacy. They also show that politicians cannot always be relied upon to change behaviour that suits them by exhortation, and that institutional changes – the establishment of ALBs and/or hard or soft law – may be needed to reinforce compliance with new standards. However, these provisions cannot guarantee that politicians will refrain from applying what influence and pressure they can on the exercise of these functions: the Public Bodies Act offers opportunities for ministers to abolish ALBs, thus removing the barriers to 'bad politics' in relation to their functions under cover of the need to bring the functions within Parliament's oversight through the conventions of ministerial responsibility.

III. POLITICIANS: THE EXECUTIVE AND PARLIAMENTARIANS

Increasingly, activities of politicians and of third parties dealing or negotiating with them are subject to restraints, many of them in the form of self-regulation, for instance in codes, conventions, guidance, formulae, memorandums and other formal though not 'legal' or justiciable documents, and in the standing orders and resolutions of the two Houses of Parliament. Many of these are directed to restraining the exercise of party-political power by party leaders and to prioritising the

---

[30] *Tribunals for Users: One System, One Service*, Department of Constitutional Affairs (2004); this was followed by a White Paper in July 2004, *Transforming Public Services: Complaints, Redress and Tribunals*, on which the 2007 Act was based.

promotion of public interests in decision making. Breaches or allegations of breaches of these requirements give rise to criticism from the press, the public and opposition parties, and to loss of trust, status and respect – the very pressures that brought about the restraints in the first place. While the existence and content of these documents are widely known, I suggest that their implications in the development of non-political dimensions to the UK's political constitution are not widely appreciated.

A. The Executive

Restrictions on party politicking and partisanship in government go back much earlier than 1979 when Griffith's article was published: the Northcote Trevelyan Report of 1854[31] led to the establishment of a permanent, professional Civil Service appointed on merit and separated from politics. Examples of how this affects the exercise of power by ministers are given below.

Many of the restrictions and other rules affecting the executive were secret until the mid-1990s. The recent trend – including the passing of the Freedom of Information Act 2000 – has been to publish the many guidelines that regulate governmental activity, and to develop and publish new ones. The very fact of publication of these documents attracts accountability since it provides accountability criteria: these are largely non-political. While breaches of the norms in these documents do not expose government to judicial review, they do generate other sanctions – parliamentary, political, public – which are more or less effective to secure that the reach of party politics and associated party political manoeuvring into government is inhibited in various ways. I shall illustrate these points by reference to the Ministerial Code and the Cabinet Manual, but these are examples from a large number of soft law documents which regulate governmental activity – including those issued by the Committee on Standards in Public Life and the Commissioner for Public Appointments which were discussed in section II. of this chapter.

i. The Ministerial Code

Written guidance for British Cabinet ministers began as *Questions of Procedure for Ministers* (QPM), a confidential document prepared by the Cabinet Office to assist ministers. It dates to at least the 1980s. It became the Ministerial Code and was first published by Prime Minister John Major in 1992. It is revised by each incoming government, taking into account lessons, experience and changes since the previous edition. The current version was published shortly after the general election in May 2010.

---

[31] Available at <www.civilservant.org.uk/northcotetrevelyan.pdf >.

The Code states that the overarching duty of ministers is to comply with the law, including international law and treaty obligations, to uphold the administration of justice and to protect the integrity of public life[32]; they must ensure that no conflict arises, or appears to arise, between their public duties and their private interests – a strong example of restrictions on how conflicts may be resolved[33]; they must not use government resources for party-political purposes.[34]

Ministers must uphold the political impartiality of the Civil Service[35]; they have a duty to ensure that influence over Civil Service and public appointments is not abused for partisan purposes[36]; they are personally responsible for the management and conduct of their political advisers, and the advisers are responsible to the Government as a whole.[37]

Facilities provided to ministers at government expense to enable them to carry out their official duties should not be used for party or constituency work[38]; official facilities and resources may not be used for the dissemination of material which is essentially party-political.[39]

Where ministers have to take decisions without their departments which might have an impact on their own constituencies, they must take particular care to avoid any possible conflict of interest.[40]

On taking office, ministers should give up membership or chairmanship of a select committee or all-party parliamentary group[41]; they should arrange their affairs so as to avoid any suggestion that a union of which they are members has any undue influence.[42]

ii. The Cabinet Manual

The Cabinet Manual, first published in 2010, reiterates some of the provisions of the Ministerial Code and seeks to summarise common understandings as to the operation of the Cabinet system. A draft was examined by the Justice Committee of the House of Commons before the general election of 2010. A revised version was published after the election. A number of parliamentary select committees reported on the draft and, later, the Manual.[43] It sets out the constraints on

---

[32] Ministerial Code, s 1.2.
[33] *Ibid*, s 1.2.f.
[34] *Ibid*, s 1.2.i.
[35] *Ibid*, s 1.2.j.
[36] *Ibid*, s 3.1.
[37] *Ibid*, s 3.3.
[38] *Ibid*, s 6.1.
[39] *Ibid*, s 6.3.
[40] *Ibid*, s 6.4.
[41] *Ibid*, s 7.14.
[42] *Ibid*, s 7.15. This is particularly important given the historical links between trade unions, the Labour Party and MPs, enshrined in the Party's constitution.
[43] See Report of the Justice Committee HC 396, 2009–2010; Constitution Committee, 12th report (2010–12): *The Cabinet Manual* (HL Paper 107); Public Administration Select Committee, 8th Report (2010–12): *Cabinet Manual* (HC 900); the Political and Constitutional Reform Committee, 6th Report (2010–12): *Constitutional implications of the Cabinet Manual* (HC 73).

decision making in government at various stages of the electoral cycle and in a whole range of circumstances, as the following examples show.

a. Post-election constraints

If no party has a Commons majority after a general election the Prime Minister may allow civil servants to support the political parties in negotiations for the formation of a government, but this support should be focused and provided on an equal basis to all parties involved.[44] Thus the public interest in the formation of an effective government – rather than the interests of particular parties – is promoted.

b. In-government constraints

Access to papers of a previous administration of a different political party that indicate the views of their predecessors is not normally permitted.[45] Thus personalised party political vendettas are restricted.

Ministers must ensure that no conflict arises or appears to arise between their public duties and their private interests – in which are included party-political ones.[46] At the discretion of the Prime Minister, however, members of Cabinet may meet to discuss party-political matters in a 'political Cabinet'. Such meetings may take place in the Cabinet Room as usual, but they are not attended by officials and the conclusions of the discussion are not recorded in minutes.[47] Thus the Civil Service is kept out of party politicking.

Ministers are required to uphold the political impartiality of the Civil Service and not to ask civil servants to act in any way that would conflict with the Civil Service Code or the requirements of the Constitutional Reform and Governance Act 2010.[48] The Civil Service Code includes requirements of impartiality, including political impartiality.[49] In addition, civil servants should not be asked to engage in activities likely to call into question their political impartiality or give rise to criticism that resources paid from public funds are being used for party-political purposes.[50]

On the face of it the employment of special advisers[51] goes against the trend of constraining party politics. The Cabinet Manual states that their employment adds a political dimension to the advice and assistance available to ministers, while reinforcing the political impartiality of the permanent Civil Service.[52] The

---

[44] Cabinet Manual, para 2.14.
[45] *Ibid*, para 11.23
[46] *Ibid*, para 3.46. See also Ministerial Code.
[47] *Ibid*, para 4.8.
[48] *Ibid*, para 7.2
[49] *Ibid*, para 7.4.
[50] *Ibid*, para 7.3.
[51] *Ibid*, para 7.11ff; and see the *Code of Conduct for Special Advisers*, Cabinet Office, June 2010.
[52] *Ibid*, para 7.13.

House of Lords Constitution Committee, in its Report on the Accountability of Civil Servants, emphasised that ministers are responsible for the actions of their special advisers. Ministers have a duty to ensure their special advisers abide by the Code of Conduct for Special Advisers at all times.[53] And they will be responsible to Parliament for these matters.

Ministerial patronage has been curtailed by the arrangements for the making of public appointments, discussed above. Under the Coalition Government's Civil Service Reform Plan of 2012,[54] ministers will have a greater role than hitherto in the appointment of Permanent Secretaries in their departments, subject to consultation over procedures for this with the Civil Service Commission: this consultation, in addition to the role of the Commissioner for Public Appointments, should limit the scope for such powers to be used for partisan or party-political purposes by ministers.

c. Election campaign constraints

During the general election campaign and until a new government is formed, the Government, though it remains in office, does so as a caretaker.[55] It is customary for ministers to observe discretion in initiating any action of a continuing or long-term character.[56] Pre-election contact by civil servants with opposition parties may be permitted by the Prime Minister. Meetings are confidential and ministers do not receive reports of them. Senior civil servants may ask questions about opposition parties' policy statements.[57]

B. Parliamentarians

We now turn to ways in which – counter-intuitively perhaps – Members of the House of Commons are required to act in a non-partisan fashion.

i. Select Committees of the House of Commons

Party leaders – perhaps because each party leader is a Prime Minister or a Leader of an Opposition in waiting to be Prime Minister, and is therefore interested in the position of opposition parties – have long acknowledged the need to share positions in Parliament between the parties rather than allowing the majority party to use its advantage to claim all such positions: some counter-majoritarian traditions are strong in the Chamber. Thus the chairs of departmental select committees are allocated according to the balance of the parties in the House. Certain

---

[53] HL 61 (2012–13), para 59.
[54] <www.civilservice.gov.uk/wp-content/uploas/2012/06/civil-service-reform-plan-acc-final.pdf >
[55] Cabinet Manual, para 2.27ff.
[56] *Ibid*, paras 2.29 and 2.30.
[57] *Ibid*, para 2.21.

committees are chaired by members of the main Opposition party – notably the powerful Committee for Public Accounts.[58]

Since 2010, in implementation of recommendations made by the Public Administration Select Committee in the 2005–10 Parliament and by the Select Committee on the Reform of the House of Commons chaired by Tony Wright MP in 2010[59] in *Rebuilding the House*,[60] the chairs and members of select committees are elected in secret ballots by MPs rather than being chosen by their party whips, as had been the practice until then; they retain their position for the duration of the Parliament. Normally only backbenchers may be members of these committees. The Government's control of parliamentary time and the agenda has been loosened by the formation of the new Back Bench Business Committee in 2010. There were plans to move to a House Business Committee in the third year of a Coalition Government.

Select committees[61] and their members enjoy far greater independence from the executive and from party politics than MPs involved in debates and legislative processes on the floor of the House or in public bill committees. It has become acceptable, indeed expected, for backbench MPs to assert some independence from the party whips in relation to their work in select committees: the fact of working together in committee may generate its own sense of group loyalty, providing a counter-balance to party loyalty. The culture in select committees is to seek consensus between the members in order to increase the authority of their reports. Negotiation may take place between members of the committees in order to produce an agreed report. Politics, in Griffith's sense of compromise and negotiation between politicians, are never far away, but 'bad politics' is weaker in committees than in many other aspects of parliamentary activity.

ii. *Individual Backbench Members of Parliament*

Although the activities of MPs in the House of Commons are in many respects dominated by party discipline and are thus highly party-political, especially during ministers' question times and other proceedings in plenary sessions in the Chamber, the long-established basic position is that MPs are under duties to uphold the law and to act in the interests of the nation as a whole and their constituents in particular.[62] They should not, therefore, promote partisan or sectional interests unless they are able to justify doing so in terms of national or constituency interest. The trend

---

[58] Indeed, the National Audit Act of 1983 established the Comptroller and Auditor General as an Officer of Parliament, independent of the Government, and in charge of the National Audit Office, thus reinforcing the depoliticisation of this aspect of the Constitution. The Comptroller and Auditor General answers to the Committee for Public Accounts.

[59] See Erskine May, *Parliamentary Practice*, 24th edn (London, Butterworths, 2010) 842.

[60] HC 1117 (2008–2009).

[61] See generally Erskine May, above n 59, ch 37.

[62] House of Commons, *Code of Conduct* (which is drawn up by the HC Committee on Standards and Privileges) and *Guide to the Rules relating to the Conduct of Members*, June 2009. See Erskine May, above n 59, 75ff.

over many years, as seen in the Standing Orders of the House of Commons, in the reports of select committees and in parliamentary resolutions, has been to depoliticise much backbench activity, or at least to immunise it from excessive partisan, party-political and executive influence.

The House has resolved in a number of contempt and breach-of-privilege cases that MPs should be free from mandate, punishment or harassment by outside bodies in the discharge of their functions which would reduce their freedom of action and exercise of judgment in, for instance – since this is where Griffith's theory comes in – the development of policy designed to resolve conflicts. For example, in November 1995 the House resolved:

> It is inconsistent with the dignity of the House, with the duty of a Member to his constituents, and with the maintenance of the privilege of freedom of speech, for any Member . . . to enter into any contractual agreement with an outside body, controlling or limiting the Member's complete independence and freedom of action in Parliament or stipulating that he shall act in any way as the representative of such outside body . . .; the duty of a Member being to his constituents and to the country as a whole, rather than to any particular section thereof . . .[63]

This resolution was passed in view of concerns over the years about the influence of outside bodies[64] wishing to promote their own interests where these were in conflict with existing public policies, or to prevent changes in policy that might be in conflict with their own interests.

It was not just the general public but most members of the House of Commons themselves who were outraged at the MPs' expenses scandal of 2009, as they had been at the 'cash for questions' scandal in 1995, which led to the formation of the CSPL, noted in section II.B. above. The 2009 scandal led to legislation to establish the Independent Parliamentary Standards Authority (IPSA) to take over the management of MPs' expenses and their salaries. Both scandals illustrate how public opinion and long-standing parliamentary law and custom come together to condemn self-serving activities by MPs on the basis that their function is to promote the general good and public interest.

Is not the whip system in the House inconsistent with this approach?[65]Although the operation of the whip system inevitably interferes with the ability or willingness of MPs to formulate and follow their own judgements on matters of public

---

[63] *Ibid*, 79. This reiterated the resolution of the House on the WJ Brown affair, in which the question was whether a sponsoring union was entitled to mandate an MP as to how he should vote in the House or punish him for failing to do as it wished: Committee of Privileges Report, HC 118 (1946–47), paras 11–15. And see the dicta in the *Osborne* case, discussed in section IV.A. below, in which Lord Shaw of Dunfermline indicated that any other position would be contrary to the Constitution.

[64] Eg, commercial companies seeking information about their competitors from the Government or seeking to lobby ministers, or trade unions sponsoring MPs.

[65] Each party's wishes as to how its MPs should vote are conveyed to them in the form of letters known as 'whips'. They outline the parliamentary schedule, with a sentence such as 'Your attendance is absolutely essential' next to each debate in which there will be a vote, underlined one, two or three times according to the severity of the whip. An MP who disobeys a three-line whip runs the risk of losing the prospect of a career on the front benches, being expelled temporarily or permanently from the parliamentary party, and losing the party's nomination for the seat at the next election.

policy against the policy of their party leaders, 'whips' – the documents distributed to MPs encouraging them to vote in specified ways – are not regarded as direct external mandates to MPs – which would breach their privilege – but are considered to be merely internal arrangements within the parliamentary parties and thus part of the internal operation of the House of Commons.

C. Comments

In both the Cabinet Manual and the Ministerial Code, conflicts between the duties of ministers and the interests of their political parties and supporters are required to be avoided so as to ensure that ministers prioritise the public or general interest. Thus one of the forums in which the conflicts with which Griffith was concerned emerge and might be expected to be resolved, the political parties, are to be excluded from dominating the policy-making process. And ministers must avoid finding themselves committed to other interests which might seek to influence their actions – which, in other words, might be in conflict with government.[66] The Civil Service is protected from involvement in politics by many of the provisions in the Cabinet Manual and the Ministerial Code, as it is also by the Constitutional Reform and Governance Act 2010, chapter 1, which places it on a statutory footing. And MPs and select committees are protected by the standing orders of the House of Commons from excessive control by the government of the day.

There remain, however, a number of gaps or weaknesses in the exclusion of 'bad politics' from government. The powers of ministers in relation to appointments of permanent secretaries and special advisers leave room for patronage.[67] The position in relation to the latter was noted above. The House of Lords Constitution Committee recommended:

> However the existing appointments process for permanent secretaries may be modified, it must continue to conform fully with the constitutional principles of integrity, honesty, objectivity and impartiality. In particular, any modified process should protect the principle of appointment on merit, on the basis of fair and open competition.[68]

---

[66] A problem during the 1974–79 Parliament was that the Government, through the Labour Party, had institutional and financial links with trade unions which affected, or appeared to affect, its ability and willingness to control trade union activity that was damaging to the country's economy. Trade union links with the party became particularly controversial during the period of the Campaign for Labour Party Democracy in the early 1980s: see D Oliver, 'The constitutional implications of the Labour Party reforms' [1981] *Public Law* 151.

[67] See House of Lords Constitution Committee, Sixth Report, *The Accountability of Civil Servants*, HL 61 (2012–13).

[68] *Ibid*, para 28.

IV. THE COURTS

The decision-making processes of public bodies have been increasingly regulated by decisions of the courts in judicial review cases, in which statutory provisions are interpreted or exercises of common law royal prerogative powers are reviewed.[69] Broadly, the judicial review case law sterilises much public decision making against party politics and partisanship, while at the same time allowing ministers to implement their policy preferences. There follow some examples of the approach taken by the courts.

A. The Role of Political Parties

A recurring issue in the case law has been the degree to which ministers, MPs or elected councillors in local authorities may be dictated to or influenced by their party organisations or other supporting organisations such as sponsors. The position of the courts has been consistently that elected decision makers owe duties to their constituents and to the general public, and must act independently as representatives of the voters and not as their delegates or delegates of their parties or sponsors. This mirrors the position taken by the House of Commons as set out in the resolution of November 1995, discussed in section III.B.ii. above,[70] and the principles set out in the Cabinet Manual and the Ministerial Code, and in many other soft-law documents.

In an early case, *Amalgamated Society of Railway Servants v Osborne*,[71] one of the issues was the legal effect of a contractual relationship between an MP and his party or sponsors – in that case the Amalgamated Society of Railway Servants, a trade union. Lord Shaw noted that '[u]nless a member becomes bound to the society and to the Labour party by these conditions, and shapes his parliamentary action in conformity therewith, and with the decision of the parliamentary party, he has broken his bargain,' and held:

> I do not think that such a subjection is compatible either with the spirit of our parliamentary constitution or with that independence and freedom which have hitherto been held to lie at the basis of representative government in the United Kingdom.[72]

It is worth noting that the House of Commons adopted a similar approach in the WJ Brown case which was discussed in section III. above, in which the House of

---

[69] See AW Bradley and KD Ewing, *Constitutional and Administrative Law*, 15th edn (Gosport, Longman, 2011) for an account of judicial review.

[70] See Erskine May, above n 59, 75ff.

[71] *Amalgamated Society of Railway Servants v Osborne* [1910] AC 87.

[72] *Ibid*, at 111. These comments were made obiter, as the main issue in that case was that trade unions were not permitted by the Trade Union Acts of that time to administer political funds or to levy contributions from their members for political purposes. The Trade Union Act 1913 reversed that position and legitimated contributions and political funds.

Commons' Privileges Committee found that it would be a contempt of Parliament for a sponsor to demand that the MP accept instructions as to his actions in Parliament and for a sponsor to punish an MP for failing to obey instructions.

Bromley London Borough Council v Greater London Council[73] is the best-known case in which the courts have dealt with the issue of the legality of decisions in which members of local authorities have felt themselves bound by decisions of their local party organisations. A major question was whether and to what extent the elected Labour Party members of the Greater London Council were bound by the policy of the London Labour Party, which it had developed before the election. Lord Diplock maintained that the elected members of the Greater London Council had 'a collective legal duty to make choices of policy and of action that they believe to be in the best interests (weighing, where necessary, one against the other) of all those categories of persons to whom their collective duty is owed' and that 'A council member once elected is not the delegate of those who voted in his favour only; he is representative of all the electors.'[74]

A number of cases have turned on the degree to which the courts have been prepared to give the political decision maker the benefit of the doubt and to find as a fact that, despite pressures from the local party or other outside bodies, the decision maker has exercised its own independent judgement. Thus in a number of cases the courts have accepted, in the absence of evidence to the contrary, that councillors have acted in accordance with their duties of objectivity and fairness even where party-political motivations have been influential. Thus in *R v Amber Valley District Council, ex p Jackson*,[75] the Council had contracted with a company to manage a proposed development, and was obliged by the contract to use its best endeavours to obtain the necessary planning permissions: failure to do so would result in the Council incurring liability in damages. The local party group having political control of the Council resolved to support the company's planning application. An objector sought judicial review on the basis that in light of the contractual terms the Council's decision was likely to be biased and unfair, contrary to its statutory duty. It was held by Woolf J (as he then was) that the Council had a general duty to act fairly and a statutory duty to consider the applicant's representations, and that the mere fact that the majority group was predisposed in favour of the applicant did not disqualify it from participating in the decision. In the absence of other evidence that the Council would fail to consider the planning application and representations on their merits, there were no grounds for the court to intervene.

In *R v Waltham Forest London Borough Council, ex p Baxter and others*,[76] the members of the majority group on the Council had met before the meeting at which the rate would be determined. The standing orders of the group required

---

[73] *Bromley London Borough Council v Greater London Council* [1983] 1 AC 768.

[74] *Ibid*, at 107. The decision in *Bromley* is open to criticism on the basis that the courts did not fully understand transport policy, but the quotation above is in line with established principles.

[75] *R v Amber Valley District Council, ex p Jackson* [1985] 1 WLR 298.

[76] *R v Waltham Forest London Borough Council, ex p Baxter and others* [1988] 2 WLR 257, 259–60.

members to refrain from voting in opposition to the decisions of the group on pain of withdrawal of the party whip. A number of ratepayers applied for judicial review of the Council's rate decision on the basis that members of the majority group had voted in favour of the new rate despite the fact that at the time of the earlier meeting they had opposed it. It was held that these matters were not evidence that the councillors' discretion had been fettered; party loyalty or party policy were relevant considerations for the councillors as long as they did not dominate; and the evidence showed that the councillors who had initially opposed the decision had voted after making up their own minds, and their freedom to vote as they thought fit had not been fettered. The case illustrates the fine balance that politicians are expected to achieve between party loyalty and their own inclinations. The point for us is that the decision upholds the principle against mandate or interference with the freedom to exercise their own judgement in line with their statutory duties.

B. Policy Preferences

A pair of cases deals with the position where a minister is predisposed to exercise a discretionary decision on a matter of broad public policy in a certain way. In both cases the courts have upheld the right of ministers to make what may be political decisions. Both are about the planning system. The issue in *Franklin v Minister of Town and Country Planning*[77] was the grant of permission for the building of Stevenage new town. The minister had declared publicly that the new town would go ahead with or without the cooperation of local people, and he later confirmed the order authorising the development. It was alleged that he had not exercised his power fairly and open-mindedly. It was held that this was not a departure from any duty of even-handed justice by those making judicial or quasi-judicial decisions.

The issue in *R (Alconbury Developments Ltd) v Environment Secretary*[78] was whether the involvement of a minister in a major planning application was inconsistent with Article 6 of the European Convention on Human Rights, which entitles a person to access to an independent and impartial tribunal when his civil rights – in this case property rights – are at stake. The House of Lords held that the minister should not be treated as if he were a judge and that he was thus entitled to make the decision in question. The Inspector who had held the inquiry into the application and reported to the minister had been obliged by the relevant Act of Parliament to apply the minister's policy; he did not have to be 'independent and impartial'. The minister was in same position. Access to a court is required by Article 6, and judicial review meets the requirement.

---

[77]　*Franklin v Minister of Town and Country Planning* [1948] AC 86.
[78]　*R (Alconbury Developments Ltd) v Environment Secretary* [2001] 2 WLR 1389 (HL).

Thus the courts have been relatively reluctant to intervene in decision making by politicians, unless it is clear that their willingness or ability to exercise their judgements and discretions fairly and objectively has been restricted by external pressures; they have upheld the rights of politicians to make and give effect to their own political value judgements.

C. Wooing the Voters

What about decisions influenced by the fact of forthcoming elections, and the desire of candidates and parties to win votes by making a popular decision or to prevent the opposition from pursing a different policy if elected? In *Persimmon Homes v R (Lewis)*,[79] a local planning authority made what it knew to be a politically controversial planning decision and signed a development agreement during the pre-election period. The Court of Appeal did not intervene because it was conceded that minds were open and there was 'little evidence . . . that members of the Committee were any more politically motivated than would normally be expected from elected policy makers'. So some political motivation is acceptable.[80]

Political parties and candidates may well be convinced that it would be in the public interest that their party – party A – should win a forthcoming election and that party B should not do so, and that this consideration justifies party A in taking certain decisions that would increase their chance of election or decrease those of party B. This was an issue in the *Waltham Forest* case, discussed in section IV.A. above, in which the party's belief that it was in the public interest for it to win the forthcoming election was held not to invalidate the Council's decision on the rate. However, this does not mean that politicians have carte blanche to engage in politicking before an election. In *Magill v Porter*,[81] it was held that selling council-owned flats to purchasers who were likely to be Conservative supporters in order to increase the Conservative vote in particular areas was unlawful. Lord Bingham observed:

> Elected politicians of course wish to act in a manner which will commend them and their party (when, as is now usual, they belong to one) to the electorate. Such an ambition is the life blood of democracy and a potent spur to responsible decision-taking and administration. Councillors do not act improperly or unlawfully if, exercising public powers for a public purpose for which such powers were conferred, they hope that such exercise will earn the gratitude and support of the electorate and thus strengthen their electoral position. The law would indeed part company with the realities of party politics if it were to hold otherwise. But a public power is not exercised lawfully if it is exercised not for a

---

[79] *Persimmon Homes v R (Lewis)* [2008] EWCA Civ 746.

[80] Compare the majority and minority judgments in *R v Hammersmith and Fulham LBC, ex p Beddowes* [1987] 2 WLR 263, in which a decision by a council just before an election to grant contracts for the development of land the existence of which would prevent the opposition party, if it won the election, from pursuing a different policy, was upheld by the majority. Compare also the provision in the Cabinet Manual, discussed in section III.A.ii. above, requiring a government to act as a caretaker and not to take new initiatives during an election campaign.

[81] *Magill v Porter* [2001] UKHL 67.

public purpose for which the power was conferred but in order to promote the electoral advantage of a political party. The power at issue in the present case is section 32 of the Housing Act 1985, which conferred power on local authorities to dispose of land held by them subject to conditions specified in the Act. Thus a local authority could dispose of its property, subject to the provisions of the Act, to promote any public purpose for which such power was conferred, but could not lawfully do so for the purpose of promoting the electoral advantage of any party represented on the council.[82]

Lord Scott agreed, and added:

> This is a case about political corruption. The corruption was not money corruption. No one took a bribe. No one sought or received money for political favours. But there are other forms of corruption, often less easily detectable and therefore more insidious. Gerrymandering, the manipulation of constituency boundaries for party political advantage is a clear form of political corruption. So, too, would be any misuse of municipal powers, intended for use in the general public interest but used instead for party political advantage. Who can doubt that the selective use of municipal powers in order to obtain party political advantage represents political corruption? Political corruption, if unchecked, engenders cynicism about elections, about politicians and their motives and damages the reputation of democratic government.[83]

In sum, the courts accept that the party or partisan interests of elected politicians do not necessarily equate with the public or general interest, and will quash decisions if, but only if, they are satisfied that party or partisan interests have dominated over considerations of public interest or that the minds of decision makers have been closed.

V. REFLECTIONS AND CONCLUSIONS

Distrust of politicians and politics and the practice of bad politics exist in most Western democracies. The UK is not alone in this. And regulating the behaviour of politicians does not stop them from being politicians: they will always be tempted to indulge in 'bad politics'; they will often get away with it, especially since the UK system rests largely on self-regulation and lacks many sanctions.

Bearing in mind then that the system in the UK is not watertight and that more needs to be done, say, in relation to lobbyists, I suggest that the trend towards the depoliticisation of decision making in areas previously politicised responds to the fact that the British electorate, and political parties when in opposition, will deny legitimacy to a policy or a decision maker which they consider to be inappropriately party-political or partisan. As some of the examples in sections II. and III. have shown, public opinion and opposition concerns have been strong among the pressures resulting in the development of new public institutions and the hard- and soft-law regulation of party-political activity. These are responses to significant

---

[82] *Ibid* [21].
[83] *Ibid* [132].

changes in public and political culture. Kellner, discussing the results of a YouGov survey in October 2012, commented:

> It's not just the ideological divide that has melted away. So, too, to a large extent, has the culture divide that used to separate working-class from middle-class voters. The range of shared experiences is far greater than it was in the heyday of class voting.[84]

While it remains the case that the political parties in the UK are very adversarial and competitive in their attitudes to politics and to other political parties, public opinion[85] in England, Scotland and Wales [86] no longer tolerates or endorses purely authoritarian, majoritarian political, party-political or partisan justifications for policy. This is an aspect of the shift from a culture of authority to one of justification[87] in public expectations and in public law that is taking place in a number of western democracies: it is a counter-majoritarian trend. The culture of authority entailed acceptance that what Parliament states to be the law and what the Government considers itself entitled to do were to be accepted without the need for public interest justifications to be offered to the courts or to the people. A culture of justification means

> a culture in which every exercise of power is expected to be justified; in which the leadership given by government rests on the cogency of the case offered in defence of its decisions, not the fear inspired by the force at its command.[88]

In the UK a government that was required to justify its decisions would not feel able to state or admit that they were based not on that government's assessment of the public interest or of how the general welfare might be promoted, but instead upon deals of the kind to which Griffith and Crick referred – deals done with sectional interests in society or overseas – the banks, the unions, the CBI, the extra-parliamentary party, the European Commission or the International Monetary Fund; nor would government nowadays feel able to assert as a justification for its policies that it is entitled simply by virtue of its majority, its position of authority or its technical legal powers to use public resources (including the Civil Service) as it wishes or to promote its own interests and the interests of its supporters, without reference to the public interest or general well-being. Its decisions would be denied legitimacy by most of the public and by opposition politicians if it were to act, for instance, for the benefit of its party or the personal advantage of a minister, or if it claimed the right to impose its own moral convictions on others. Government will

---

[84] P Kellner, 'Labour's lost votes', *Prospect*, November 2012, at 40. For the survey results, see <http://cdn.yougov.com/cumulus_uploads/document/ic8lcj9svf/YG-Archives-Pol-ST-results%20-%20121019.pdf> (accessed 20 October 2012). And see discussion of the State as a social group dedicated to the general well-being in Barber, above n 5.

[85] See, eg, the biannual surveys of public perceptions of standards by the Committee on Standards in Public Life.

[86] Note that the position is different in Northern Ireland, where two communities remain divided and mistrustful of one another and their leaders.

[87] This expression was coined by E Mureinik in 'A bridge to where? Introducing the interim Bill of Rights' in (1994) 10 *South African Journal of Human Rights* 31, at 32.

[88] *Ibid*, 32.

feel compelled to assert that its decisions are based upon its honest judgement of where on balance the public interest lies. It may have to be frank that pressures from outside, eg from the International Monetary Fund,[89] force it to adopt certain policies; but it will be expected to state that, in the circumstances and on balance, acceptance of the terms in question is in the general interest. It is, in my view, only because politicians know or believe that the population at large generally expects them to do their best to promote general and shared interests rather than partisan ones that politics operates legitimately in the UK.[90] Of course there are and always will be differences of opinion about where the public interest lies. Politicians may claim that their policies and actions are in the public interest in order to cover up a partisan preference. No amount of soft law can prevent that. But some hard law can, as in the cases of the ALBs discussed above, and a number of disincentives to bad politics have come into operation over the years, including freedom of information, investigative journalism, and a mature and highly suspicious and sceptical public.

Thus a maturing public culture and public opinion have stimulated the carving out of non-political pockets in the UK's constitutional arrangements. This trend in the UK, and in Scotland and Wales in relation to devolution issues, provides evidence for the development of a sense of common, non party-politically-based interests among the affected population. This has profound influences on political behaviour. It is this culture that has given rise not only to legal reforms, but also to the political norms of a non-legal kind that have been discussed in this chapter: these are derived from public opinion and pressure on government that have been discussed above, rather than from spontaneous, altruistic, rational, public-spirited initiatives taken by politicians. Griffith's focus on raw politics in opposition to law as underpinning politics neglects another dimension to public life. Nowadays – and things have changed since the late 1970s – the electorate itself generally dislikes party politicking and expects its representatives to act – in a spirit of public service – for the general welfare as they conceive it to be. Politicians in Great Britain know and care about this fact. Politicians who do not conform to these public expectations are liable – if found out – to forfeit the trust and respect of voters.

Alongside the political constitution, below the radar, a non-political dimension to the British Constitution has developed. This trend may be symptomatic of a shift towards 'post-party' politics – still politics and still the process of conflict resolution as Griffith and Crick saw it, but less 'party' based. The formation of a Coalition Government after the general election of 2010 may have been an example of this: the Prime Minister stated that the priority of the coalition was the promotion of the general or national interest in dealing with the economic crisis; leaders in both parties had to abandon some of their parties' policy preferences in the bargaining that produced and maintains the Coalition Programme for

[89] As in the last couple of years of the Parliament of 1974–79, when public expenditure cuts were required by the IMF as the price for its financial support.
[90] I speculate that it is because of the weakening of assumptions of interests shared with the rest of the UK in Scotland, and their absence among some of the population of Northern Ireland, that the legitimacy of the UK system has been called in question in those territories.

Government[91]: the terms of this agreement and subsequent policy initiatives and compromises represent the outcomes of conflicts over policy priorities between and within the Coalition parties (welfare and health service reforms, university tuition fees, constitutional reform and many other areas of disagreement between the parties) outside – and within – Parliament.

Thus Griffith's political constitution is still going strong: but within the Coalition it is less party-based[92] and less secret than it was. Among backbenchers and party members, party politics and partisanship remain strong.

I suggest that awareness of the trend in public opinion is reflected in the rhetoric with which the main parties address the public: the Conservative Party's advocacy of 'The Big Society'[93] and 'common ground',[94] and the Labour Party's 'One Nation Labour'[95] of its annual conference in October 2012, all seek to appeal to public perceptions of shared (rather than conflicting) communal interests and to convince the public that they are concerned with the general well-being. (Saying so does not of course make it so. And whether the general public understands or is convinced by these parties' commitments to these values is of course another matter. But it must surely approve of the idea.) The 'public interest' rhetoric itself may have a unifying effect, which may well undermine support for a party that is in other respects aggressively partisan and political.

What, if anything, will fill the void left by a weakening of public support for party-based politics in government is hard to predict. It may lead to much more consensual politics, with coalitions and pacts between parties being forced on politicians by election results and thus becoming more common; it may lead to wider use of petitions and citizen initiatives in policy development: we may already be witnessing the development of processes outside the political parties for the aggregation of interests in the name of the public interest or general well-being.

But of course the broadly-based senses of shared interests and beliefs that the fundamental duty of government is to promote the general well-being which have emerged in recent years are not immutable. It is entirely possible that British politics may come to be dominated by divisions among the population which challenge these cultures: nationalistic or national identity pressures, as in Scotland and Wales in relations with the UK; or – and this would be the worst possible result of the inability of parties to reflect and promote senses of shared interests – by racial, xenophobic, sectarian, religious or ideological divisions which assert the duty of the State to promote the interests of certain sections of society over others, or deny that sections of the population 'belong'.

---

[91] <www.cabinetoffice.gov.uk/media/409088/pfg_coalition.pdf >.

[92] See R Hazell and B Yong, *The Politics of Coalition: How the Conservative–Liberal Democrat Government Works* (Oxford, Hart Publishing, 2012).

[93] See J Norman, *The Big Society: The Anatomy of the New Politics* (Buckingham, Buckingham University Press, 2010).

[94] David Cameron's speech at the Conservative Party conference on 10 October 2012. Note also the statement by President Barak Obama in his election victory speech on 7 November 2012, that 'we are an American family, and we rise or fall together as one nation and one people'.

[95] Is this an oxymoron?

6

Constitutional Conventions

DAVID FELDMAN

A S SOMEONE WHO understands law's distinctive logic and its capacity to shape as well as be shaped by political processes, Vernon Bogdanor is a particularly perceptive commentator on constitutional law. He generously supports and collaborates with lawyers, and as one who has benefited greatly from his kindness, I am delighted to have this opportunity to offer this token of my respect and gratitude.

I. WHAT MAKES CONSTITUTIONAL CONVENTIONS CONSTITUTIONAL?

Constitutional conventions are of interest to political scientists, historians and lawyers. They can be found in all constitutions. They are rooted in politics and political theory, so lawyers tend to feel that they have an uncertain grasp on them. In 1885, Dicey observed that a system of 'conventions, understandings, habits or practices' operated alongside the law of what he persisted in calling the 'English' Constitution, 'which, though they may regulate the conduct of the several members of the sovereign power, of the Ministry, or of other officials, are not in reality laws at all since they are not enforced by the Courts'.[1] The ultimate object of all these 'understandings or practices which though commonly observed are not laws in any true sense of that word at all,' or 'maxims which make up our body of constitutional morality'[2] was, Dicey thought, to bring the forms and legal rules of the Constitution (including the royal prerogatives and the legal sovereignty of the Queen in Parliament) into line with the political principle which, by 1885, Dicey considered to be fundamental legitimising principle of the Constitution, that is,

> to secure that Parliament, or the Cabinet which is indirectly appointed by Parliament, shall in the long run give effect to the will of that power which in modern England is the true political sovereign of the state – the majority of the electors, or (to use popular though not quite accurate language) the nation.[3]

[1] AV Dicey, *Lectures Introductory to the Study of the Law of the Constitution* (London, Macmillan, 1885) 25.
[2] *Ibid*, 347. See also *ibid*, 12. Dicey enumerated some of the important ones *ibid*, at 27, 354.
[3] *Ibid*, 356–57. See also *ibid*, 350.

This is not a definition of constitutional conventions, though he explained what they were not, namely, legally enforceable norms. With a gentle dig at the academic fields of two professorial colleagues, Dicey suggested that responsibility for teaching the non-legal customs of the Constitution

> should . . . be transferred either to my friend the Professor of Jurisprudence, because it is his vocation to deal with the oddities or the outlying portions of legal science, or to my friend the Professor of International Law, because he being a teacher of law which is not law, and being accustomed to expound those rules of public ethics, which are miscalled international law, will find himself at home in expounding political ethics which, on the hypothesis under consideration, are miscalled constitutional law.[4]

Nevertheless, Dicey understood that they were important for politics, law and a proper understanding of the workings of the Constitution generally. This is as true in 2013 as it was in 1885. Dicey appreciated Walter Bagehot's account in *The English Constitution* of the non-legal, constitutional principles and practices which shaped the efficient part of the Constitution (whereas law was often concerned only with the dignified part).[5] Many constitutional conventions save legal rules from irrelevancy by allowing them to operate in practice compatibly with prevailing principles of constitutional morality. But what makes these non-legal norms *constitutional?* To answer this question, we must have an adequate conception of 'constitution'. The following characteristics of constitutions provide a starting-point.[6]

First, constitutions essentially create and shape *institutions* of States. Constitutional conventions are those conventions which contribute to this task.

Secondly, constitutions are concerned with managing disagreement and tension between institutions. Each institution builds up its own picture of the constitution as viewed from its own position within it, and tends to give centrality in the picture to its own institutional functions and aims over those of other institutions. This generates a number of conflicting conceptions of the constitution and its fundamental values. Such conflicts are inevitable and essential in a constitutional democracy; they are the driving force behind constitutional dynamism. Constitutional conventions are among the instruments for managing those conflicts, as well as for implementing consensus on the occasions (rare in democracies) when it can be found.

Thirdly, and as a result, conventions are of different *types.* Some cater for disagreements, or reflect them by being contested; others reflect consensus, usually

---

[4] *Ibid*, 23. The two Oxford professors to whom Dicey referred were, respectively, Sir Frederick Pollock, the Corpus Professor of Jurisprudence, and Sir Thomas Erskine Holland, the Chichele Professor of International Law, who had been a friend of Dicey since their early days in Oxford; they had both been members of the Old Mortality Society.

[5] *Ibid*, 20. Dicey noted that Bagehot's work 'is so full of brightness, originality, and wit, that few students notice how full it is also of knowledge, of wisdom, and of insight'.

[6] D Feldman, 'None, one or several? Perspectives on the UK's constitution(s)' [2005] *Cambridge Law Journal* 329; D Feldman, '"Which in Your Case You Have Not Got": Constitutionalism at Home and Abroad' (2011) 64 *Current Legal Problems* 117.

at a high level of abstraction and generality, perhaps concealing disagreement over the some or all of the details. They help people who strongly disagree to cooperate (most of the time) in making constitutional practices work.

Fourthly, constitutional conventions have different *functions*. Some are instruments of constitutional change; others provide predictability and consistency. Some regulate particular institutions; others regulate relationships between institutions. Some contribute to stability, some to efficiency, some to change, some to legitimacy and some to more than one of them.

Against the background of this understanding of constitutions, how should we conceive of non-legal, constitutional norms?[7] Peter Morton has provided a particularly perceptive analysis.[8] He argued that discussion of constitutional conventions had typically failed to take sufficient account of three matters. First, conventions arise from and operate within a constitutional tradition which, in the UK, is one of respect for fundamental values, including government by consent, individual freedom, diversity of opinion, contestation as the essence of political life and ethical standards of behaviour in politics. The UK is peculiar in that the values of this tradition are generally accepted without conscious thought, and deviations from them are regarded as pathological rather than normal behaviour. The institutions, laws, conventions, forms and rituals of the Constitution are made and change within that principled tradition. It is this tradition, not law, which is the core and essence of the Constitution. Constitutional conventions are a key expression of that tradition, and they provide legitimacy to the Constitution. They are far more than descriptions of general practices or flesh clothing legal bones of the Constitution, or what he calls 'footpath conventions', identifying pragmatically convenient ways of doing business.[9] It is equally wrong to think that they are obeyed (when they are obeyed) because of a threat of unwelcome consequences on disobedience. They are obeyed because they encapsulate right behaviour. Disobedience is likely to precipitate criticism on the ground that the behaviour is seriously unconstitutional because it is regarded as wrong. The wrongness justifies the sanction; the sanction does not establish the wrongness.[10]

Secondly, Morton criticised the view that conventions are essentially similar to law. He contrasted the systematic and formally uniform character of laws with the 'formidable miscellany' of non-legal rules of which conventions are part; the relative certainty of legal rules and deep uncertainty of many non-legal rules; and the fixity of legal rules with the contingency and malleability of non-legal norms.[11] He also noted that legal norms 'exist' by reason of their incorporation

---

[7] I have examined the position of legal, constitutional norms in D Feldman, 'The nature and significance of "constitutional" legislation' (2013) 129 *LQR*, forthcoming.

[8] P Morton, 'Conventions of the British constitution' (1991-1992) 15 *Holdsworth Law Review* 114. I am grateful to him for a number of illuminating discussions of these and other matters when we were colleagues at the University of Birmingham. In retrospect, I see that his influence on my thinking was even more profound than I realised at the time.

[9] *Ibid*, 117–25.

[10] *Ibid*, 125–30, 140–41.

[11] *Ibid*, 130–38.

into a functioning legal system in accordance with the rules of that system governing such incorporation. Non-legal norms, by contrast, 'exist' only if they are regarded by people within society as proper standards for guiding and criticising behaviour.[12]

Thirdly, Morton saw a constitution essentially as an 'institutional complex'. A constitutional framework is a structure of institutions. There are two major types of institutions: *associational*, where individuals are involved as members of a group or organisation, and *practical*, where individuals engage 'not as members of an association but as participants in an activity or procedure'.[13] The first, constitutive task of a constitution is to form the institutions of the State. This is not done by prescriptive (duty-imposing) norms. Instead, drawing on HLA Hart's distinction between primary and secondary rules, Morton pointed out that many non-legal, constitutional norms are constitutive, secondary rules, not primary rules imposing duties on people to behave in particularly ways. 'In constitutional affairs the duties [of individuals] (and indeed the rights and powers of individuals) have their meaning and significance only within the institutional structures of the constitution.'[14] Institutions are

> the basic building blocks of the constitution . . . We could no more speak of a constitution without institutions than we could of a capital city without buildings and streets. Institutions are not just the background to, or the focus for, our norms; they are the chunks of bedrock *within which* constitutional norms have their existence. The constitutional rules exist only within or between the institutional forms of life.[15]

Non-legal norms form institutions (such as the Cabinet), provide their internal structures and modes of operation, and govern their relationships with other institutions, each of which has an existence, authority and principled objectives of its own, quite apart from any that other institutions seek to impose on it.[16] Some of these are merely footpath conventions, of little or no principled (and so constitutional) importance. Others are fundamental to constitutional principles.[17] This can be seen in collections of non-legal, constitutional norms such as the Cabinet Manual and the Ministerial Code, discussed in section II. below.

Settlements between institutions are always temporary. They may be formal or informal, written or unwritten. They may arise out of practice based on tacit assent by members or participants, formal codes or instructions promulgated by hierarchically superior members or participants (the hierarchy itself being established, perhaps, by non-legal norms) and negotiated settlements between actors or institutions. Legal norms may also contribute, but only alongside, not in a manner superior to or more fundamental than, non-legal norms, as the effect and effectiveness of legal norms depends, ultimately, on how members of and parti-

---

[12] *Ibid*, 138–44.
[13] *Ibid*, 148.
[14] *Ibid*, 147.
[15] *Ibid*, 152.
[16] *Ibid*, 156–58, 166.
[17] *Ibid*, 161–62.

cipants in institutions interpret and implement them. Both non-legal and legal norms are always subject to, and are usually in a continual process of, renegotiation and adjustment as circumstances and institutional priorities change.[18] Non-legal norms which prescribe behaviour are most similar to primary legal rules; those which shape institutions and facilitate cooperation are least like legal rules, bearing in mind that secondary rules are usually social rules which take their meaning from their social and institutional contexts rather than from posited, positive legal prescription. To be conventions, however, Morton considers that they must be sufficiently concrete to be useful in resolving disputes, as conventions are, he considers, dispute-orientated, concerning disputes which courts will not be called on to settle.[19] Constitutional conventions, he concludes, 'are the unenacted norms whose breach will raise questions of principle'. They are not rules, as they lack the all-or-nothing character of rules. They are principles, or 'principled norms of varying degrees of particularity,'[20] so not every deviation from a convention amounts to an unconstitutional act.[21]

This richly-textured understanding of constitutional conventions is a major improvement on models which present them as a practice or a rule, or as ancillary to laws. It shows when norms can properly be regarded as constitutional (when they help to resolve tensions or conflicts over constitutional principles) and why they are not necessarily clear or determinate (because they are not rules but principles which may conflict with other non-legal norms, may not be fully articulated but are part of a constitutional tradition, have differing levels of particularity, and exist in institutional and inter-institutional settings where they are always subject to renegotiation). That also explains how they are different from legal norms, and why they cannot be judicially determined (except for those norms which contribute to the internal structure and working of the judiciary): only members of or participants in institutions with a principled interest in the operation of a non-legal norm can negotiate its meaning and operation.

Morton's analysis illuminates two sets of connections. The first is between *types* and *functions* of non-legal, constitutional norms. People naturally choose or fashion instruments appropriate to the job in hand. The second link is between constitutional *conventions* and constitutional *principles*: constitutional principles provide the normative justification for any argument concerning constitutional conventions.[22] Together with more pragmatic or prudential considerations, they help to provide the reasons which, as Jennings pointed out, are important both to recognising conventions and to making them effective.[23] We can understand constitutional conventions as normative expressions of constitutionalism or fundamental values

---

[18] *Ibid*, 162–63, 166–73.

[19] *Ibid*, 163.

[20] *Ibid*, 173, 174. Morton draws on Ronald Dworkin's work for the distinction between rules and principles: *ibid*, 175.

[21] *Ibid*, 175–76.

[22] Dicey, above n 1, 25.

[23] Sir Ivor Jennings, *The Law and the Constitution*, 5th edn (London, University of London Press, 1959) ch III.

of the constitution;[24] as Turpin and Tomkins put it, they 'are part of the constitutional order, interwoven with but distinguishable from rules of law. On this view, breach of a constitutional convention is every bit as unconstitutional as a breach of constitutional law.'[25]

As Marshall pointed out, this gives rise to two possible ways in which constitutional conventions may be connected with morality:

> One is that conventions are what we might call the positive morality of the Constitution – the beliefs that the major participants in the political process as a matter of fact have about what is required of them. On this view the existence of a convention is a question of historical and sociological fact. The alternative possibility is that conventions are the rules that the political actors *ought* to feel obliged by, if they have considered the precedents and reasons correctly. This permits us to think of conventions as the critical morality of the Constitution.[26]

For Wheare, conventions were the positive morality of the Constitution; for Jennings, they were its critical morality.[27] Marshall preferred Jennings's approach, because it left room for critics and commentators to disagree with those who are subject to a convention as to what the Constitution requires them to do in given circumstances.[28] If we follow Wheare, political actors, in circumstances where they are bound only by conventions, would be free to interpret their constitutional obligations in accordance with their own best interests. This would make it hard to maintain that a convention is obligatory in any non-trivial sense. Lord Wilson of Dinton, who as Cabinet Secretary had the task of trying to ensure that ministers respected conventions in their day-to-day work, was very conscious of this.[29]

A critical morality is not purely aspirational. To provide a sound basis for criticism, its standards must be attainable. Unlike moral philosophers, who are free to imagine critical moralities unattached to the practices of real people, constitutional critics and commentators who offer interpretations of conventions must ensure that their interpretations have secure roots in the soil of political and governmental reality and practical possibility. If the critical morality of constitutional conventions is divorced from the history and sociology of the constitutional system, it will lose credibility and the capacity to induce a sense of obligation among constitutional actors. To put it another way, while precedents might not be needed for a convention to arise, and must in any case always be aligned with good constitutional reasons before they can be taken to reflect a constitu-

---

[24] A McHarg, 'Reforming the United Kingdom constitution: law, convention, soft law' (2008) 71 *MLR* 853, 857.

[25] C Turpin and A Tomkins, *British Government and the Constitution*, 7th edn (Cambridge, Cambridge University Press, 2011) 182.

[26] G Marshall, *Constitutional Conventions: the Rules and Forms of Political Accountability* (Oxford, Clarendon Press, 1984) 11–12.

[27] Sir Kenneth Wheare, *Modern Constitutions* (Oxford, Oxford University Press, 1951) 179–80.

[28] Marshall, above n 26, 12.

[29] Lord Wilson of Dinton, 'The robustness of conventions in a time of modernisation and change' [2004] *Public Law* 407, 409.

tional convention, good reasons for acting in a particular way do not without more make a convention.

One of the main reasons for the success of Morton's account is that it is based on a clearly articulated model of constitutions as being institutional, and of the nature of law as essentially linked to the institutions of any State which a Constitution, including its conventional part, establishes. He developed his argument about this in a subsequent monograph.[30] For present purposes, the important point is that any coherent notion of constitutional principles or conventions or law in any State relies on a conception of its Constitution, and Morton grounds his notion in such a conception. It clarifies enough basic ideas sufficiently to allow us to focus on more specific matters: first, the relationship between consensus, disagreement and form in constitutional conventions; secondly, the relationship between constitutional conventions and constitutional laws.

II. CONSENSUS, UNCERTAINTY AND DISAGREEMENT

How can we tell whether a convention exists? How do conventions arise? The questions overlap. Sir Kenneth Wheare, for example, identified two different ways in which conventions may arise which, if exhaustive, might also serve as criteria for deciding whether a particular convention exists: a series of actions or decisions which, over time, are accepted by those concerned in the working of the constitution as reflecting an obligatory rule of behaviour; and a conscious agreement between people at a particular time to deal with a problem in a specific way for the foreseeable future.[31] Sir Ivor Jennings argued that one had to take account, when deciding whether a convention had arisen, of three factors: the presence or absence of precedents; the belief (if any) on the part of those acting in the precedents that they were bound by an obligatory rule; and whether there was a reason for the rule.[32]

Both Wheare and Jennings regarded precedents as evidence of the existence of a convention but not a necessary condition for it.[33] Yet it is not always easy to find appropriate precedents. Lord Wilson of Dinton has recounted that, as Cabinet Secretary, he had custody of

> the Precedent Book, seven loose-leaf folders covered in tatty red plastic, full of loose slips of paper which have to be kept carefully in place, which each Secretary of the Cabinet hands on to his successor. I consulted this collection frequently and almost always failed to find the answer to whatever point concerned me.[34]

[30] P Morton, *An Institutional Theory of Law: Keeping Law in its Place* (Oxford, Clarendon Press, 1998).
[31] Wheare, above n 27, 179–80.
[32] Jennings, above n 23. I am grateful to Professor Patrick Birkinshaw for pointing out to me that this makes conventions a form of the customary interaction which, according to Unger, is law: Roberto Mangabeira Unger, *Law in Modern Society: Towards a Criticism of Social Theory* (New York: The Free Press, 1977) 49.
[33] R Brazier, *Constitutional Practice: The Foundations of British Government*, 3rd edn (Oxford, Oxford University Press, 1999), provides plentiful examples of sources of precedents.
[34] Wilson, above n 29, 408.

Quite apart from the difficulty of finding a precedent suitable to guide one through novel and challenging circumstances, Jennings's original insight, that *reasons* are important, suggests that neither the existence of precedents nor a consensus that one is bound by a rule is sufficient to establish a constitutional convention. There must be a *constitutional* justification for treating a practice as reflecting an obligatory rule of conduct. If a convention exists, it is not because of precedents which are consistent with it. Constitutional principle makes constitutional obligations, and may do so even without precedents. As Wheare recognised, a convention may be created by a negotiated agreement to cope with an unprecedented problem or anticipated conflicts. In the UK, this occurred when the system of devolution, introduced under the Government of Wales Act 1998, Northern Ireland Act 1998 and Scotland Act 1998, was being brought into operation. It was necessary to reach agreements between devolved institutions and Whitehall to forestall conflicts over how to proceed when the different bodies implementing the legislation were dealing with matters in which they had shared competences, or when it was unclear where the dividing line between their respective competences fell. Discussions (largely at official-to-official level) led to fairly detailed, written agreements, or concordats, which are bodies of non-legal, constitutional norms some of which reflect constitutional principles while others are what Morton called 'footpath conventions'.[35]

Another example of a freshly minted convention is that relating to the role of the Civil Service in relation to negotiations between potential partners in a coalition government following an indecisive general election. The precedent for an express convention to avoid uncertainty over what should happen in a possible, future eventuality was set by Gordon Brown, the Prime Minister before and immediately after the 2010 general election. He agreed that the Civil Service should, on the Prime Minister's authorisation, offer support to all parties to a potential coalition with a view to constructing a government which could command the confidence of the House of Commons. The terms of the new convention were published before the election in the form of a draft of chapter 6 of the Draft Cabinet Manual, and it was put into effect after the election.[36]

Non-legal, constitutional norms can thus be found in written documents. Examples of this sort of norm have proliferated. Lord Wilson described the proliferating Codes – the Ministerial Code, the Civil Service Code, the Civil Service Commissioners' Recruitment Code, the Guidance on the Work of the Government Information Service and the Code of Conduct for Special Advisers, to which we may now add the Cabinet Manual – as reflecting a body of practice which is not itself constitutive of conventions but has 'accumulated over the years to translate the conventions into everyday rules and guidance'. The Ministerial Code, for instance, can be altered by the Prime Minister, and may but need not reflect more widely shared understandings of proper behaviour. The Cabinet Manual, first

---

[35] R Rawlings, 'Concordats of the constitution' (2000) 116 *LQR* 257.
[36] See now Cabinet Office, *The Cabinet Manual: A Guide to Laws, Conventions and Rules on the Operation of Government* (October 2011), 2.14.

published by the Cabinet Office with Cabinet approval in October 2011, does not claim to be a statement of norms the authority of which depends on the Prime Minister or Cabinet. It contains an articulation of legal rules and non-legal norms as a guide to current understanding of existing practices in government, together with a statement of practices in government as were thought by the Cabinet to stand on the day of publication. The Manual was intended as a record rather than 'a driver of change', and a work of reference for the internal working of government rather than a norm-creating document.[37] The word 'guidance' is important. Codes and manuals are intended as practical, concrete guides to which ministers, officials and others may refer if in doubt. Because they are written down, they are more flexible and easier to change in response to circumstances than conventions.[38] However, it would be wrong to regard them as *mere* records of practices. They include normative standards with which people are expected to comply. As they are relatively concrete in form, it is relatively easy to say what people *ought* to do and whether someone has breached those standards. The range of activities covered by such codes is vast: Professor Patrick Birkinshaw points to the secret code on the role of the 'Crown' which allows Prince Charles, for example, to be consulted in relation to legislation affecting their official interests.[39]

Written snapshots of non-legal, constitutional norms rarely say anything about consequences of breach. This is understandable. Such norms work through acceptance, and need for any enforcement should be exceptional and arises only when a norm is flouted or challenged. Guidance in the Codes is, if necessary, enforceable: the Prime Minister can discipline (and in extreme cases dismiss) ministers who flout the Ministerial Code, and civil servants are subject to disciplinary processes on the basis of the Civil Service Code and the Civil Service Management Code.[40] Even the purportedly descriptive Cabinet Manual occasionally sets out consequences of non-compliance. An example, perhaps reflecting the importance of the norm, is the statement (whether factual, normative or both it is hard to say), 'Ministers who knowingly mislead Parliament will be expected to offer their resignation to the Prime Minister.'[41] It is not clear whether the Prime Minister can be expected accept the resignation, or to dismiss a minister who does

---

[37] Sir Gus O'Donnell, 'Speech on the Cabinet Manual: Constitution Unit Event', 24 February 2011, paras 2 and 4, accessible at <http://www.cabinetoffice.gov.uk/resource-library/cabinet-manual>. The implications of the Manual are perceptively analysed by A Blick, 'The Cabinet Manual and the codification of conventions' (published on-line, 15 July 2012) *Parliamentary Affairs* 1.

[38] Wilson, above n 29, 410.

[39] This was revealed through a freedom-of-information request. See the Information Commissioner's decision notice FS50425063 21 August 2012, available at http://www.ico.gov.uk/enforcement/decision_notices.aspx, and *R Evans v Information Commissioner* [2012] UKUT 313 (AAC), in which the Upper Tribunal's decision that correspondence with Prince Charles concerning legislative proposals, held by a Government Department, should be disclosed under the Freedom of Information Act 2000 was followed by a ministerial 'veto' under s 53 of that Act. I am grateful to Professor Birkinshaw for allowing me pre-publication access to his discussion of these matters in a forthcoming article, 'Valuing transparency in Government and media'.

[40] Civil Service Code and Civil Service Management Code are both accessible at <http://www.civil-service.gov.uk/about/values>.

[41] Cabinet Manual, above n 36, 5.6.

not offer to resign. The Cabinet Secretary as head of the home Civil Service can decide, or give advice as to, whether a particular act or omission breaches a provision of a Code. In short, the rules make up a body of standards round which specific institutions are organised, consisting of practices (some written down) regarded as obligatory by those subject to them, and having good constitutional reasons (the maintenance of governmental institutions and of standards of ethics and propriety in government) justifying their observance and, if necessary, sanctions for their violation.

If it is to be seen as accurately recording a non-legal norm or norms, a written formulation must command a certain level of consensus and acceptance among those whose behaviour it affects. As noted above, Sir Kenneth Wheare observed that conventions, when not a product of negotiation on a specific occasion, were norms *accepted by those concerned in the working of the constitution* as reflecting an obligatory rule of behaviour. Even when norms are consciously created, there is a need for acceptance, if at any rate there is no enforcement mechanism. We might illustrate this by reference to the Ministerial Code and the Cabinet Manual. The Ministerial Code is issued on the authority of the Prime Minister in cooperation with the Cabinet Secretary to guide the conduct of ministers. As the Prime Minister can dismiss a minister at any time, ministers have a strong prudential reason for complying, but the Prime Minister can do so only as long as he is in a strong position vis-à-vis that minister and there is no compelling reason of political reputation or loyalty for retaining the services of the minister. (For instance, Tony Blair could not realistically have removed Gordon Brown from the Chancellorship of the Exchequer.) In normal circumstances, therefore, there is no great need for ministers to feel an obligation of political morality in order for them to comply with the Ministerial Code.

The Cabinet Manual is rather different, as it expresses not the will of the Prime Minister but a collection of norms (some legal, others not) which are said to be accepted by actors in the constitutional machinery. It is 'owned' by and issued under the authority of the Cabinet, not the Prime Minister alone, but the Cabinet could hardly take action to enforce it. Considerable care was therefore taken to secure wide agreement to the formulation of the norms, particularly where they state important, constitutional principles or affect relations between government and Parliament or other institutions. (This was of less importance in relation to what Morton called 'footpath' norms, relating to ordinary, day-to-day work within government.) A draft was issued for consultation. Several parliamentary select committees were among those who commented extensively on it, and the Government published detailed responses to the comments and suggestions, some of which were adopted in the final version of the Manual. When it turned out that a formulation was contested, that was generally taken into account.[42]

---

[42] House of Commons Justice Committee, *Constitutional Processes Following a General Election*, 5th Report of 2009–10, HC 396 (on the draft chapter published before the 2010 General Election); House of Lords Constitution Committee, *The Cabinet Manual*, 12th Report of 2010–12, HL Paper 107, House of Commons Political and Constitutional Reform Committee, *Constitutional Implications of the*

If there is uncertainty as to whether there is sufficient evidence of an appropriate level of acceptance for a norm to be regarded as a convention, Dr Aileen McHarg suggests that it should be regarded as a type of constitutional soft law.[43] This would imply that these norms have law-like qualities, or aspire to law-likeness. It is better, as Morton puts it, to regard them as examples of a wide range of non-legal, constitutional norms, some of which may turn out to be recognisably conventions. Whatever one calls the norms, the document might not long remain an accurate encapsulation of the convention. In the light of practice, disagreement and continued discussion and negotiation, the accepted norm is likely to move away from the written version. The Cabinet Secretary, Sir Gus O'Donnell, recognised this in his Preface to the Cabinet Manual: 'If the Cabinet Manual is to continue to play a useful role as a guide to the operations and procedures of government it will need to be updated periodically to reflect such developments.'[44]

Negotiated and recorded norms are naturally likely to be at least certain enough for their purposes and to command a reasonable level of consensus. Some norms which have grown rather than been created are also likely to be accepted without question. These are likely to be those most strongly grounded in a constitutional tradition and its fundamental principles. As it usually becomes necessary to clarify the content of an evolved, non-legal norm only when there is a challenge to it, the higher the level of acceptance of a norm the less likely it is that the parameters of the norm will have been crystallised. Marshall suggested, for instance, that

> the most obvious and undisputed convention of the British constitutional system is that Parliament does not use its sovereign power in an oppressive or tyrannical way. That is a vague but clearly accepted constitutional rule resting on the principle of constitutionalism and the rule of law.[45]

Later he described this as

> a good example of a convention that is both general in its formulation and founded on principle rather than precedent. That the Queen in Parliament's powers are not used (as Leslie Stephen said that they lawfully might be) to provide for the execution of all blue-eyed babies, or in pursuance of policies of an equally immoderate character, is not a notion derived from previous instances. It plainly does not rest upon any series of unsuccessful arbitrary legislative attempts on the lives of helpless infants or randomly chosen minorities.[46]

Cabinet Manual, 6th Report of 2010–12, HC 734, and House of Commons Public Administration Committee, *Cabinet Manual*, 8th Report of 2010–12, HC 900 (on the full draft published in December 2010); *Government Response to the House of Lords Constitution Committee, Political and Constitutional Reform Committee and Public Administration Select Committee on the Cabinet Manual Committee Reports of Session 2010–12*, Cm 8213 (2011); *Government Response to Comments Received on the Draft Cabinet Manual* (2011).

[43] McHarg, above n 24, 857–63.
[44] Sir Gus O'Donnell, 'Preface by the Cabinet Secretary' in Cabinet Manual, above n 36, iv.
[45] Marshall, above n 26, 9. (By 'does not use' Marshall meant also 'should not use': he was using the verb '[not] to do' in the normative sense of 'not the done thing'.)
[46] *Ibid*, 201.

One might alternatively say that there was a consistent (negative) practice sustained by an unarticulated but widely-shared belief that it would have been improper to attempt to legislate for the killing of helpless infants. An absence of counter-examples may in these circumstances be evidence of the weight of a principle as powerful as any number of occasions on which attempts to act inconsistently with the principle have been rebuffed for principled reasons. Nevertheless, the lack of direct challenge to the general principle against oppressive or tyrannical legislation has left the scope of the principle vague. The uncertain and contestable meanings of 'oppressive' and 'tyrannical', as well as the range of competing models of constitutionalism and the rule of law, make it hard to assert the principle in argument. We have seen that Morton, whose general view that constitutional conventions arise from fundamental constitutional principles is consistent with Marshall's, thought it too vague to be a convention: conventions, Morton thought, were principles orientated towards resolving tension and conflict, and the principle formulated by Marshall was insufficiently precise to be useful in resolving a dispute about whether or not the Queen in Parliament acted unconstitutionally in enacting particular pieces of legislation. It was an example of a non-legal, constitutional principle, but probably not a convention, although Morton deprecated attempts to distinguish conventions from other non-legal, constitutional norms.[47]

Marshall acknowledged that the vagueness of many non-legal, constitutional norms presents problems of formulation and application. There may be very great disagreement as to whether a provision in proposed legislation is oppressive. Disagreement is yet more likely when, as in the UK over the last 100 years, people have been entering Parliament (in both Houses) from a wider range of social, economic and educational backgrounds than previously. When these people have not been brought up with common values and a shared understanding of what is simply not done in polite society, it is not surprising that they are less inhibited than their predecessors about legislating in ways which would previously have been regarded as unacceptably repressive interferences with liberty. In Morton's terms, political behaviour is less likely to be shaped by the UK's constitutional tradition, because people in power are not sufficiently educated or steeped in that tradition. The great American constitutional historian Charles Howard McIlwain saw that risk starting to materialise as early as 1938.[48] Where this happens, people who want to limit the risk of oppression can no longer rely on respect for constitutional principles and other non-legal, constitutional norms. They have to argue for constraints on legislative power to be imposed by institutions external to the legislature, perhaps including courts. It is unlikely to be mere chance that the breakdown of common standards among parliamentarians as to what measures

---

[47] Morton, above n 8, at 164 fn 112, and 176.

[48] CH McIlwain, *Constitutionalism: Ancient and Modern* (Indianapolis, Ind, Liberty Fund, 2007) 18–21. The book is based on the Messenger Lectures on the Evolution of Civilization which McIlwain delivered at Cornell University in 1938–39. They were first published by Cornell University Press in 1940; a revised edition was published in 1947, and the book was republished by the Liberty Fund in 2007.

should simply not be taken because they would be unacceptable in a civilised society (or at least in this civilized society) in the twentieth century coincided with a rebirth of interest in legal, doctrinal limits on parliamentary sovereignty, whether of the 'manner and form' kind, proposals for an entrenched, codified constitution, or doctrines such as common-law constitutionalism.

Nevertheless, little attention has been paid to the matters in relation to which consensus is needed, or the mechanisms by which such consensus arises. If one burrows down into particular conventions, it becomes clear that while some agreement is necessary at a fairly high level of generality (for example, that there is a convention of ministerial responsibility to the Houses of Parliament), at a more detailed level conventions are ways of handling disagreement rather than encapsulating agreement. For instance, there is significant disagreement as to what information a minister is required to provide to the two Houses by virtue of that convention. This matter is discussed below. Key issues over which there is conflict are usually left to be the subject of continuous argument between protagonists within the groups that operate the convention. That is what makes conventions, like constitutional arrangements generally, dynamic rather than static.

How much disagreement can be tolerated before we need to reconsider the existence of the convention? How are such disagreements to be resolved, if indeed they need to be resolved at all? The answers to these questions depend on the nature of the particular convention which we are examining. We can draw a distinction for this purpose between two kinds of constitutional convention: those which govern the existence, role and internal regulation of single institutions, and impose obligations on particular institutions in the constitutional system and their members or participants; and those which are concerned with relations between institutions.

Conventions of the first kind guide the operation of an institution and the relations between the institution and its members or participants. In this context, the relationship between Her Majesty and her Prime Minister is of this kind. Both are members of the institution known in constitutional law in the UK as 'the Crown'. In most cases, both the existence of these internal, institutional conventions and the behaviour which they require are clear. For example, before 2010 there was no doubt that where a general election produced an overall majority in the House of Commons for one party, the Queen should invite the leader of that party to form a government (subject to the possibility that when this would lead to a change of government, the incumbent Prime Minister should be allowed some time to try to form a coalition that would secure majority support in the Commons for him or her). When unusual circumstances arise, however, the requirements of the convention may be less clear. At this stage, there may be discussion to try to produce a common understanding of what would be done in specified circumstances. The discussions preceding the general election in 2010, when a hung Parliament was a possibility (which eventuated), provide an unusual example of prior negotiation rather than the more usual discussion when the problem arises. An agreement was reduced to writing and (as noted earlier) published in the form of a draft of chapter 6 of the draft Cabinet Manual, which later became chapter 2 of the Cabinet Manual.

Another example of the first kind of convention limits the royal prerogative so that the Queen, in exercising her power to dissolve Parliament, must act on the advice (effectively the instructions) of her Prime Minister. The applicability of the convention has been narrowed by the Fixed-term Parliaments Act 2011 and the Coalition Agreement, but the principle that Her Majesty acts on her Prime Minister's advice is effectively unchanged. Other values change: in place of the previous refusal of successive Prime Ministers to reveal anything about Cabinet committees, their structure and membership are now freely available on the Cabinet Office website, reflecting enhanced commitment in government to openness and transparency.[49]

The offices of ministers of the Crown, Her Majesty's Loyal Opposition and the existence of the Cabinet as an organ of government all have their foundations in constitutional conventions, although these are complemented by legal rules allowing (for example) for salaries to be paid to up to 109 ministers of the Crown and for the receipt of a salary as a minister not to disqualify a person from membership of the House of Commons as the holder of an office of profit under the Crown as long as the total number of paid and unpaid ministers in the House does not exceed 95.[50] From this viewpoint, the convention of collective ministerial responsibility can be seen as a rule imposing duties owed by ministers to each other, and more particularly to the Prime Minister who has the effective power to appoint and dismiss them.

Such conventions govern the internal working of institutions, so they can easily be established and changed. Social pressure can secure compliance with them, and where necessary sanctions may be imposed for breach, through the ordinary, formal and informal structures of the institution in question. For example, many of the rules governing the conduct of ministers are contained in the Ministerial Code, given authority by the Prime Minister, taking account of the principles of conduct in public life settled by the Committee on Standards in Public Life. The Ministerial Code is enforced partly by the Prime Minister and partly by civil servants, for whom it offers protection against being required by ministers to take action which is more political than governmental (although the dividing line between them can, of course, never be drawn with complete clarity).

---

[49] Cabinet Manual, 1.1, 2.1, 2.22, 2.24, 3.4. Principles for forming a government are contained in the Cabinet Manual, 2.7–2.20; see also Cabinet Manual, 4.9–4.11, Coalition Agreement, 3.1, and David Cameron's 'Introduction' to the Cabinet Manual and David Cameron's and Nick Clegg's joint 'Foreword' to *The Coalition: Our Programme for Government* (2010), 7 and also 20–21. On conventions concerning the monarch, see V Bogdanor, *The Monarchy and the Constitution* (Oxford, Oxford University Press, 1995) chs 5 and 6.

[50] Ministerial and Other Salaries Act 1975, s 1(1) and sch 1; House of Commons Disqualification Act 1975, s 1(4). Stewardship of the Chiltern Hundreds remains an office of profit under the Crown which disqualifies a person from membership of the House of Commons (House of Commons Disqualification Act 1975, s 4), so applying for Stewardship is still the conventional route by which MPs may resign their seats.

In normal cases, at least, the existence of a convention of this sort is beyond doubt, and the corresponding obligation is concrete and unambiguous. The Queen and the Prime Minister face no difficulty in deciding what is permitted or required in their respective roles. There is accordingly little or no room for disagreement as to the content or effect of the convention, and the fact that nobody has authority to determine disputes about it presents no problem.

Sometimes, on the other hand, there will be disagreement between two institutions as to the limits of their respective obligations and rights. This is particularly likely where a convention concerns a relationship between two or more institutions. We might take as examples two conventions relating to the idea of responsible government: the collective responsibility of a government to Parliament (particularly the House of Commons, which can in theory remove an entire government by a vote of no confidence); and the individual accountability of every minister to one or other House for the activities of his or her department.[51]

Collective Cabinet responsibility involves ministers in presenting a united front to Parliament over decisions of the Cabinet. Dissenting in Cabinet does not permit a minister to depart from the approved line in public. This has obvious political advantages for the party or parties in government; it makes it easier for the Prime Minister to maintain party discipline in Parliament and prevents opposition parties presenting the Government as internally divided. A minister may restore his or her freedom of speech by resigning from Government, a public act of dissent which the former minister traditionally explains in a statement to the House, although disclosure of Cabinet proceedings must, by convention, be agreed with Her Majesty (via the Prime Minister) in advance. A notable example was Sir Geoffrey Howe's speech in November 1990 after resigning from his position as Mrs Thatcher's Deputy Prime Minister over her refusal to agree to a timetable for entering the European Exchange Rate Mechanism (ERM).[52] In retrospect, we know that Mrs Thatcher's scepticism about the ERM was well founded. Nevertheless, Sir Geoffrey's speech is widely thought to have been instrumental in bringing her down.

At first sight, this looks like a norm concerning the internal working of the institution of Cabinet government, one of Morton's 'footpath conventions'. Marshall suggested that it does not seem to impose obligations owed towards other institutions or individuals. Neither House of Parliament has any right that

---

[51] See generally P Hennessy, *Cabinet* (Oxford, Blackwell, 1986); V Bogdanor, 'The Civil Service' in V Bogdanor (ed), *The British Constitution in the Twentieth Century* (Oxford, Oxford University Press, 2003) ch 7; G Drewry, 'The executive: towards accountable government and effective governance?' in J Jowell and D Oliver (eds), *The Changing Constitution*, 7th edn (Oxford, Oxford University Press, 2011) ch 7; H Fenwick and G Phillipson, *Text, Cases and Materials on Public Law & Human Rights*, 3rd edn (Abingdon, Routledge, 2011) 627–64; G Marshall, 'The evolving practice of parliamentary accountability: writing down the rules' (1991) 44(4) *Parliamentary Affairs* 460; D Oliver, 'Parliament, ministers and the law' (1994) 47(4) *Parliamentary Affairs* 630; D Woodhouse, *Ministers and Parliament: Accountability in Theory and Practice* (Oxford, Clarendon Press, 1994); D Woodhouse, 'Ministerial responsibility' in V Bogdanor (ed), *The British Constitution in the Twentieth Century* (Oxford, Oxford University Press, 2003) ch 8.

[52] *Official Report*, HC Deb, 13 November 1990, vol 180, cols 461–65.

collective ministerial responsibility be maintained, so when Prime Ministers suspend it, as Harold Wilson did in 1975 to allow ministers to express their views on both sides of the debate leading up to a referendum on continued membership of the European Economic Community (EEC), it was hard to regard that as a breach of a constitutional convention.[53] This conclusion is correct for another reason. Wilson's action in 1975 may be seen as a renegotiation or adaptation of the convention in response to a new political situation which made the convention as previously understood practically impossible to maintain. The scope of obligations under the convention changes and in some unexpected ways crystallises. The notion of breach is as elastic as the obligations of the convention. The agreement between the Conservative Prime Minister and the Liberal Democrat Deputy Prime Minister about the scope of collective responsibility in the Coalition Government after the 2010 general election offers an example of a similar phenomenon.[54]

From another perspective, however, this may be seen as offering only a partial picture. The norm is not concerned with the internal working of government alone. It also helps to define the relationship between the Government and Parliament, particularly the House of Commons. Only if the Government maintains its solidarity can the House of Commons ensure the collective responsibility of the Government to Parliament. The House of Commons, on a vote of no confidence, may by convention require the Government to resign *en bloc*, resulting either in a general election or in Her Majesty inviting someone to form a new government and seek the support of the House of Commons. If the Government were publicly divided, the House would find it even harder than, politically, it now is to hold it collectively to account. In relation to this aspect of the convention's operation it deserves to be classified as a principled, non-legal, constitutional norm. The same norm may have both internal and inter-institutional significance; the categories are not mutually exclusive.

Collective governmental responsibility to the Commons is a key feature of the UK's Constitution because it regulates relationships of power, responsibility and accountability between different institutions. This aspect of the convention cannot be altered by agreement within just one of the institutions. From a constitutional perspective, the House of Commons does have a constitutional right to the maintenance of collective responsibility of the Government, because it is necessary to its control over the executive. If the convention were to change, either the Government would no longer be accountable in that way to the Commons or the Commons would have to assert some other way of securing governmental accountability; in other words, a new convention would have to be developed.

There is another reason for rejecting a sharp dichotomy between norms governing an institution internally and those arising from relationships between

---

[53] Marshall, above n 26, 7–8.
[54] See *Coalition Agreement for Stability and Reform*, 2.1: 'The principle of collective responsibility, save where it is explicitly set aside, continues to apply to all Government Ministers.'

institutions. As Morton points out, institutions are complex unities. An institution is irreducible in that it cannot be reduced to its members or participants. It has authority, responsibilities, powers and objectives which are not in any way an aggregation of those of individuals working in it. (This is why the notion that the 'intention of Parliament' as expressed in legislation is a reflection of the ideas or purposes of individual parliamentarians or groups of them is misguided.) At the same time, many institutions are themselves collections of institutions. The Queen in Parliament is a constitutional institution (the UK's top legislature) but is composed of three separate institutions (the monarch, the House of Lords and the House of Commons). Each of these has its own, internal norms, and other norms (mainly non-legal, but in a few cases legal) concerning the relationship between them when they work together as constituent parts of the Queen in Parliament.

Despite (or perhaps because of) its importance, obligations arising under this aspect of collective Cabinet responsibility are subject to considerable disagreement. Not every defeat in the House of Commons requires a Government to resign. 'The ability of a government to command the confidence of the elected House of Commons is central to its authority to govern. It is tested by votes on motions of confidence, or no confidence.'[55] Before the Fixed-term Parliaments Act 2011, the effect of a government's losing a confidence vote was governed by convention, and was to some degree uncertain. In particular, it was previously not clear whether the convention required the government to resign at once. A practice had developed of a government responding to its defeat on a particular issue by returning to the House for a debate on a motion of confidence in the government in relation to its whole programme, and continuing in office if it mustered a majority in the lobbies after that debate. Members in opposition typically regarded this second bite at the cherry as a breach of the convention, but when in government they took the equally principled view that if one was to dismiss an entire government, it should be done on its record as a whole, not on a single issue. This demonstrates the uncertain and contested character of a convention which, though not often deployed, was fundamental to the tradition of responsible, parliamentary government which underpins the UK's Constitution. There was agreement on the tradition and on the existence of a convention of collective responsibility, but significant disagreement about the more concrete obligations which arise under the norm and how it should be put into practice. It became necessary to resolve the issue (in this case, by legislation) only when the Fixed-term Parliaments Act 2011 introduced a fixed term of five years for parliaments, so that the consequences of the Government being defeated during that term had to be settled for the statute to function.

The 2011 Act has now superseded convention, providing that a government falls only if defeated on a motion that 'this House has no confidence in Her Majesty's Government'. The sitting government is then allowed up to 14 days to seek to regain the confidence of the House of Commons through a debate on a

---

[55] Cabinet Manual, 2.7.

motion 'that this House has confidence in Her Majesty's Government'.[56] When the Bill was before Parliament, the Government did not need to make great efforts to secure consensus on the matter; it could use its majority in the two Houses to force its own view of the appropriate norm into law.

Another tension between the constitutional interests of different institutions arises in relation to the convention of individual ministerial responsibility to Parliament. The Westminster system is based on the idea of responsible government: that is, the Government and its ministers are responsible to the two Houses of Parliament, and particularly the House of Commons, for their decisions, policies and actions, and those of their departments. Ministers sit in one House or the other and are full members of it. As such they are subject to the discipline of the House and also enjoy its privileges. This can produce a peculiarly close relationship between ministers and one of the Houses, but one in which each party has a distinct institutional role. What is more, their different roles are not always in harmony with each other. Nevertheless, they are mutually dependent: neither can achieve its purposes without at least a measure of cooperation from the other. Disagreements cannot be allowed to develop to the point at which either party withdraws cooperation entirely. To do so would make it impossible for the Government to make progress with its legislative programme. It would also make it impossible for the two Houses to perform their roles in scrutinising government action: to do that effectively they need information which can only be provided by government itself.

These circumstances shape the conventions which govern the relationship between ministers and the two Houses, and also make for a lack of consensus as to the content of the conventions. It is in the interests of each House to maximise the available information about the work of government, but ministers and departments have an interest in denying or limiting access to certain information. The principles of individual ministerial responsibility are today said to involve two main elements:

(a) *the duty to give an account* to Parliament of policies and actions of departments, and to answer questions from Members;
(b) *a duty to accept responsibility* when things go wrong, which may include sometimes a duty to resign.

As a complement to these duties there is a duty not 'knowingly' to mislead Parliament.[57] Yet some senior civil servants and many ministers consider that it is permissible to withhold some information from Parliament without telling Parliament that it is being withheld, arguing that half the story can be true and not misleading even if it gives a different impression from the whole story. Indeed, Sir Robin Butler, when he was Cabinet Secretary, argued that sometimes it is essential

---

[56] Fixed-term Parliaments Act 2011, s 2(3). See also Cabinet Manual, 2.31.

[57] See Ministerial Code, accessible at <http://www.cabinetoffice.gov.uk/propriety_and_ethics/ministers/ministerial_code/>; Public Service Committee, Second Report of 1995–96, HC 313; Government's Response, Public Service Committee, First Special Report of 1996–97, HC 67.

not to supply answers in order to protect security, government negotiations with people or bodies inside or outside the UK, or the economic well-being of the country (for example, in relation to information about a forthcoming devaluation of the currency). There are occasions when the harm done by lying to one of the Houses has to be balanced against the harm that would result from telling the truth.[58]

It is said to follow that a minister or civil servant may withhold information when answering a question, being (as Alan Clark called it on 10 November 1992, when giving evidence in the prosecution of directors of Matrix Churchill for selling to Iraq items which could be used make weapons) economical with the *actualité*.[59] In such circumstances, the minister or civil servant is usually required to say that some information is being withheld, but it may sometimes be possible to give an incomplete answer which is correct as far as it goes and is not actively misleading to listeners. In that case, it is said not to breach the Ministerial Code to be economical with the truth without admitting that information is being withheld. In other cases, the greater good is sometimes said (by ministers and civil servants) to justify withholding information even if that creates a misleading impression. Parliament and its select committees, however, do not accept this. Nor could they, without compromising their position on the general principle of ministerial accountability to Parliament:

> When I was working for the Joint Parliamentary Select Committee on Human Rights one of my tasks was to draft letters from the Chair of the Committee, the Rt Hon Jean Corston MP, to ministers asking for information or replies to the Committee's questions about the compatibility of Bills or draft Bills with human rights. Initially, being polite and well brought up, I couched these letters in polite (some would say obsequious) terms: 'The Committee would be most grateful . . .', or 'The Committee would greatly appreciate a reply by . . .'. These expressions were ruthlessly excised by the Lords and Commons Clerks of the Committee, who reminded me that the ministers are accountable to Parliament, not the other way round: the two Houses are the boss, and ministers must do as they are told. Language in a letter that suggested otherwise would be constitutionally inappropriate, and might lead ministers to get ideas above their stations. It is unlikely that quite the same view is held within government Departments, but that does not mean that the attitude of parliamentarians is wrong. It is just that different perspectives produce different views of the relative significance of various institutions of the state.[60]

Tensions between institutions mean that some disagreement as to the scope and applicability of relevant principles is inevitable and, for strategic or tactical reasons,

[58] See Treasury and Civil Service Committee, Fifth Report of 1993–94, HC 27, paras 124–26, and the Minutes of Evidence (Sir Robin Butler); Ministerial Code, para 1.2; House of Commons, *Official Report*, vol 292, cols 1046–47 (19 March 1997); Cabinet Manual, 5.6 (third bullet-point).

[59] Sir Richard Scott, *Return to an Address of the Honourable the House of Commons dated 15th February 1996 for the Report of the Inquiry into the Export of Dual-use Goods to Iraq and Related Prosecutions*, HC 115 (London, HMSO, 1996), 5 vols and index; A Tomkins, *The Constitution after Scott* (Oxford, Clarendon Press, 1998) esp 3–6 and ch 1; A Clark, *The Last Diaries: In and Out of the Wilderness* (ed I Trewin) (London, Weidenfeld & Nicolson, 2002) 61.

[60] Feldman, 'None, one or several?', above n 6, 344–45.

irresolvable. There are times when it is not clear whether an institution is asserting that there is a convention or arguing for a new convention. An example is the suggestion that there now is, or should be, a convention that the UK's armed forces will not embark on a military campaign without parliamentary approval[61]: in the end, the two Houses are likely to act in any case as if it had been accepted, whether or not the government of the day considers itself to be under an obligation to act in accordance with it. In this way, conventions are as much (no less but no more) foci for principled disagreement and statements of negotiating positions as reflections of persistent consensus.

III. CONVENTION AND LAW

We began by noting Dicey's distinction between the law of the Constitution and non-legal, constitutional norms, and his view that the latter serve almost entirely to ensure that the royal prerogative is exercised in ways which preserve the political sovereignty of the electorate. Even in 1885 this was too narrow an understanding. Relationships between important institutions, such as the House of Commons and the House of Lords, were regulated by non-legal understandings; in large part they still are, subject to the invocation of the Parliament Acts 1911 and 1949. Maintaining the political sovereignty of the electorate is one of the purposes of those understandings. On the other hand, there were understandings which served the purpose of facilitating efficient government by encouraging civil servants to give frank advice, such as the convention that such advice would not be disclosed to the public. Lastly, there were understandings that restricted the ultimate sovereignty of the electorate in order to protect other values, including the understanding (noted earlier) that the Queen in Parliament would not legislate oppressively.

It has been said that conventions are like or indistinguishable from laws even to the point where they may be legally enforceable, or that they clothe the legal skeleton of the Constitution.[62] This chapter concludes by identifying two reasons why this misrepresents the nature of these norms. First, important conventions often contradict rather than complement the formal, legal rules. Secondly, when lawyers make use of conventions, they do not blur the distinction between norms which are identifiably legal as having been made by a legally-authorised institution and those which are not; their roles are quite distinct.

We have already seen how the law of the royal prerogative is contradicted by conventions which effectively prevent Her Majesty from exercising her legal

---

[61] House of Lords Select Committee on the Constitution, *Waging War: Parliament's Role and Responsibility*, 15th Report of 2005–06, HL Paper 236-I, paras 85–96, 108–10.

[62] Jennings, above n 23, 81–82, 117–18; TRS Allan, *Law, Liberty, and Justice: The Legal Foundations of British Constitutionalism* (Oxford, Clarendon Press, 1993) ch 10; TRS Allan, *Constitutional Justice: A Liberal Theory of the Rule of Law* (Oxford, Oxford University Press, 2001) 179–86; NW Barber, 'Laws and Constitutional Conventions' (2009) 125 *LQR* 294.

powers, and how the non-legal norm against oppressive use of legislative power contradicts the law of parliamentary sovereignty in the UK, at least as Dicey understood it. (There is, of course, controversy as to whether Dicey was correct and whether his formulation is accurate today.) In important respects, the bones of the real Constitution, the Constitution as it operates in practice, bear no relationship to the legal constitution. This is not a peculiarity of an uncodified constitution. It is true to a greater or lesser extent of all constitutions, including codified constitutional documents (at any rate once they have operated for a period after their making).

The US Constitution exemplifies this. Article II § 1 sets out the procedure for electing the President of the USA. In each state, the legislature provides for appointment of electors, the number of whom is equal to the combined representation of that state in the Senate and House of Representatives. Electors in each state meet and vote by ballot for two people, at least one of whom must not be an inhabitant of that state. The result is sent to the President of the Senate, who opens all the certificates. The person with the largest number of votes, if that be an overall majority, is thereby elected President, and the person with the second highest number is elected Vice-President. In the event of two or more people having an overall majority and an equal number of votes, the House of Representatives elects a President from among them, and if there is a tie for second place the Senate elects a Vice-President, with the representatives of each state together casting one vote.

Anyone who has taken an interest in modern elections for the Presidency will immediately see that these provisions of constitutional law have next to no similarity to today's reality. The objectives of the legal arrangements – avoiding faction, ensuring that electors are those who best understand government and are most familiar with the merits of leading statesmen, and so on – are no longer the purposes of the system. Instead, the guiding values are electoral democracy on the basis of universal adult franchise. Avoidance of faction has been replaced with a straight, popular choice between factions. This has been given effect through a mixture of state legislation and constitutional conventions about methods of appointing electors in such a way as to make them responsive to popular opinion expressed through ballots, and conventions and financial realities which make political parties' machines dominant in selecting candidates and campaigning for them.

Dicey recognised this gap between constitutional law and constitutional reality, noting that

> the 'electors' have become a mere means of voting for a particular candidate; they are no more than so many ballots cast for the Republican or Democratic nominee. The understanding that an elector is not really to elect, has now become so firmly established, that for him to exercise his legal power of choice is considered a breach of political honour too gross to be committed by the most unscrupulous of politicians. . . . Under a written, therefore, as under an unwritten constitution, we find in full existence the distinction between the law and the conventions of the constitution.[63]

---

[63] Dicey, above n 1, 29–30.

Dicey said little about how conventions arise, or how we can identify them as such and ascertain the obligations which they embody. He did, however, say something about the sanctions by which conventions are enforced. He recognised that the threat of impeachment and the force of public opinion might have some residual or current power to impress the importance of conventions on the minds of politicians, but the most compelling reason to follow conventions was, he thought, 'the fact that the breach of these principles and of the these conventions will almost immediately bring the offender into conflict with the law of the land'.[64] Failing to summon Parliament annually would make it impossible for the necessary annual legislation to be passed to allow the army to be controlled by law, taxes to be levied lawfully and, one might add, expenditure authorised. Conventions worked because they operated in the shadow of the law.

To understand the relationship of law to convention we need to keep in mind that the US example does not show conventions operating in a manner ancillary to constitutional law. They do not clothe the bare bones of constitutional law, as Jennings suggested, or fill gaps between legal norms. They make the legal norms wholly irrelevant for practical purposes. They provide an alternative constitutional skeleton in a wholly different shape, to the point at which anyone attempting to give practical effect to the provisions of constitutional law will be acting wholly unconstitutionally. One might even say that any attempt to give practical effect to the law would tend to undermine the legitimacy of the Constitution, divorcing it from what are now regarded as principles of political morality on which its legitimacy depends. The Constitution could then be saved only by radically amending its legal provisions to bring them into line with constitutional propriety. The gap between law and the real Constitution is one reason for finding it surprising that federal courts felt able to play a significant role in determining the result of the presidential election fought by George W Bush and Al Gore in 2000.[65]

Of course, not all constitutional conventions directly contradict or displace legal provisions. As we have seen, some are glosses on or ways of implementing the law. Conventions are of different kinds, have different effects and stand in different relationships to law. The subtleties of the relationship between legal and non-legal constitutional norms may be illustrated by examining an aspect of the convention of collective Cabinet responsibility which restricts the freedom of ministers to disclose what goes on during Cabinet meetings.

In 1975, the Attorney-General sought injunctions to restrain the literary executors of Richard Crossman, a former Cabinet Minister, and the *Sunday Times* from publishing Crossman's diaries, or extracts from them, which disclosed disagreements between ministers in Cabinet during Harold Wilson's Labour Government of 1964–70. The Attorney advanced his claim in *Attorney-General v Jonathan Cape Ltd and another*[66] on three grounds. First, he asserted that he had a duty to protect the public interest in litigation. This went to his *locus standi*. He went on to argue

---

[64] *Ibid*, 374.
[65] *Bush v Gore*, 121 S Ct 525 (2000), US SC.
[66] *Attorney-General v Jonathan Cape Ltd and another* [1976] QB 752.

that a court could, at the Attorney's suit, restrain a disclosure, in the same way as it could refuse to order disclosure in legal proceedings, in order

> to protect the public interest in good government of which collective responsibility is a major pillar . . . The public interest in non-disclosure must be weighed against disclosure in the interests of justice. . . . The courts should recognise that even if injustice to an individual results there is a higher public interest in relation to the protection of a certain class of material. In the present case the public interest in the citizen being informed clashes with the interests of the machinery of government.[67]

For the defendants, James Comyn QC and Brian Neill QC denied that an act being contrary to the public interest gave rise to any legal cause of action, and that collective Cabinet responsibility was not a legal norm and so could not be a recognised basis of legal liability.[68] Lord Widgery CJ seems to have accepted this argument, at least for cases where national security was not affected.[69]

The Attorney-General based his alternative argument on the then relatively undeveloped principle that courts would prevent a person from profiting from unauthorised disclosure of information received in circumstances which impart confidentiality to the information. He tried to show that information about conflicting views expressed in Cabinet, advice given by civil servants, and discussion of transfer and promotion of civil servants, was permanently confidential on account of the operation of the convention of collective Cabinet responsibility: 'Confidentiality is an inherent and essential part of the administrative machinery of government.'[70] Lord Widgery thought that it would be difficult to establish such long-lasting confidentiality on the basis of the convention, because there was disagreement among former Cabinet ministers as to what, in concrete terms, the convention required. Furthermore, when the Attorney-General, rather than a private party, was asserting a duty of confidentiality in respect of governmental information, he had to show that a recognised public interest required a court not only to treat the information as confidential, but also to restrain publication indefinitely, outweighing the powerful interest in freedom of expression. Lord Widgery accepted that, as a matter of law:

> . . . when a Cabinet Minister receives information in confidence the improper publication of such information can be restrained by the court, and his obligation is not merely to observe a gentleman's agreement to refrain from publication. . . .
>
> The Attorney-General must show (a) that such publication would be a breach of confidence; (b) that the public interest requires that the publication be restrained, and (c) that there are no other facts of the public interest contradictory of and more compelling than that relied upon. Moreover, the court, when asked to restrain such a publication, must closely examine the extent to which relief is necessary to ensure that restrictions are not imposed beyond the strict requirement of public need.[71]

---

[67] *Ibid*, 755.
[68] *Ibid*, 756, 758.
[69] *Ibid*, 768G–H.
[70] *Ibid*, 756C.
[71] *Ibid*, 770A–771A.

Lord Widgery had already said that he was far from convinced that, when balanced against the public interest in freedom of speech, the public interest in restraining publication had the necessary weight.[72] When he came to apply the above principles to the facts of the case, Lord Widgery concluded:

> In my judgment, the Attorney-General has made out his claim that the expression of individual opinions by Cabinet Ministers in the course of Cabinet discussion are matters of confidence, the publication of which can be restrained by the court when this is clearly necessary in the public interest.
>
> The maintenance of the doctrine of joint responsibility within the Cabinet is in the public interest, and the application of that doctrine might be prejudiced by premature disclosure of the views of individual Ministers.
>
> There must, however, be a limit in time after which the confidential character of the information, and the duty of the court to restrain publication, will lapse. Since the conclusion of the hearing in this case I have had the opportunity to read the whole of volume one of the Diaries, and my considered view is that I cannot believe that the publication at this interval of anything in volume one would inhibit free discussion in the Cabinet of today, even though the individuals involved are the same, and the national problems have a distressing similarity with those of a decade ago.[73]

What, then, was the status of the convention? Lord Widgery accepted that the evidence established that joint Cabinet responsibility was at the heart of the working of responsible government, which could be prejudiced by premature disclosure of the views of individual ministers. That established a duty of confidentiality and a public interest in upholding it. The Attorney-General had not proved, however, that the convention required long-term non-disclosure. In any case, from the point of view of the law of breach of confidence, the question was what the balance of public interests required by way of legal restraint, not what the convention required of Mr Crossman as a matter of good taste or good sense. While accepting that the public interest against disclosure might be compelling over a period of weeks or months, Lord Widgery doubted that it required legal protection for Cabinet confidences over a period of years.[74]

Thus, so far as evidence supported the existence of a convention requiring confidentiality, the law of breach of confidence took it as establishing that the circumstances were such as to impart a quality of confidentiality to information about Cabinet proceedings. But other legal questions remained to be answered. Lord Widgery had to decide, as a matter of law, whether the public interest in permanently protecting the confidentiality outweighed competing public interests, such as freedom of expression and information. Legal remedies restricting disclosure should not be available beyond the point at which the balance of public interests clearly demanded non-disclosure. Deciding whether that time had passed involved the judge in an exercise of judgement; it was a legal, not a political or conventional, assessment. Neither directly nor indirectly did Lord Widgery decide

---

[72] *Ibid*, 767B.
[73] *Ibid.* 771A–D.
[74] *Ibid*, 768, 771.

to enforce or not enforce a convention as such. Evidence about the convention was important in helping to establish that two of the requirements for a remedy had been satisfied.

This shows that non-legal constitutional norms cannot on their own form the basis of a legal claim. But sometimes a public body raises a convention by way of a defence in legal proceedings. For example, ministers have frequently asserted their collective or individual responsibility to Parliament to argue that courts should not subject ministerial judgements on politically controversial matters of policy to scrutiny on grounds such as unreasonableness, or grant remedies in respect of political acts; the reasonableness of political judgements is said to be the business of political rather than legal methods of accountability. Courts have been particularly willing to accept such arguments when judges have felt out of their depth in dealing with the issues, for example in relation to the formidably complex politics and mathematical calculations surrounding efforts by the Thatcher Government to cap levels of rates and expenditure by left-wing local authorities in the 1980s. This is not an example of judges enforcing a convention in any sense, but only of their restricting the exercise of their jurisdiction to leave appropriate space for the operation of a convention.[75] In fact, it is unreal to believe that the two Houses of Parliament exercise effective control over the merits of subordinate legislation. When a government commands the confidence of the House of Commons, ministerial responsibility to Parliament for such decisions is very weak. As Farwell LJ said in December 1910, in connection with the Government's attempt to prevent a taxpayer from seeking a declaration that an attempt to gather tax without legislative authority was unlawful, 'If ministerial responsibility were more than the mere shadow of a name, the matter would be less important, but as it is, the Courts are the only defence of the liberty of the subject against departmental aggression.'[76]

Of course, the use by a court of part of a convention for its own purpose does not affect the convention. This is evident from developments after the judgment in *Attorney-General v. Jonathan Cape*. The Government reasserted its view of the convention in the form of a statement of principles set out in a report by a committee of Privy Councillors chaired by Lord Radcliffe, subsequently incorporated into the Ministerial Code by reference. The Ministerial Code provides:

> The principle of collective responsibility, save where it is explicitly set aside, requires that Ministers should be able to express their views frankly in the expectation that they can argue freely in private while maintaining a united front when decisions have been reached. This in turn requires that the privacy of opinions expressed in Cabinet and Ministerial Committees, including in correspondence, should be maintained.[77]
>
> Former Ministers intending to publish their memoirs are required to submit the draft manuscript in good time before publication to the Cabinet Secretary and to conform to the principles set out in the Radcliffe report of 1976 (Cmnd 6386).[78]

[75] See eg *R v Secretary of State for the Environment, ex p Nottinghamshire County Council* [1986] AC 240 (HL).

[76] *Dyson v Bank of England (No 1)* [1911] 1 KB 410 (CA) per Farwell LJ at 423–24.

[77] Ministerial Code, 2.1.

[78] *Ibid*, 8.10.

The principles are set out in the Directory of Civil Service Guidance.[79] They are both more concrete and therefore certain than the evidence put before Lord Widgery, and more restrictive than the requirements of the legal obligation of confidentiality as Lord Widgery held them to be: for example, Key Principle 1.iii allows a former minister to regard the restrictions on disclosure as lifted after 15 years in non-security cases (far longer than had elapsed in Crossman's case). Key principle 3 notes that 'established principles of law do not provide a system which can protect and enforce those rules of reticence that the Committee regard as called for when ex-Ministers compose their memoirs of Ministerial life'. This is the clearest possible recognition that the law and the conventions are quite separate, and are not congruent with each other.[80]

The last point to note is that all aspects of the convention may be adjusted, at least temporarily, on the *ipse dixit* of the Prime Minister, normally following negotiation or at least consultation with other affected parties. We have already mentioned that Harold Wilson suspended the convention so that ministers could publicly debate the merits of membership of the EEC before the referendum on membership in 1975. Further adjustments were made to redefine the conventions for the Coalition Government after the general election in 2010.[81] For good or ill, non-legal, constitutional norms are always subject to political renegotiation or, if they affect only one institution, revision by an authorised officer of the institution. Courts can make use for legal purposes, when relevant, of evidence as to what a relevant norm may be, but no decision of a court can change or authoritatively state such a norm, unless it concerns the judiciary or relations between the courts and other institutions.

IV. CONCLUSIONS

What lessons can we draw from these reflections? I suggest the following, using 'convention' to mean the whole gamut of non-legal, constitutional norms operating within a particular constitutional tradition:

(a) The classical concept of 'convention' covers a wide range of types of non-legal norms and statements of useful practices. They are constitutional if they concern institutions of the State, whether by constituting them (as in the case of the Cabinet), managing them or guiding their relationships with other institutions of the State. A constitutional convention is rooted in a constitutional tradition: important ones represent judgements as to the weighting of conflicting, constitutional principles; less important ones (such

---

[79] Directory of Civil Service Guidance, available at <http://www.cabinetoffice.gov.uk/resource-library/directory-civil-service-guidance>, vol 2, 41–43.

[80] See the discussion in House of Commons Select Committee on Public Administration, *Whitehall Confidential? The Publication of Political Memoirs*, Fifth Report of 2005–06, HC 689, 2 vols.

[81] Coalition Agreement for Stability and Reform, May 2010, para 2.1, available at <http://www.cabinetoffice.gov.uk/news/coalition-documents>.

as statements of efficient working practices) are neutral as between constitutional principles.

(b) Any constitutional norm will attract both a degree of consensus as to the significance of constitutional principles on which it draws and disagreement, typically between institutions, as to the application and scope of those principles. Disagreement is made more likely when a convention is relatively vague or general, ie closer to a principle than a rule of conduct. Attempts to codify conventions can, to some extent, limit their vagueness, but cannot secure acceptance on which conventions ultimately rely. For that, there must be either principled engagement of all who are affected by it or an authoritative officer, such as the Prime Minister or Cabinet Secretary, with power to make the convention stick.

(c) Conventions are essentially different and separate from laws. They operate in different institutional settings. Each may draw on the other, but a judicial institution can never arrive at a statement of a convention which could be authoritative from the perspective of officers and members of other institutions, because non-legal norms are the product of discussion between or tacit acceptance by members of the institutions which are affected. Unlike constitutional laws, important constitutional conventions must be rooted in constitutional principles arising from the constitutional tradition of the State, and the principles which form part of that tradition.

(d) It follows that whilst there is clear conceptual water between legal and non-legal constitutional norms (despite their occasional overlaps), there is no clear water between different kinds of non-legal, constitutional norms, and there is no point in trying to separate them systematically.

7

Continuity and Change in Constitutional Conventions

JOSEPH JACONELLI

I. INTRODUCTION

N O PART OF the Constitution of the United Kingdom illuminates the related themes of the present volume, continuity and change, as vividly as that of constitutional conventions. It is intrinsic to the very nature of such conventions that they are capable of ready adaptation to both changing circumstances and evolving political ideas. Yet, at the same time, the characteristic motif in reasoning by reference to constitutional convention is appeal to past precedents as exerting a determining influence on how a present-day problem is to be resolved. This contribution examines that nature in the light of the three defining phases in the life of constitutional conventions: their coming into existence (section II); their adaptation to changing conditions (section III); and their ceasing to exist (section IV).

The most frequently-cited definitions have two different points of departure. First is the type of definition which concentrates on the role played by constitutional conventions: that they are rules of political accountability,[1] or that their purpose is to control the manner in which the royal prerogative is exercised.[2] Each of these has its shortcomings. Certainly, the conventional rules that limit the functions of the House of Lords and of the Queen in the legislative process accord well with the former perspective, since they promote the predominance of the elected component of the legislature. At the same time, however, the approach marginalises the whole array of legal rules (in legislation such as the Representation of the People Acts) that strive to ensure the same end. In the same way, to focus the definition on questions of control of the royal prerogative is to concentrate merely on the executive branch of government, while ignoring the substantial role

---

[1] G Marshall, *Constitutional Conventions* (Oxford, Oxford University Press, 1984) is subtitled *The Rules and Forms of Political Accountability*.
[2] AV Dicey, *Introduction to the Study of the Law of the Constitution*, 10th edn (London, Macmillan, 1959) 429.

performed by conventions such as the Salisbury–Addison convention (in assisting to secure the primacy of the House of Commons generally) and the Sewel convention (in maintaining the primacy of the Scottish Parliament over matters devolved to Scotland).

Secondly, a definition may eschew issues of the functions of constitutional conventions and focus instead on the practical tests to be applied in determining whether a particular constitutional convention does indeed exist. The prime example in this category is that of Jennings' three-part inquiry, 'first, what are the precedents; secondly, did the actors in the precedents believe that they were bound by a rule; and thirdly, is there a reason for the rule?'[3]

The application of this tripartite test necessarily requires an answer to the prior question of whether or not the area under investigation in this way is truly an area properly characterised as subject to the province of constitutional conventions. Nevertheless, even if one accepts this series of tests on their face value, the way in which they are expressed harbours a number of critical ambiguities. The first limb, for example, does not distinguish between recent precedents and precedents that have long since been discarded; between those that may be regarded as applicable to today's circumstances and those which are merely of historical interest. The third limb, in searching for a 'reason' for the supposed rule, obscures an important difference: between what we might call 'historical' reasons for a convention and the reasons 'of principle' which underpin it. The former is an investigation of the factors that originally came together in shaping the rule at its inception. The latter, by contrast, asks how the supposed rule – irrespective of its origins – may be fitted today into the constitutional system as a whole in a way that gives that system some coherence.

II. INSTANTANEOUSLY CREATED CONVENTIONS: CONSTITUTIONAL UNDERSTANDINGS AND THE INNER LOGIC OF THE CONSTITUTION

Of the three elements listed by Jennings, it is clear that the first – the existence of one or more precedents – is of primary importance. With the second and third elements the inquiry shifts to secondary considerations: the beliefs of the participants in the precedents; and the reasons for the phenomenon (which has now developed from a precedent or precedents into a 'rule'). In one important respect, therefore, the application of constitutional conventions shares a characteristic with the adjudication of cases at common law: the appeal to the past as a determining consideration in the correct resolution of a present problem. Yet in both systems of practical reasoning situations can arise where there is quite simply no precedent that is even remotely applicable. This is an unusual event in developed common law systems that are in possession of an established stock of case law. Its

---

[3] I Jennings, *The Law and the Constitution*, 5th edn (London, University of London Press, 1959) 119–20.

occurrence in the more sparsely occupied areas of constitutional practice, however, is not so rare an occurrence.

Sometimes, therefore, a claim as to what is the proper mode of conduct in the field of constitutional matters is advanced on nothing more than what may be termed the 'inner logic' of the Constitution. In time, given repetition in essentials of the same situation, it may develop into a fully-fledged constitutional convention with its characteristic appeal to the authority of that originating event and the manner of its resolution. However, it is possible, in view of the rarity of the circumstances, that there will only ever be a single instance. Some examples will help to clarify the point.

The first is based on an episode in the negotiations of the Anglo-Irish Treaty. In 1921, Sir Gordon Hewart, who was Attorney-General at the time, was involved in the legal aspects of those negotiations. The following year he was appointed to the post of Lord Chief Justice – a transition facilitated by the then convention that, should the post of Lord Chief Justice fall vacant, the Attorney-General of the day had the right of first refusal of the post. The propriety of a judge being involved in continuing negotiations with the Irish Provisional Government was questioned in Parliament. Lord Cecil asked 'why this departure from constitutional practice was made,' adding 'there are objections to a judge, who may have to decide judicially questions arising out of [the Treaty] even appearing to be in consultation with Ministers on the matter'. This was clearly an objection of principle, ultimately founded on considerations of judicial impartiality or the separation of powers. It could have developed into a constitutional convention in the normal sense in the extremely unlikely event of repetition of this unusual situation. That it was not as yet transposed into the realm of convention was emphasised in the reply: 'The task undertaken by Lord Hewart can hardly be described as a departure from constitutional practice, inasmuch as no precedent is believed to exist for the occasion on which his assistance was requested.'[4]

A more topical example of the scope for instantaneous creation of a constitutional convention is likely to arise from the West Lothian Question or (as it is now better known) the English Question. According to a frequently-canvassed solution to the problem, Scottish MPs would be debarred from voting at Westminster on bills regarding purely English matters – defined as bills which, had they pertained to Scotland, would have fallen within the legislative competence of the Scottish Parliament.[5] It could be argued that, as a result of such a restriction, it would be impermissible for an MP sitting for a Scottish constituency ever again to become Prime Minister or to hold one of the principal offices of State. On the other hand, that view could be said to rest on the confusion between the legislative and executive roles of such persons as the Prime Minister, Chancellor of the Exchequer and Home Secretary. A Scottish constituency-based holder of these offices would not be able to vote on purely English matters, but would not be

---

[4] HC Deb 14 June 1922, vol 155, cols 354–55.
[5] An example would have been s 66 of the Scotland Act 1978, which never entered into force.

debarred from discussing or debating them within the forum of Westminster.[6] However, if the disqualification were to apply, it would surely be applicable at the point when an MP sitting for a Scottish seat was seeking the leadership of his party. Once he were elected as such, it would be impossible for the Monarch to refuse him the position of Prime Minister if he were to lead his party to a general election victory. And he, in his turn, would find it very difficult to deny one of the principal offices of State to a colleague for no better reason than the location of the constituency which returned him to Westminster.

The idea of an instantaneous convention – one that is created on the basis of nothing more than the inner logic of existing constitutional arrangements – could be viewed as having been subsumed already in Dicey's compendious list of 'conventions, understandings, habits, or practices'. [7] Three of these items are instances of social practice. 'Understandings', however, stand somewhat apart from those three since they may have a dual role. They may assist in the interpretation of social practice, but they may equally consist of unspoken but generally shared assumptions which have yet to be manifested in a practical resolution to a concrete problem.

III. SOME INSTANCES OF THE EVOLUTION OF PARTICULAR CONVENTIONS

This section examines four areas of transition in the evolution of conventions. The first two focus on the Prime Minister, as a member of the Government who is now necessarily recruited from the House of Commons and as the person who in recent times (but perhaps for not much longer) has had sole responsibility for deciding the date for the dissolution of Parliament that is to be tendered to the Monarch. The second pairing brings together the related conventions governing the duration of grants of revenue to the Crown and the consequences of interruption in that revenue for the survival in office of the Government.

A. The Prime Minister (and Others) as Necessarily a Member of the House of Commons

This first example considers the evolution of the conventional rule that the Prime Minister is required to occupy a seat in the House of Commons. The key dates in this context are 1902 (the termination of the premiership of Lord Salisbury, the last Prime Minister to discharge that office throughout from the House of Lords) and 1963 (when Lord Home was required to renounce his peerage on being appointed Prime Minister by the Queen). Between those years there were two

---

[6] The idea of a member of either House being permitted to sit and speak (but not vote) is not totally unknown. It was suggested as one among several arrangements to accommodate a peer in the post of Chancellor of the Exchequer. See n 19 below.

[7] Dicey, above n 2, 24.

occasions on which a member of the House of Lords was closely considered for appointment as Prime Minister: in 1923, when Lord Curzon was passed over in favour of Stanley Baldwin; and in 1940, when the choice lay, realistically, between Lord Halifax and Winston Churchill. Each of these occasions is instructive in the evolution of constitutional conventions, though for different reasons. The pairings, however, are recounted in the literature without any indication as to why it was that the choice was confined to the two sets of individuals in the first place.

A number of factors are offered by Vernon Bogdanor as to why Lord Curzon was not appointed Prime Minister. Some of these are personal (his haughty personality). Others are constitutional in nature (that he was tied to a seat in the House of Lords, whether as a consideration in itself or allied to the fact that the official Labour Opposition had no representation there and/or that the House of Lords already had a high number of members of the Cabinet).[8] As for the reason why the selection lay between Curzon and Baldwin, he refers only to the respective positions held by them at the time (Foreign Secretary in the one case, and Chancellor of the Exchequer and leader of the House of Commons in the other).[9] The established practice in 1923 was that the major parties had two leaders, one in each House of Parliament. The leadership of the party, when it was out of office, went into abeyance as between these two individuals, unless one of them was a former Prime Minister (in which case he was usually regarded as the leader of the whole party). If there was no such person, the Monarch could choose as Prime Minister the leader in either House.[10] In accordance with this rule, Lord Curzon was eligible for consideration since he was leader of the House of Lords (a position that he held from late 1916 until 22 January 1924). He combined that post with that of Foreign Secretary, though this was constitutionally irrelevant. The contest of 1923 lay on the cusp of the evolving convention that the Prime Minister must occupy a seat in the House of Commons. A number of significant changes in the statute book since the time when Lord Salisbury had laid down office had propelled forward this new 'understanding': in particular, the truncation of the legislative powers of the House of Lords by the Parliament Act 1911 and the extension of the franchise. When two, prima facie applicable, conventions are in conflict, there is no routine way of according supremacy to one over the other (as there is, for example, in regard to laws). Those charged with administering the relevant part of the Constitution must arrive at a judgement as to where the balance lies between the respective rules.

To turn to the second episode, the position of Lord Halifax did not exactly correspond to that of Lord Curzon 17 years earlier. One point of difference is that Lord Halifax ruled himself out by reason of his sitting in the House of Lords. In doing so, however, he could simply have been erecting a barrier that might well

---

[8] V Bogdanor, *The Monarchy and the Constitution* (Oxford, Oxford University Press, 1995) 90–93.
[9] *Ibid*, 90. Likewise, D Gilmour, *Curzon* (London, John Murray, 1994) 579–85 does not advert to the question why Baldwin was in the running in the first place.
[10] See V Bogdanor, *Politics and the Constitution: Essays on British Government* (Aldershot, Dartmouth, 1996) 47.

have been raised against him by the King in the event that he had decided to press his claims. He was Foreign Secretary in the National Government, but again that was constitutionally irrelevant. More in point, he happened at the precise time not to be leader of the House of Lords – a post which was undergoing rapid turn-over at the time but on the critical date, 10 May 1940, was occupied by Earl Stanhope. The factors that would have weighed in support of any claim advanced by Halifax were his occupation of a senior post in government together with the fact that he was between two periods of occupancy of the position of leader of the Lords (1935–38, and October–December 1940). Churchill was at the time First Lord of the Admiralty, and therefore outside the two posts from which the Prime Minister was traditionally to be recruited.[11]

The overriding point of difference with the first of our episodes, of course, is that the country was at war. It emerges from the events of May 1940 that the choice was minimally constrained by pre-existing constitutional rules according to the posts occupied by the various persons. Not only was the range of candidates considerably larger than usual, the country was willing to consider a peer in the role of Prime Minister. In view of the exigencies of national survival, the only real consideration in determining the choice of Prime Minister was the person most likely to lead the country to victory. Jennings does not quite put his finger on the point in saying 'The arguments against a peer would be less strong in such an all-party coalition as that of 1940–5.'[12] The decisive factor was not the coalition nature of the Government (there had been a National Government since 1931), but rather the existence of a war-time emergency.

A question may be posed about this instance. The departure from the normal constitutional rule was generally considered entirely legitimate. Why, then, does it matter how it is characterised by constitutional scholars: whether as a breach of convention, or as falling within the scope of an exception to the general conven-tional rule? It is significant, and for this reason. If there is no exception pertaining to war-time or conditions of emergency, it would count as an example of counter-conventional conduct – as an instance that could count in favour of the view that the convention was losing its force *even in peace-time conditions*. If, on the other hand, there is such an exception, the instance is not an example of counter-conventional conduct at all.

There can be few constitutional rules that can be considered more basic today than that the Prime Minister is to be recruited from the House of Commons. Yet the status of that rule has of late undergone a significant change. In so far as the only parties that are likely to possess a majority of seats in the Commons are par-ties the internal rules of which permit only an MP to stand for the position of leader, to that extent the conventional rule that the Prime Minister must hold a seat in the Commons has been transformed, albeit surreptitiously, into a legal

[11] As Andrew Roberts indicates, there were even more candidates who were considered for the post, including Leo Amery and the Home Secretary, Sir John Anderson. See A Roberts, *'The Holy Fox': A Biography of Lord Halifax* (London, Weidenfeld & Nicolson, 1991) 199.

[12] I Jennings, *Cabinet Government*, 3rd edn (Cambridge, Cambridge University Press, 1959) 24, fn 1.

rule. That rule is derived, not from a grand constitutional text, but from the most humble of areas of private law – the law of unincorporated associations and similar structures – which forms the basis upon which internal rules of party organisation are founded.

The existence of an exception in time of war to the normal rule applicable to the selection of Prime Minister prompts the question of whether the same exception could be found to apply to lesser ministerial offices. Examples, though of lower profile, are to be found. In 1942 Winston Churchill announced in the House of Commons the appointment of Australian politician, Richard Casey, as Minister of State in the Middle East and member of the British War Cabinet. Questions were asked about Casey's position: would he become a member of the Commons or the Lords; would he retain his seat in the Australian Parliament; would a minister reply for him in the British House of Commons? Churchill explained that 'there are precedents in time of war for Ministers who are His Majesty's subjects from the Empire holding office in this country without being Members of either House of Parliament'.[13] It even emerges that while serving in this capacity Casey participated in the discussion of purely domestic matters unrelated to the conduct of the war.[14]

The precedent to which Churchill appeared to be appealing was the appointment in 1917 to the British War Cabinet of South African, General Jan Smuts. The constitutional propriety of Lloyd George's selection, as one which was then without precedent, was questioned at the time. There was an attempt to fudge the position with the claim that Smuts was attending, without being a member of, the War Cabinet. Irrespective of such niceties, it appears that Lloyd George did try, without success, to persuade him to contest a seat in the House of Commons.[15] An irony that appears to have gone unnoticed was that the terms of Smuts's home jurisdiction would have forbidden an arrangement whereby a person (whether South African or not) sought to hold ministerial office without occupying a seat in Parliament.[16] This precedent was not confined to those from the wider Empire. Most noteworthy among British appointments other than from the ranks of serving MPs at the time was that of Neville Chamberlain to the key ministerial post of Director-General of National Service.[17]

There would appear, however, to have been offices which were beyond the scope of the war-time exception. In the early months of the Second World War, the Prime Minister, Neville Chamberlain, became increasingly dissatisfied with

---

[13] HC Deb 19 March 1942, vol 378, cols 1664–65.

[14] See RG Casey, *Personal Experience 1939–1946* (London, Constable & Co, 1962) 167–68 (entry for 13 July 1943), from which it is apparent that Casey was privy even to the discussion of the White Paper presented by RA Butler that foreshadowed the Education Act 1944.

[15] See WK Hancock, *Smuts: The Sanguine Years 1870–1919* (Cambridge, Cambridge University Press, 1962) 436.

[16] The South Africa Act 1909, s 14, stipulated that 'no minister shall hold office for a longer period than three months unless he is or becomes a member of either House of Parliament'.

[17] See D Dilks, *Neville Chamberlain: Vol 1 Pioneering and reform 1869–1929* (Cambridge, Cambridge University Press, 1984) 196, 191 and 222, for some indication of the difficulties arising from the fact that Chamberlain did not, at the time, hold a seat in Parliament.

the performance of Sir John Simon as Chancellor of the Exchequer. He approached Josiah Stamp, by then ennobled as Baron Stamp, to ask whether he would be willing and able to assume that post.[18] Stamp raised many of the same objections that would have told against Lord Halifax in the position of the Prime Minister. He could not resign his peerage, nor could the King 'unmake' him in that capacity. The idea of Stamp being 'dis-peered' by Act of Parliament was floated, as was the idea of a more limited bill which would enable a peer to sit in the House of Commons. All these ideas came to nothing, and the issue was never tested.[19] What emerges from this little-known episode is that the objections to a Chancellor of the Exchequer sitting in the House of Lords were, if anything, even greater than those telling against a Prime Minister sitting in that place. Nor should this be surprising. The supremacy of the House of Commons in money matters had been long established, even before the Parliament Act 1911 had set the legislative seal on that supremacy. It would have been extremely odd for a Chancellor to be conducting the finances of the nation from a seat in the legislative chamber which had minimal powers over national income and expenditure.[20] Indeed, as recently as August 1923, Reginald McKenna had agreed to return to the post of Chancellor of the Exchequer – a position he had occupied during Asquith's Coalition Government (May 1915–December 1916). However, his failure to find a seat led to him being passed over in favour of Neville Chamberlain. Apparently, the idea that he should be granted a peerage and a seat in the House of Lords, if it was entertained at all, was promptly discarded.

B. Choosing a Dissolution Date: Statute, Cabinet, Prime Minister, and Monarch

The start and conclusion of the past 150 years' history of the dissolution of Parliament are marked by two significant pieces of legislation. The Representation of the People Act 1867 stipulates that the death of the Monarch no longer requires a dissolution.[21] The Fixed-term Parliaments Act 2011 lays down the date for the next general election (7 May 2015)[22] and, of greater significance, it envisages successive general elections at intervals of five years. The rules governing the dissolution of Parliament have traditionally been a patchwork of statute, royal prerogative and convention – in descending order of their importance in the hierarchy of

---

[18] See JH Jones, *Josiah Stamp, Public Servant: The Life of the First Baron Stamp of Shortlands* (London, Pitman, 1964) 337–39.

[19] For a full account of the possible solutions and their respective difficulties, see the paper prepared by Granville Ram: National Archives PREM 5/170. Particularly interesting was the suggestion that Stamp be accorded rights of sitting and speaking, but not of voting, in the House of Commons. The paper observes, in the familiar spirit of reasoning by reference to constitutional conventions, that there were 'no exact precedents for what is contemplated'.

[20] The same position, with the same reasons, would surely hold as a matter of constitutional logic in regard to the principal members, at least, of the rest of the Treasury team. This would be particularly so in regard to the Chief Secretary to the Treasury, a post that has been in existence only since 1961.

[21] Representation of the People Act 1867, s 51.

[22] Fixed-term Parliaments Act 2011, s 1(2).

sources. It is convention that is the predominant concern of this chapter, and that element makes its presence felt on two issues: on the source of the advice to the Monarch to dissolve Parliament; and the circumstances (if any) in which it would be proper for the Monarch to decline to follow advice on the question of whether or not to dissolve.

It has been a long-standing convention that it is the Prime Minister alone, not (as formerly) the Cabinet as a whole, who decides on a date for the dissolution of Parliament that is to be tendered to the Monarch. In this regard the decisive shift from Cabinet to Prime Minister occurred under the premiership of David Lloyd George. An historical account of the convention would say that the shift was due to the occupation of the post of Prime Minister by a particularly forceful individual, and one whose prestige at the relevant time, 1918, was at its highest as a result of his having led the nation to victory in the First World War. An ancillary reason would be the fact that Lloyd George headed a coalition government and, therefore, one in which there was no clear party interest that would determine the date to be tendered. The explanation would go on to say that the pivotal role of the Prime Minister continued into an era of less forceful occupants of that office and at the head of single-party governments. An argument of principle, by contrast, would be rather more difficult to construct. There appears to be no argument that could be so founded that would count in favour of the Prime Minister, in contrast to the Cabinet as a whole, being empowered to decide on the dissolution date to be communicated to the Monarch.

Geoffrey Marshall suggests that it was imprecision in a memorandum submitted by Lord Haldane to George V in 1916 that created the precedent responsible for transferring the power to recommend a dissolution date from the Cabinet to the Prime Minister alone. The crucial words – 'The only minister who can properly give advice as to a dissolution of Parliament is the Prime Minister' – were written against the background of a possible successor to Asquith as Prime Minister making it a condition of his acceptance of office that Parliament first be dissolved.[23] This shows that, as in reasoning by reference to precedent at common law, utterances made by the constitutional actors must be interpreted in the context of the relevant background dispute that requires resolution. Certainly, similarities may be identified between reasoning on the basis of common law and the exercise of extracting from constitutional events of the past what is required to be done in a present-day situation. The role played by precedent is of central importance in both. Yet precedent functions in different ways as between case law and conventions. A judicial precedent that is reached without taking account of relevant decided case law – the typical instance of a precedent reached *per incuriam* – is a weak authority that is likely to be discarded. A social rule that is founded on erroneous assumptions is, nevertheless, still a social rule.[24]

---

[23] Marshall, above n 1, 48–51.

[24] See J Jaconelli, 'The nature of constitutional convention' (1999) 19 *Legal Studies* 24, 28–31, for the submission that constitutional conventions are, in essence, a species of social rule as defined in HLA Hart, *The Concept of Law* 2nd edn (Oxford, Oxford University Press, 1994) 50–58.

In regard to the second issue, the precedents appear to point in the same direction. As far as the United Kingdom (at least) is concerned, there is no instance of a Prime Minister (or, under the former arrangements, the Cabinet) being refused a request to dissolve Parliament. That, as Vernon Bogdanor points out, may demonstrate no more than that every such request has properly been made.[25] In concluding that there are such circumstances he abandons precedent as a guide and offers a situation based (to use our terminology) on the inner logic of the Constitution: that is, where the Prime Minister lacks the support of his party or Cabinet. Such a situation would be highly unusual but, no matter how serious the consequences for the Prime Minister (especially if he has miscalculated in choosing to go to the country), it is surely a matter of intra-party concern only and therefore lacking in constitutional significance.

It is submitted that a more appropriate example of a legitimate refusal of a Prime Minister's request for a dissolution would be one in which he was seeking to exploit a situation where the main Opposition party was in the process of electing a new leader. In her capacity as 'constitutional umpire' the Queen would surely be entitled to defer the general election until such time as a new leader was in post. Quite apart from considerations of fair play, there would be a very practical reason for the Queen to take such an approach: the new party leader might, after all, turn out to be the new Prime Minister. Certainly, the great majority of party leaders tend to retire as such, other than in the case of illness, in the immediate aftermath of a general election defeat. It would then be plainly ridiculous to hold another election within such a short period of time. Sometimes, however, a leader resigns a considerable time into a parliamentary term in response to pressures from his party. An example in this vein is the resignation of Iain Duncan Smith as Conservative leader in 2003, mid-way through the Parliament of 2001/2005. Any attempt by the Prime Minister, Tony Blair, to take advantage of that situation by seeking an early dissolution would have been correctly rebuffed by the Queen, even though there could not be said to have been any precedent in point for such a decision.

C. The Raising of Revenue: Conventional Constraints and Economic Considerations

The contrast that we have drawn between historical reasons and reasons that are grounded in principle may be illustrated by the conventional rule that Parliament votes major sources of revenue for one year at a time only. Historically, the reason for the rule was founded in Parliament's grant of authority to tax for limited periods – a limitation which exerted pressure on the Monarch to summon Parliament (the consent of which is necessary to impose taxation) on a regular basis. In contrast, there are several diverse reasons of principle that may be advanced for the practice.

---

[25] See his treatment of the issues in Bogdanor, above n 8, 79–83.

It should be noted at the outset that the present-day position is a curious half-way house. There is standing authorisation to impose numerically the greater number of taxes. In the two cases of income tax and corporation tax, however, authority is granted by Parliament for a year at a time only.[26] This could be justified on principle as a compromise between two extreme positions. One approach would place all taxes on a permanent footing (with the need for legislation only to alter the chargeable rate or to change the tax base). The other approach would limit the duration of all taxes to one year (or a similar short period). Both extremes would appear, for different reasons, to be unsatisfactory. The latter would be too risky for the sound conduct of the public finances in general, if (for whatever reason) no Finance Act could be enacted in any particular year. The former, by contrast, would undermine the financial means whereby the House of Commons could remove a government from office. In any event, the status of the present rule limiting the principal two taxes to a period of one year at a time as a conventional rule has been obscured by the fact that it is embodied in law, specifically in successive Finance Acts. It has thus been treated as a matter outside the province of constitutional conventions. However, once the point is taken that there may be conventions regulating such matters as the period of duration of laws, it becomes apparent that this is a neglected instance of an important constitutional convention.

Taxation, as a matter of general principle, serves several functions, only some of which are linked to the need for frequent Finance Acts. The first factor is the element of compiling a set of accounts and ascertaining how income and expenditure relate to each other over a given period. Fundamentally this purpose is little different – other than on the score of magnitude of the sums – to the compilation of accounts for any economic unit (whether it be a household, a club, or a company). A second major role of taxation is that of redistribution of wealth – a purpose to which the frequent imposition of taxation is scarcely relevant at all. It is the third, and most modern, end served by taxation which points up the need for frequent Finance Acts. The rationale here is the Keynesian one of managing the economy so as to achieve the goals of growth, low inflation and a strong balance of payments.

Fiscal means have been used in conjunction with monetary controls in striving to balance these objectives. In a comparative appraisal of the two means of managing the economy, it has been said that the central difficulty with income tax is that it is 'impossible . . . to raise in mid-year'.[27] It would have been more accurate to say that it is impossible to vary income tax without a Finance Act. Certainly, legislation could have been enacted which would have authorised the Government to vary the rate of income tax in between Budgets by subordinate legislation. This would have

[26] The taxes that have been cast in this temporary role have varied over time. Previously tea duty and sugar duty served the same purpose. Once corporation tax was introduced by the Finance Act 1965 it easily slipped into this role, since it replaced the previous regime whereby companies paid income tax on their profits.

[27] J Dow, 'Fiscal Policy and Monetary Policy as Instruments of Economic Control' (1960) *Westminster Bank Review*, pt II, 9.

been a facility similar to the 'regulator', by which indirect taxation – originally purchase tax, now value added tax – is varied, up or down, by Treasury Order within a given percentage range without the need for primary legislation. The obstacle to such a change would lie in the deep-rooted constitutional convention that adjustments in the scope and rates of such a major tax as income tax should be imposed by nothing less than primary legislation. The point is well illustrated by the Finance (Income Tax Reliefs) Act 1977. A supplementary statute enacted mid-way through the financial year, it consisted of only two operative sections that effected increases in personal reliefs. It is the sort of mid-term adjustment that, but for that convention, could easily have been made the province of delegated legislation.

Once inflation occurred on any significant scale – as it did in the 1970s – a further reason for the regular incidence of Finance Acts could have been given. If monetary thresholds were not adjusted in line with the loss of purchasing power of money, people would be lifted into higher tax brackets or, indeed, would be liable to pay tax when previously they had escaped such liability. The reason is to be found in the principle of nominalism – the fundamental rule that monetary obligations are to be discharged in accordance with the nominal (or face) value of the sums stipulated, irrespective of changes in the purchasing power of the currency since the date on which the sum was fixed. That principle, in periods of inflation, leads to a situation where taxation is imposed without (in effect) the authority of Parliament. This is clearly contrary to the spirit of both Article 4 of the Bill of Rights 1689[28] and the general principle that the coercive power of the State may be exercised only through law.[29] One possible solution to the problem, one which would have circumvented the need for annual review, would have been to provide for automatic indexation of the relevant limits in the tax legislation. The approach that has been adopted is to provide that indexation, though presumed, may be set aside in any year.[30] In the event, then, the constitutional convention that required annual review was respected, together with the need for the Government to come out into the open and acknowledge the non-indexation of the allowances as, in effect, a tax increase.[31]

D. The Loss of Revenue and Loss of Office

Moreover, allied to the financial and economic reasons of principle for frequent legislative authorisation of taxation is what has emerged as a constitutional ration-

[28] Art 4 reads: 'That levying money for or to the use of the Crown by pretence of prerogative without grant of Parliament for longer time or in other manner than the same is or shall be granted is illegal.'

[29] At its worst it can lead to a situation where failure to take account of inflation fundamentally changes the nature of the tax. See *Secretan v Hart* [1969] 3 All ER 1196. The result of this case, in not allowing for changes in the value of money, was that nominal capital gains were being taxed, thereby changing a capital gains tax into a capital levy.

[30] Finance Act 1977, s 22(2); and Finance Act 1980, s 24.

[31] For a practical instance, see Finance Act 1981, s 23(1): 'Section 24(5) of the Finance Act 1980 (increase of personal reliefs) shall not apply for the year 1981–82.'

ale. Defeat on the Budget is traditionally viewed as one means of voting the Government out of office. Vernon Bogdanor lists that event together with defeat on a Confidence vote or on the Queen's Speech as comprising occasions that 'must involve the government's resignation'.[32] The classic instance is the resignation of the Liberal Government in 1909 as a result of the defeat of the 'People's Budget' in the House of Lords. It is not a particularly illuminating precedent, partly because it involved the extreme case of the rejection of the Budget in total, and partly because it cannot be repeated as long as the powers of that House remain constrained by the Parliament Act 1911.

That Supply is essential to the continued existence of a government is reflected in the arrangement for stable government, falling short of a full coalition, known as a 'Confidence and Supply agreement'. Strictly, since Supply relates to the funding of government, it is the passage of the Appropriation Act that is of primary importance. But that serves little purpose if the public coffers are not being replenished. This explains the greater, if derivative, importance of legislation that imposes taxes. Dicey's account of threats to the lawful survival in office of governments vacillates between authorisation of taxation and expenditure, in other words between the Finance Act and the Appropriation Act, as integral to their continuation in office. He instances the former when recounting the consequences of not summoning Parliament at least once a year,[33] and the latter when explaining why a government that refuses to resign on losing a confidence vote will be forced to leave office.[34]

The two types of legislation, however, do not stand on an equal footing. Taxation, being coercive, is more readily open to challenge in the courts than expenditure if it is not lawfully imposed.[35] Furthermore, although Appropriation Acts have been an established feature of the central government finances since the eighteenth century, it has been rare for them to be amended in point of detail on their way to the statute book. Yet it is not uncommon for even quite important items in the Chancellor's revenue plans, in the form of provisions of the Finance Bill, to be defeated.

It is therefore necessary to raise the question of what is meant by a defeat on the Budget, and why exactly it poses a threat to the viability of the Government. For even a total rejection of the Budget would leave in force the permanent taxes, though at their previously set rates. Income tax and corporation tax, as annual taxes, would be lost, for the time being at least. But what of defeat of important items in the package, whether in the form of particular Budget resolutions or key clauses in the

---

[32] V Bogdanor, *The Coalition and the Constitution* (Oxford, Hart Publishing, 2011) 112.
[33] Dicey, above n 2, 447.
[34] *Ibid*, 450.
[35] For a firm statement that government expenditure must be authorised by law, see *Auckland Harbour Board v The King* [1924] AC 318, 326–27. However, the difficulty of bringing a successful challenge based on the terms of the Appropriation Act is illustrated by *R (Friends of the Earth) v Secretary of State for Environment and Climate Change* [2009] EWCA Civ 810, [2010] HLR 313. See especially [43] and also [46], where apprehension is expressed about 'a wholly undesirable judicialisation of public spending priorities'.

Finance Bill? It is not immediately obvious why this should entail the resignation of the Government. There are two possible approaches to this situation. Defeat on key features of the Budget could be treated as a matter of defeat on what amounts to a Confidence motion in all but name. It betokens, in itself, that the Government is no longer entitled to remain in office. On the other hand, it could be treated purely as a matter of financial strategy. If the Government is still capable of soldiering on despite the loss of revenue then it is entitled to do so – until such time, if any, as it becomes apparent that it is no longer able effectively to run the country.

The principal precedents are almost a century apart. On 8 June 1885, an amendment successfully moved in the House of Commons to the Liberal Government's Budget (incidentally on beer duty, a matter of indirect taxation) led to its resignation. Yet on 8 May 1978, the successful moving of an amendment to the Finance Bill that reduced the rate of income tax envisaged by the Labour Government had no constitutional consequence whatsoever. This was despite the size of the ensuing cost to the Treasury (estimated at over £300 million for 1978–79) and the undoubted accuracy of the observation that 'nothing could be more central to the policy of any government than the rate at which direct taxation is levied'.[36]

The latter period, marked as it was by the precarious existence of the Government of James Callaghan and its dependence on Liberal support, is replete with statements about the constitutional consequences of lost votes on the Budget. Support can be gleaned for both of the positions set out above. Doubtless some of those in the first category will have been uttered, not as considered statements of the constitutional position, but rather with an eye (in part, at least) to keeping the support of the Liberals and avoiding an early general election. In the context of the 1977 Budget, for example, their then leader, David Steel, quotes Callaghan as saying, 'no government could lose its budget resolutions and stay in office'.[37] The second approach is less predictable in its application. Despite the loss of the vote on the rate of income tax, the following year the Chancellor, Denis Healey, was quoted as stating that the critical point was the amount of the loss to the Exchequer occasioned by the defeat. A drop of 1 penny in the pound was said not to matter, while a drop of 2 pence would have 'ruined [his] strategy'.[38]

Statements such as these, however, are to be treated with caution. At the root of the system of constitutional conventions lies the issue of what actually happened in the past (recall Jennings' first test: 'what are the precedents?'). Propositions uttered outside such a factual context, even by the leading constitutional actors, are of persuasive value only.[39] Indeed, to find an example of a major defeat on the

[36] Professor Max Beloff in a letter to *The Times*, 13 May 1978, 13.

[37] D Steel, *A House Divided: The Lib-Lab Pact and the Future of British Politics* (London, Weidenfeld & Nicolson, 1980) 48. It emerges from a memorandum of 30 March 1977, reproduced at 167–68, para 7, that this phrase is to be read in the context of two resolutions only which impinged on motoring costs.

[38] A Michie and S Hoggart, *The Pact: The Inside Story of the Lib-Lab Government, 1977–8* (London, Quartet Books, 1978) 171.

[39] In this respect there is a similarity with common law adjudication, where the only binding part of a decision is the part required to decide the dispute before the court. Statements made other than for that purpose are given obiter (by the way) and are persuasive only.

Budget one need go no further back than 6 December 1994, when the Conservative Government lost the vote on the Budget resolution which formed the first step in increasing from 8 per cent to 17.5 per cent the rate of value added tax on fuel. The only consequence was that the Chancellor, Kenneth Clarke, returned to the House a few days later with plans to make up the resulting shortfall – about £1 billion – in revenue.[40]

Any government that fails to raise the amount of revenue that it looks to collect on the basis of the Budget statement has a number of ways in which to make up the shortfall. Like any economic unit, it may respond to the presence of the gap either by borrowing or by cutting its expenditure. In the short term, at least, the latter is quite difficult to implement. As regards the former, there has occurred a marked shift in recent years in the financial assumptions on which public policy is formulated, leading to a severe tightening of controls on public borrowing. The new economic climate is reflected in the Fiscal Responsibility Act 2010, which lays down a (non legally-enforceable) duty to effect progressive reductions in public sector borrowing for the financial years 2011–16, and the Budget Responsibility and National Audit Act 2011. It is reasonable to assume, therefore, that there has been a narrowing of the limits within which governments may today survive crucial defeats on the Budget by resort to increased borrowing.

To sum up, it is clear that Budget defeats today would not necessarily possess that 'sudden death' element that is to be found in defeats on Confidence motions or defeats on the Queen's Speech. Some defeats on economic matters are more disruptive of the Government's policy than others. In any event, there exist several means of making up a shortfall in government revenue, although some of these – in particular, resort to increased borrowing – are today viewed very differently by comparison with former times.

IV. THE MODIFICATION AND TRANSFORMATION OF CONSTITUTIONAL CONVENTIONS

Many of the same considerations that apply to determine the birth of constitutional conventions apply equally to decide the question of their continued existence. Once again, the inner logic of the Constitution may be the driving force for change. Legislative or institutional changes may compel the abandonment, reconsideration or adaptation of even well-established conventions.

In this connection it would be appropriate to recall a lecture given by Vernon Bogdanor in 1993, in which he discussed the consequences for the traditional notion of ministerial responsibility of the growth of executive agencies. One of his themes was that ministers would lose the means of exerting overall control, which was the traditional justification for requiring their resignation in the event of a

---

[40] HC Deb 6 December 1994, vol 251, col 243.

departmental error of sufficient magnitude.[41] For this purpose two examples may be cited of the new approach to issues of ministerial responsibility. In neither case, despite the considerable gravity of the errors, was the issue raised of the potential resignation of the relevant minister. In October 2007, a package containing two CDs sent out by HM Revenue and Customs (HMRC) was lost. Containing details of 25 million individuals, the CDs would be a rich source of information to potential fraudsters. Although the Chancellor, Alistair Darling, was accountable for HMRC, it was not thought appropriate that he should resign.[42] In fact, this conclusion owed nothing to the new arrangements, since the line of responsibility between the Treasury and the Inland Revenue has long been indirect so as to accord a degree of autonomy to the latter. The second instance, however, illustrates in full the new approach. In 2009, the Justice Secretary, Jack Straw, apologised to the families of two students murdered by persons who were at large because of failings of the Probation Service. He was reported as taking full responsibility for those failings but it was not considered that they warranted his resignation. The persons who lost their jobs in these episodes were, respectively, the chairman of HMRC and the Chief Probation Officer for London.

Discussion of the convention of ministerial responsibility is traditionally centred on instances of failings, real or alleged, that culminate in the resignation of the relevant minister. As these two examples bear out, a full discussion of the subject should also include instances of errors of comparable gravity where no question has been raised of the departure from office of the minister. The inclusion of the latter perspective bears particularly on the issue of the continued existence, or modification, of the convention.

Unlike the position at the start of its life, a convention may be transposed at the end of its life into a different level of existence. It continues in force, but thereafter as a legal rule. There exist two principal ways of transposing constitutional conventions into law (for this purpose 'law' is to be taken as meaning statute law). Special emphasis will be placed on the second method since it raises issues of the continuing relevance and application of the practices that delineate the convention.

The first method is to spell out the understanding of what the demands of the convention are. The amount of detail might be considerable, as is the case with the delineation in section 1 of the Parliament Act 1911 of the category of Money Bills and the circumscribed powers of the House of Lords in regard to them. Or the detail might be minimal, as with section 4 of the Statute of Westminster 1931:

> No Act of Parliament of the United Kingdom passed after the commencement of this Act shall extend, or be deemed to extend, to a Dominion . . . unless it is expressly declared in that Act that that Dominion has requested, and consented to, the enactment thereof.

---

[41] V Bogdanor, 'Ministers, Civil Servants and the Constitution: A Revolution in Whitehall?' *Institute of Advanced Legal Studies Bulletin*, 15 October 1993, 10.
[42] A Darling, *Back from the Brink* (London, Atlantic Books, 2011) 49–53.

Irrespective of the degree of detail, the question may well be raised as to whether the written formulation, even at the time of enactment, fully corresponds to the extent of the convention. Undoubtedly the operative convention at the time of the Statute of Westminster, to take that example, was that the Imperial Parliament should not legislate for a Dominion without the latter's consent. A mere recital in the legislation, however false, that the Dominion had consented would not have accorded with the convention.

The second method is for the statute to refer in general terms to the relevant practice, at the same time changing its normative status into that of law. There is no attempt to spell out, however minimally, what is entailed by the practice, which is consequently incorporated into law by reference. An example in point is the legislative transformation of the position of Ireland into Dominion status under Article 41 of the Irish Free State Constitution Act 1922. This provided that the representative of the Crown 'shall . . . act in accordance with the law, practice and constitutional usage governing the like withholding of assent or reservation in the Dominion of Canada'. There are several noteworthy points about this provision. It incorporated into law an amalgamation of the previous law (of necessity, the law of another legal system) and practice. It did not – indeed, it could not – incorporate practice and usage simply as practice and usage. These exist only in the realm of social practice. Most importantly of all, it raised the question of whether changes in practice and usage from the early 1920s onwards would be reflected in a changed legal position. In other words, should the position of the Irish State be frozen in perpetuity in the shape of the legal status enjoyed by Canada in 1921? Or would changes in the position of Canada be carried over, via Article 41, into that of the Irish Free State?

A third method, of hitherto limited use, is exemplified by section 36(2)(a)(i) of the Freedom of Information Act 2000, which sets out an exception to the duty, imposed by the statute, to disclose information held by a 'public authority'. This provision does so by reference to the issue of whether disclosure would, or would be likely to, prejudice 'the maintenance of the convention of collective responsibility'. This is a variation on the second method, referring *by title* to the constitutional convention in question. It has the potential to raise several points that are relevant to the theme of this chapter. Once again, would the scope of this legal provision change as the demands imposed by the convention shift and change? And would it, too, be waived in line with occasions on which the convention – or, at least, the unanimity limb of the convention – is itself announced as not applying? In this context there has been too ready an acceptance at its face value of the statement made by James Callaghan, that collective responsibility applies 'except in cases where I announce that it does not'.[43] But it is erroneous to suggest, as this does, that a decision as to whether a constitutional convention may be suspended is to be taken in the unfettered discretion of an official, however important he may be. The waiver decision is itself regulated by constitutional conventions. It

---

[43] HC Deb 16 June 1977, vol 933, col 552.

presupposes a set of 'second-order' conventions identifying the following matters: which 'first-order' conventions may be waived; the person(s) by whom they may be waived; and the circumstances in which waiver is deemed permissible.

In private law there are instances of statutory incorporation, by reference, of social phenomena that have been variously designated by words such as the 'practice', 'custom' or 'usage' prevailing in certain groups. Some representative examples may be given. Section 47 of the Marriage Act 1949 prescribes the conditions for the validity of marriages conducted 'according to the usages' of the Society of Friends. The Supreme Court Act 1981, section 67, after laying down the general rule that business is to be conducted in open court, stipulates some exceptions to the rule, including one that is defined by reference to 'the practice of the court'. The Barristers (Qualification for Office) Act 1961 refers indifferently to any statutory provision or 'custom' whereby the qualification of a barrister for holding an office depends on his having been called to the Bar for a given period. And section 22(1) of the Sale of Goods Act 1979 stipulates as a condition, 'where goods are sold in market overt, according to the usage of the market'.

In contrast to the above, there are instances which identify the point in time by reference to which the practice is to be identified. Section 1(1) of the Royal Assent Act 1967 lays down that the required procedure is the 'form and manner customary *before the passing of this Act*' (emphasis added). In the same way, section 33(2) of the Taxes Management Act 1970 renders the operative practice that 'which was generally prevailing *at the time*' when the income tax return in question was made (emphasis added). Are the last two provisions expressly spelling out a limitation which is implicit in those listed above? There is much to be said, in all these instances, for the view that the 'custom', 'practice' or 'usage' to which reference is being made should be fixed in regard to a particular point in time. Otherwise, the law on the matter would change automatically in line with each alteration in practice or custom. There would, in effect, be a delegation of legislative power to whichever person, body or group is identified by the legislation for the purpose of the relevant practices. On the other hand, if the possibility of ready adaptation to changed circumstances is the hallmark of conventional arrangements, that essence should be replicated when the transition to legal form is effected.

V. CONCLUDING COMMENT

This chapter has sought to delineate, by reference to some leading instances, the ways in which constitutional conventions have responded to changing circumstances. Sometimes the driving force is change in background ideology (the advance of democracy). Sometimes the impetus is nothing more than the presence of extraordinary conditions (war or other emergency) which were absent at the beginnings of the convention, but where it can plausibly be argued that, properly understood, the convention always contained within itself the seeds of an exception to accommodate those conditions. These themes predominate in the two selected areas that focus on the position of the Prime Minister. The conventions that concern the raising of revenue are different in that they evince a confluence of factors. Behind the unchanging outward norm of the annual planning of public finance lie various underpinning rationales which have varied in force over time. As all the selected instances show, the analysis of constitutional conventions rests on a study of both historical factors and arguments based on principle. It is this combination which gives the subject its peculiar fascination.

8

'The Three Hundred and Seven Year Itch': Scotland and the 2014 Independence Referendum

STEPHEN TIERNEY

I N JANUARY 2012 the Scottish Government announced its intention to hold
a referendum on independence in the Autumn of 2014. A draft Referendum
Bill to this effect was published which asserted the authority of the Scottish
Parliament to hold such a referendum, while a public consultation exercise was
embarked upon.[1] Although the United Kingdom Government immediately challenged the legislative competence of the Scottish Parliament to pass this Bill, and
in doing so launched its own consultation process,[2] to the surprise of many, on 15
October an agreement ('The Edinburgh Agreement'[3]) was reached between the
two governments. A draft Order in Council was attached to the Agreement. This
has now been passed[4] and will, in terms of section 30 of the Scotland Act 1998,
devolve to the Scottish Parliament the competence to legislate for a referendum to
be held before the end of 2014 on whether Scotland should become independent
of the rest of the United Kingdom, paving the way for the referendum to be
organised through legislation of the Scottish Parliament on 18 September 2014.
Over the next year the constitution of the United Kingdom, to the study of which
Vernon Bogdanor has dedicated his scholarly career, faces perhaps its greatest
internal challenge since the 1920s, with the possibility that the parliamentary
union secured in 1707 might, after 307 years, come to an end.

But although we should correctly identify this as a possible moment of crisis for
the British Constitution, the recent process also highlights some of its strengths,
in particular the flexibility to adjust to such a challenge and the capacity also to
recognise the multinational character of the State which underpins the political

---

[1] <http://www.scotland.gov.uk/Publications/2012/01/1006>.
[2] <http://www.scotlandoffice.gov.uk/scotlandoffice/files/17779-Cm-8203.pdf>.
[3] *Agreement between the United Kingdom Government and the Scottish Government on a referendum on
independence for Scotland*, available at <http://www.scotland.gov.uk/About/Government/concordats/
Referendum-on-independence>.
[4] The Scotland Act 1988 (Modification of Schedule 5) Order 2013.

aspirations of its different peoples. Although the very existence of the State is challenged, it is of great significance to amicable constitutional relations across the UK that this challenge will be faced against the backdrop of agreement as to the referendum process and the acceptance by the UK Government of the fundamental principle that the Scottish people have the right, by way of referendum, to determine whether or not they will remain within the United Kingdom. This is a particularly notable concession when compared with other potentially secessionist situations around the world, and one which tells us much about a century during which the United Kingdom has gradually decentralised its constitutional apparatus in appreciation of the different identities and traditions which compose it.

As we take stock at this crucial turning point in the country's history, Vernon Bogdanor's ground-breaking treatment of devolution, dating back to the 1970s,[5] offers us historically contextualised insights with which to reflect upon how we have reached this moment and where the referendum period might lead us. Whereas devolution is relegated to a minor place in many treatments of the UK Constitution, Vernon has always treated the disaggregation of power as an essential part of any serious mainstream treatment of the UK Constitution, giving the subject a central place in his books,[6] and in doing so exploring how devolution of power from the centre has important consequences for fundamental constitutional doctrines such as parliamentary supremacy.

In light of Bogdanor's work on devolution, this chapter will reflect on the past four decades within which the demand for Scottish devolution first took serious shape, developed through an extra-parliamentary campaign for home rule and led to the Scotland Act 1998. This remains an on-going journey, most recently embracing the Scotland Act 2012. Secondly, it will, in the context of the 2014 process, consider the referendum itself as a vehicle for change. Vernon was also one of the first political scientists to recognise that direct democracy, first used at a pan-British level in 1975 in a consultation on membership of the Common Market,[7] was likely to become a growing feature of constitutional change, and that, accordingly, the constitutional implications of the spread of the referendum ought to be taken seriously. This prediction has been an accurate one, and in 2000 we saw the growing use of the referendum recognised by Parliament in the Political Parties, Elections and Referendums Act 2000. One decade later, in light of increasing calls for referendums in the EU context and in relation to Welsh and Scottish devolution, a full consideration of the impact of referendums upon the

---

[5] Among his notable contributions are: *Devolution* (Oxford, Oxford University Press, 1979); *Whither the Union?* (London, Goldsmiths College, 1999); *Devolution in the United Kingdom* (Oxford, Oxford University Press, 2001).

[6] V Bogdanor, *Power and the People: A Guide to Constitutional Reform* (London, Victor Gollancz, 1997) ch 2; V Bogdanor, *The New British Constitution* (Oxford, Hart Publishing, 2009) ch 4.

[7] An earlier referendum was held exclusively in Northern Ireland in 1973, discussed below. This was entirely unsuccessful in light of the widespread boycott by nationalists. As Vernon commented, in such a situation of polarised conflict, 'the referendum has little to offer'. V Bogdanor, 'Western Europe' in D Butler and A Ranney (eds), *Referendums Around the World: The Growing Use of Direct Democracy* (London, Macmillan Press, 1994) 38. See also S Tierney, *Constitutional Referendums: The Theory and Practice of Republican Deliberation* (Oxford, Oxford University Press, 2011) 73–74.

Constitution was undertaken by the House of Lords Constitution Committee in its inquiry into referendums in 2010.

It is useful to take stock and consider how the referendum itself can shape, and thereby delimit, the substantive constitutional options open to the citizen. The 2014 referendum will offer only two options; the Edinburgh Agreement makes this clear. A number of witnesses addressing the House of Commons Scottish Affairs Committee inquiry[8] into the issue, argued for a three-option referendum which would have included an option of further devolution which might have taken the UK closer to a federal or even a confederal arrangement. Towards the end of the chapter we will consider what has become of the federal solution which for over a century framed the backdrop to devolution debates and which Vernon Bogdanor, for a time at least, saw as the best solution with which to manage the UK's national diversity.

I. THE INDEPENDENCE REFERENDUM IN HISTORICAL CONTEXT: POPULAR DEMOCRACY AND THE PROCESS OF DEVOLUTION

One of the difficult questions one faces when teaching the history of devolved government to students is where, or more accurately *when*, to begin. Of course the obvious year is 1998, which saw the passage of the Scotland Act, the Government of Wales Act and the Northern Ireland Act, three pieces of legislation which have done so much to reshape the contours of our Constitution and which, with some subsequent development (eg Government of Wales 2006; Scotland Act 2012), continue to do so. But 1998 is in some sense merely a recent chapter of a much longer story, dating back to the unions of the sixteenth century (Wales and England), seventeenth and eighteenth centuries (Scotland and England) and the beginning of the nineteenth century (Great Britain and Ireland), and encompassing over one hundred years during which each of these unions has been gradually restructured. A rich element in Vernon's work is the historical perspective he brings to recent developments, for example with an important focus upon Gladstone's commitment to Irish Home Rule in 1886 and the on-going legacy of this Liberal commitment which led to a long period of constitutional change during which (most of) Ireland won her independence and the political culture of both Scotland and Wales became increasingly nationalist in outlook and aspiration; all of this serves as an important long-lens backdrop to 1998, which in some sense was the culmination of this period of recognition of sub-State national distinctiveness and the constitutional aspirations which come with such markers of difference.

One of Vernon Bogdanor's important insights is how the UK came together through historical contingencies rather than in dramatic founding moments; an

---

[8] House of Commons Select Committee on Scottish Affairs, *Report: The Referendum on Separation for Scotland*, HC 1608, 2010–12, <http://www.publications.parliament.uk/pa/cm201012/cmselect/cmscotaf/1608/1608we20.htm>.

observation which helps illuminate how, in the same way, its reorganisation has also been led by such contingencies, including inter- and in some cases inner-party competition, again piece by piece and from place to place. In so far as we can talk of the 'fissuring' of the UK, this has taken place in a contingent and gradual way, first with Ireland slowly breaking its bonds with Westminster, the Stormont regime being established (temporarily) for the remaining six counties, and 'administrative devolution' being extended in the inter-war establishment of a UK government department for Scotland and the creation of a Minister of Welsh Affairs in 1951. In this light, 1998 was another step in the same direction, whereby these three territories gradually acquired more and more responsibility for their own domestic affairs, but in a way that built upon the powers and to some extent the institutional arrangements already in place or, in Northern Ireland's case, previously tried.

As we turn our attention to the latter part of the twentieth century, another important dimension to the devolution story, particularly when we consider the close relationship that now attends the further devolution of power in the United Kingdom and the use of the referendum,[9] is the influence of civil society in the process that led to the 1998 legislation. In particular, the Scotland Act 1998 built upon an extra-parliamentary campaign for devolution within Scotland which was orchestrated by the political opposition and certain important civic institutions (local government, trades unions) through the 1980s and 1990s, largely as part of a broader campaign by the Labour movement against successive Conservative Governments. The extent to which the eventual parliamentary process towards devolution, adopted by the Labour-led UK Parliament in 1997, reflects this movement is unsurprising, given that this campaign was led in large measure by the Labour Party in Scotland. And in observing the significance of the Labour Party in shaping the 1998 Act, we must also look back to the failure of a devolution proposal put forward by the Callaghan Government in the late 1970s. Although a detailed model of devolution was enacted by Parliament in 1978, and won a small majority in a referendum in 1979, it failed to meet the requisite threshold of support in that referendum.[10] This failure, and accusations that the threshold rule was designed to frustrate the devolution proposal, continued to haunt the Scottish Labour Party in opposition. With the election of a Conservative Government in 1979 and its subsequent re-election in 1983, a push for devolution was set in train by Labour and by other opposition groups, including in due course the Liberal Democrats, who united in the view that the Conservative agenda was given to excessive centralisation. This movement continued to offer constitutional proposals throughout the next two decades.

The campaign for constitutional change began with the Campaign for a Scottish Assembly launched in 1985. This resulted in a document, *A Claim of Right for*

---

[9] Eg the referendum in 2011 on extending the law-making powers of the National Assembly for Wales, as provided for under pt IV of the Government of Wales Act 2006.

[10] 52% voted for devolution on a 64% turnout, failing to meet the requirement in the Scotland Act 1978 that at least 40% of the entire electorate should vote in favour.

Scotland, issued in 1988. What is notable about this paper and others which subsequently emerged through this process, is the extent to which they would draw upon the notion of 'union' as the fundamental constitutional principle of the UK. This had three implications. First, the *Claim of Right* asserted the distinctive national identity and cultural and institutional specificity of Scotland (each of which had to some extent been recognised in the Acts of Union 1707), and argued for the on-going constitutional relevance of this 'multinational' conception of the United Kingdom. Secondly, the document aired the grievance that the 'union state' pact stemming from 1707 had been undermined by subsequent UK constitutional practice.[11] Thirdly, the *Claim of Right* declared an entitlement to Scottish self-government based upon the notion that a distinctive national identity carries with it a legitimate, indeed inherent, political right of self-determination.

It is also notable that important elites not only set the agenda for devolution during this period, they were also heavily influential in shaping the substantive model eventually enacted in the Scotland Act 1998. The *Claim of Right* 1988 recommended that a cross-party Scottish Constitutional Convention (SCC) be established, which would have the task of drawing up a model of devolution that would generate popular support and hence 'assert the right of the Scottish people to secure the implementation of that scheme'. This SCC was inaugurated on 30 March 1989, and over the next seven years it embraced a similar constituency to that which had engaged with the *Claim* process, including not only the Labour and Liberal Democratic Parties, but also local authorities, churches and the Scottish Trades Union Congress. This resulted in a series of publications, the most important of which (*Scotland's Claim, Scotland's Right*, 1995) set out a detailed blueprint for devolution.

The level of detail in this document meant that the process by which legislation was passed after Labour came to power in 1997 was very swift. The political climate in 1997–98 was highly conducive to devolution; a Labour administration elected with a large majority in 1997 was committed to the principle, and so, heavily influenced by Scottish Labour MPs, the Government steered the devolution settlement through in the first session of the new Parliament. Upon taking office, and relying heavily upon the detail in *Scotland's Claim, Scotland's Right*, the Government issued a White Paper, *Scotland's Parliament*, which was, therefore, able quickly to set forth a comprehensive plan for devolution. Although some minor changes were made by Parliament to the devolution proposal after the referendum in 1997, the model finally enacted in the Scotland Act was in substantive terms the same as that voted for in the referendum, which in turn reflected heavily the pre-1997 deliberation.

In light of the influence of civil society in framing Scottish devolution, the three implications which I identify in the *Claim of Right* process need to be kept in mind as essential background to the Scotland Act 1998 and to the creation of the Scottish Parliament, and as such also help explain not only the current SNP

[11] OD Edwards (ed), *A Claim of Right for Scotland* (Edinburgh, Polygon, 1989) 19.

Scottish Government's conviction that the Scottish Parliament has the constitutional legitimacy to organise a referendum on independence, but also the acquiescence of the British State in this idea, as encapsulated in the Edinburgh Agreement. The Scottish Parliament was created out of a sense of Scottish popular sovereignty; and this idea has remained an important political undercurrent to recent debates. Another factor at play in making 1998 such a key focal-point of this 'self-determination' argument is that while the extra-parliamentary process was largely the preserve of elite actors and suffered from the lack of participation of both the Scottish Conservative Party, which, favouring the status quo, never took part, and indeed the Scottish National Party itself, which withdrew after early involvement, alleging a failure to address independence for Scotland as a serious constitutional option, the creation of the Scottish Parliament was in the end the direct result of a referendum in 1997, and one which saw a very high level of support for devolution.[12] In this sense again, the notion of the Scottish Parliament's legitimate right to initiate further constitutional change stems from the fact of its own credibility as a body conceived within the Scottish body politic and broader civil society, and given birth in consequence of the direct will of the people.

II. DEVOLUTION AS A JOURNEY: THE RESILIENT GRADUALISM OF BRITISH CONSTITUTIONAL CHANGE

Addressing devolution as a long-term process, and one with numerous changes since 1998, highlights two important features of the Constitution, one of which brought it about and one which has itself been shaped by this process. The first is that in structural terms the UK does not have a written constitution, and as such devolution has been created, and subsequently changed, by ordinary Acts of Parliament. Vernon Bogdanor has written about UK devolution against the backdrop of the path not taken: a more formal and definitive federal settlement. One fear for those who have favoured a model of federalism for the UK is that since the devolved settlements were created by ordinary acts of the Westminster Parliament, they can be amended or even repealed in the same simple way, whereas the danger of recentralisation which comes with this model would largely be avoided within an entrenched federal system. From another perspective, however, the flexibility of the UK model can be seen as a strength. This elasticity has offered the opportunity to create various models of devolved government in an ad hoc way through a simple parliamentary process, with scope for further changes in a relatively easy way in the future. The experience of devolution has also been very successful in that hitherto very few competence disputes of any significance have come before the courts. This raises the interesting question whether on an institutional level federalism is the only, or indeed the best, way to manage national diversity within

---

[12] On the first question: 'I agree that there should be a Scottish Parliament', 74% voted Yes; and on the second: 'I agree that a Scottish Parliament should have tax-varying powers', 63.5% voted Yes.

a multinational polity. It may be that the very complex national mix in the UK would not lend itself well to the rigidities that we associate with a federal system, where the Constitution can be very difficult to change and may require broad territorial consensus in highly-charged meta-constitutional moments; the inter-provincial conferences which in Canada proved such a failure in 1987 and 1992 are a salutary reminder that highly formalised constitutional processes, while attempting to institutionalise democratic controls, can result in stasis. In contrast to the Canadian experience, the ease with which UK devolution was created, was later suspended to meet various emergencies (Northern Ireland)[13] and has been amended to extend further devolved powers (Wales 2006, 2011 and Scotland 2012), suggests that the UK model carries considerable benefits, not least in being able to meet the complex specificities of the country's diverse demography and regionally variable constitutional aspirations.

In this context a second feature of the UK model, which flows from the first, is the deep asymmetry of the system. Since the model of devolution has been shaped in a case-by-case way to reflect the deep and complex national pluralism of the State, the result has been three very different devolved settlements. In the first place, devolution does not extend to every sub-State nation. England, in contrast to the other territories, has shown little inclination for devolution either as a whole or by region. This arguably has led to an imbalance in terms of the representation of other territories at the centre; and indeed there is no territorial chamber of Parliament as is to be found in federal systems, neither is there a legally-regulated system of inter-governmental relations at the executive level. Secondly, devolution differs greatly among Scotland, Wales and Northern Ireland, reflecting the specific history, demography, identity patterns, institutional infrastructure and constitutional aspirations of each. This means that each country got a model which was tailored to the situation at the time but which also left open the door to further change. In Northern Ireland's case, the model was always intended to develop as the Belfast Agreement was gradually implemented; the protracted delay in the devolution of policing, for example, shows the flexibility built into the system to ensure institutional arrangements align with political will. In Wales's case, the asymmetry of the system led to some degree of neighbour envy as devolutionists peered greedily at the extensive legislative powers enjoyed by the Scottish Parliament, and agitation for further change led to the 2006 Act and 2011 referendum.[14] The UK Constitution's flexibility has also been of use in extending further powers to the Scottish Parliament

---

[13] In the case of Northern Ireland, powers remained with both the UK Parliament and the UK Government to suspend operation of devolution when agreement between republicans and unionists broke down at various points between 1998 and 2006. This adaptability has been very controversial, but arguably it has allowed breathing space until a final agreement could be reached to revive the institutions on a, thus far, settled basis in 2006.
[14] R Wyn Jones and R Scully, *Wales says Yes: Devolution and the 2011 Welsh Referendum* (Cardiff, University of Wales Press, 2012). See also the Commission on Devolution in Wales (Silk Commission), <http://commissionondevolutioninwales.independent.gov.uk/>.

in 2012 without the need even for primary legislation, far less constitutional amendment.[15]

Despite this extension of powers, in Scotland more than anywhere the 1998 process has taken on an unsettled character. The election of the SNP, first as a minority government in 2007 and then with the shock result of an overall majority in 2011, has of course kick-started perhaps the most important constitutional issue facing the UK since the 1707 Union itself. But let us not forget that moves for further powers for the Scottish Parliament have been a feature of devolution from the beginning. Some of this is symbolic; it was a Labour First Minister who unofficially changed the name of the Scottish Executive to the Scottish Government, a title that has now been given legislative recognition.[16] And the 2012 Act is itself not insignificant in the new powers it accords to the Scottish Parliament, although in the context of the independence issue the implementation of this measure is largely being overlooked by commentators. This Act emerged, of course, from the Commission on Scottish Devolution (Calman Commission) which was established by a Labour Party motion passed by the Scottish Parliament on 6 December 2007, with the support of the Conservatives and Liberal Democrats, following the election of the SNP earlier that year. The Calman Commission consulted and deliberated on the issue of further devolution, and its report led to two White Papers and extensive consideration by parliamentary committees in both Parliaments.[17]

This Act brings a number of developments, particularly new fiscal powers. Among the main changes are the renaming of the finance ministers' quadrilateral meeting as Joint Ministerial Committee (Finance); a new bilateral ministerial-level body to manage operational matters involved in putting the Scotland Act changes in place; and the intention to create a 'clear line of sight' between HM Revenue & Customs (HMRC) and the Scottish Parliament to provide a degree of accountability to the latter by the former. There is also an open-ended power which will allow the UK Government to devolve further tax powers to Scotland.[18] There are, of course, intense debates as to how extensive these new powers are likely to prove and how effectively they will be implemented.

This growth of powers for Scotland is already having knock-on consequences for the stability of the devolution model as a whole. One inevitable result is that the new tax powers will stimulate further debate in Wales. Already, the Commission on Devolution in Wales ('the Silk Commission'[19]) has been reviewing existing financial and constitutional arrangements, investigating the possibility of devolving addi-

---

[15] Eg, in 2004 such an order was made under s 30(2) of the Scotland Act. Under s 63, further powers have also been extended to the Scottish Government. See also C Himsworth, 'Devolution and its Jurisdictional Asymmetries' (2007) 70 *MLR* 31.

[16] Scotland Act 2012, s 12.

[17] This was largely because the Bill required to be addressed twice by each Parliament because of the change of UK Government at the General Election in 2010.

[18] Section 23, which inserts a new s 80B into the Scotland Act 1998 which will enable Her Majesty, by Order in Council, to do this.

[19] For details, see <http://commissionondevolutioninwales.independent.gov.uk/>.

tional fiscal powers to the National Assembly for Wales. Also, as Scotland becomes more autonomous, many argue that the West Lothian question can no longer be avoided. We have seen the establishment of the Commission on the Consequences of Devolution for the House of Commons ('the McKay Commission') to consider issues arising from devolution in the United Kingdom and their effect on the workings of the House of Commons (its remit is 'To consider how the House of Commons might deal with legislation which affects only part of the United Kingdom, following the devolution of certain legislative powers to the Scottish Parliament, the Northern Ireland Assembly and the National Assembly for Wales').[20] If this suggests some model of amending the legislative procedure of Parliament in line with the principle of 'English votes for English laws', this might require substantial changes to how Parliament operates and will create different categories of MPs. It would also have a knock-on effect at executive level as departments adjust to new models of law-making.

In addition to the substantive changes which the 2012 Act is likely to bring, the long and convoluted process by which it was passed has also been instructive as to the status of the Scottish Parliament. The Scotland Act 1998 left an area of uncertainty concerning the balance of power between Westminster and Holyrood. On the one hand the Scottish Parliament has extensive legislative powers. The Scotland Act contains a 'retaining model' of devolved power, whereby those matters which are reserved to the exclusive competence of Westminster are explicitly articulated within the Scotland Act, with all other matters devolved. There is an extensive range of devolved matters (Scotland Act, sections 29 and 30 and Schedules 4 and 5) and, with few concurrent or shared powers, the Scottish Parliament effectively has exclusive competence in these areas, which extends as far as a power to repeal existing UK legislation in devolved areas of jurisdiction. Certainly there is a residual power for the UK Parliament to legislate in devolved areas (Scotland Act, section 28(7)), which is in any case arguably superfluous in light of the doctrine of parliamentary supremacy,[21] but there is now a constitutional convention to the effect that the UK Parliament will not do so without the consent of the Scottish Parliament through a Legislative Consent Motion.[22] Notably, the Scotland Bill (which became the 2012 Act) went through Holyrood twice in the quest for successive Legislative Consent Motions in line with the Sewel convention. This seems to have hardened this convention still further, when we consider that the UK Government was keen to see this Bill passed and for a long time was faced with the opposition of the Scottish Government. At no point, however, was there any effort to drive the Bill through the UK Parliament without a Legislative Consent Motion. It might be asked whether all of these

[20] <http://www.parliament.uk/documents/commons-vote-office/5-DPM-Devolution.pdf>.

[21] Note also the White Paper preceding devolution, Scotland's Parliament, Cm 3648, para 42: 'The United Kingdom is and will remain sovereign in all matters.'

[22] Hence, the 'Sewel convention', named after Lord Sewel who, speaking for the Government, suggested this process in parliamentary debate on the Scotland Bill. HL Deb 21 July 1998, vol 592, col 791.

developments have in fact moved the UK further towards a de facto federal model as discussed by Vernon in 1999.[23]

III. THE 2014 REFERENDUM: DIRECT DEMOCRACY AND CONSTITUTIONAL CHANGE

Of course, with the signing of the Edinburgh Agreement the focus is now on the referendum planned for 2014, the outcome of which might well make further discussion on alternative models of decentralised government superfluous. A major issue which has emerged since January 2012, and which was at the heart of the Edinburgh Agreement, is the process which is likely to be followed. This referendum will be part of a growing trend towards direct democracy in the UK since 1975. Vernon is one of the few constitutional analysts to take the referendum seriously as an important constitutional innovation within the British system,[24] and so when the House of Lords came to address the issue in 2010, it turned to him for evidence. In addressing the referendum Vernon has argued that it can be a legitimate method of bringing about constitutional change within a democratic system. As he once put it, 'in the last resort, the arguments against the referendum are also arguments against democracy, while acceptance of the referendum is but a logical consequence of accepting a democratic form of government'.[25]

But he has also been mindful of the democratic problems which can accompany referendum use; not the least of which is the unprincipled way in which they may be used to solve or avoid party-political problems. His work has shown that the referendum on the EEC in 1975 and those on devolution in the late 1970s were largely issue-avoidance measures by the Labour Party in the face of serious splits over these issues. When devolution was first seriously proposed in the mid-1970s, a promise of a referendum accompanied this plan. It has been observed that the referendum was a device 'that would enable Labour backbenchers opposed to devolution nevertheless to vote for it in the House of Commons while campaigning against it in the referendum'.[26] The Bill in question was withdrawn in the end in March 1977. But when the devolution proposal was revived in 1977–78, again the Labour Party was seriously divided on the issue, and so once more a referendum was proposed in 1978 'to defuse [the] issue'.[27] Referendums are far from being a panacea. In Northern Ireland, a highly controversial referendum, designed to reinforce the Union, and hence boycotted by Irish nationalists, was

---

[23] Bogdanor, *Whither the Union?*, above n 5.

[24] We find coverage of the referendum as part of the UK Constitution in V Bogdanor, *The People and the Party System: The Referendum and Electoral Reform in British Politics* (Cambridge, Cambridge University Press, 1981), pts I and II; Bogdanor, *Power and the People* 1997, above n 6, ch 5; and Bogdanor, *The New British Constitution*, above n 6, ch 7.

[25] Bogdanor, *The People and the Party System*, above n 24, 93. For a similar point, see also DC Mueller, *Constitutional Democracy* (Oxford, Oxford University Press, 1996) 189.

[26] Bogdanor, *The People and the Party System*, above n 24, 42.

[27] *Ibid*, 45.

held in 1973. This, arguably, polarised conflict – 'the referendum [had] little to offer'.[28] It did not resolve a problem, and may in fact reinforce polarisation; a referendum cannot create consensus where none exists.[29]

Of course the mainland United Kingdom cannot in any way be described as a divided society. However, with the lesson that referendums improperly designed can be divisive, it is imperative that the 2014 process be fully open and democratic. In this respect it is to be welcomed that the UK and Scottish Governments have reached agreement on how the ground-rules for the referendum process will be drawn up. As observed above, the Edinburgh Agreement lead to a section 30 Order in Council setting out certain fundamentals of the referendum process and empowering the Scottish Parliament to legislate on these and other rules.

IV. WHERE TO AFTER 2014: INDEPENDENCE OR FEDERALISM?

The referendum in 2014 of course may lead to the break-up of the UK. But in the event of a victory for the 'No' campaign, which opinion polls through 2013 suggest is very likely, constitutional restlessness among Scots is unlikely to abate. So far the impact of devolution on the central organs of the State has been minimal. And the 1998 model has served well in containing and indeed preventing competence disputes from emerging. There have been few serious political disputes concerning the nature of intra-state relations. But there is still a recognition that this state of affairs in the early years owed a great deal to the fact that from 1999–2007 the Labour Party was in power in Edinburgh as the dominant partner in a coalition government, thus helping to maintain smooth relations with the Labour Government in London.

It is widely perceived that the devolution settlement for Scotland, and indeed for Wales and Northern Ireland, is unsatisfactory in that the role of devolved governments in central decision-making through a properly formalised system of inter-governmental relations is potentially a longer-term problem. Scope remains for enduring problems based upon the institutional design of the system stemming from what is essentially the ad hoc, or some might say incomplete, nature of the settlement.

The Scotland Act 1998 actually has little to say about what in federal systems is known as intra-state federalism, with a lack of detail on how institutions to coordinate policy for the UK as a whole would be set up, far less about how these should be designed or how they should operate. And the result is that there is not a formalised, and legally protected, set of mechanisms in place for occasions where serious competence disputes arise. Instead, institutions operate largely at the behest of the centre, and therefore depend upon the goodwill of the central

---

[28] Bogdanor, above n 7, 38.
[29] Bogdanor, *The People and the Party System*, above n 24, 144; Bogdanor, above n 7, 45. See also Tierney, above n 7, 73–74.

Government and Parliament for their continuation.[30] We see this in the informal arrangements for inter-executive cooperation.[31] But in addition, the potential for tensions to be exacerbated is also evident at the level of inter-parliamentary relations between the Scottish Parliament and Westminster. One issue concerns a lack of clarity in the division of competences between legislatures, and the second is the lack of protection of the competences of the devolved legislature from the risk of central retrenchment; both of these seem to be particular to the UK's unitary model in contrast to a more highly-developed federal system. It is in the context of the former that the so-called West Lothian question arose, as discussed above (the power of Members of Parliament from Scottish, and indeed Welsh and Northern Irish, constituencies to vote on legislation and other parliamentary matters that affect only England).[32] This structural issue is being addressed by the McKay Commission, but the danger is that any proposed solution may further diminish the limited role which representatives from Scotland, Wales and Northern Ireland have at the centre of British parliamentary decision-making. Also, although the Sewel convention has been strengthened as a result of its centrality to the passage of the Scotland Act 2012, the legal relationship between the two parliaments continues to lack clarity.

Vernon Bogdanor, as a great advocate of devolution, has in his work remained aware of these structural imbalances, and it is notable that he ended his 1999 book with a proposal for a federal model for the UK. At the moment such an outcome seems unlikely, but in light of the historically-informed analysis which Vernon has brought to the study of the Constitution of the UK, it would be well to note that the race goes not to the swiftest, and that the centuries-long story of union in these islands may well have more twists to take. We do not know yet how the referendum on independence will go in 2014, but in the more likely event of a 'No' vote, we might anticipate not the end of the devolution story but rather the beginning of a new chapter in the constitutional realignment of the British unions.

---

[30] 'Memos show how Blair and Brown "ignored" McConnell', *Sunday Times* (Scottish edn), 16 September 2007, at 7.

[31] R Rawlings, 'Concordats of the Constitution' (2000) 116 *Law Quarterly Review* 257–86.

[32] The anomaly was raised in the late 1970s by Tam Dalyell, MP for West Lothian.

9

Constitutional Change and Parliamentary Sovereignty – the Impossible Dialectic

RICHARD GORDON QC

ERNON BOGDANOR HAS always been a principled critic of the doctrine of parliamentary sovereignty as being incompatible with the idea of a codified Constitution.[1] He concludes that '[i]n practice . . . if not in law, Parliamentary sovereignty is no longer the governing principle of the British constitution,'[2] and challenges the contrary opinions of Professor Jeffrey Goldsworthy, whom he considers to 'have become a prisoner' of the doctrine.[3]

Some who have directly confronted his views in print, such as Jeffrey Goldsworthy, and others who have not (the late Lord Bingham), have accused him (or, as the case may be, would accuse him) of confusing the practical with the legal. The fact that Parliament cannot do something in a practical sense, so it is observed, does not mean that it cannot do it in a legal sense. Thus, for example, no matter that in practice judicial review operates to prevent Parliament from ousting the jurisdiction of the courts; in such cases, it is suggested by adherents to the sovereignty doctrine that the judges follow what Goldsworthy terms the 'noble lie', so that 'the fact that a lie is felt to be required indicates that the judges themselves realise that their disobedience is, legally speaking, illicit'.[4]

When the divorce between constitutional theory and real life becomes as stark as this, something might be thought to be wrong with the theory. To suggest this is not, necessarily, to opt for some form of common law constitutionalism in which our most fundamental axioms are claimed to be derived from the common law. Neither is it, however, to opt for an unalloyed, hard-line Diceyan version of Parliament's sovereignty merely because (reverting to Goldsworthy's analysis) it conforms to what most of our influential constitutional players have signed up to

---

[1] V Bogdanor, *The New British Constitution* (Oxford, Hart Publishing, 2009) 13–14.

[2] *Ibid* at 283.

[3] See Vernon Bogdanor's review of J Goldsworthy, *Parliamentary Sovereignty, Contemporary Debates* (Cambridge, Cambridge University Press, 2010) in 'Imprisoned by a Doctrine: The Modern Defence of Parliamentary Sovereignty' (2012) 32(1) *Oxford Journal of Legal Studies* 179.

[4] J Goldsworthy, *The Sovereignty of Parliament* (Oxford, Clarendon Press, 1999) 252.

(in more dignified language, because it conforms to the most important of Hart's established rules of recognition).[5]

Those who support a unipolar theory either of sovereignty or common law constitutionalism appear implicitly to accept a central proposition, which is that a prevailing constitutional narrative is needed to explain all our current constitutional arrangements even if that narrative fails to accord with reality. The somewhat oxymoronic concept of a sovereignty- or common law-based narrative that does not explain the present and that seems also to falsify the past is rarely explored to test its improbable validity.

Much of our political theory is, admittedly, founded on a human need for narrative. But for most of the time, the fact that the narrative is imaginary is not significant. No one supposes that Hobbes's Leviathan or Rawls's veil of ignorance are other than philosophical constructs designed to explicate (respectively) totalitarian and liberal visions of society. There is a subtle but significant difference between these essentially normative political systems (purporting to explain how society should operate) and the doctrines of parliamentary sovereignty and common law constitutionalism that have been wrought to explain both how society is historically constituted and how contemporary political decision-making takes place.

It is not always necessary that explicatory doctrines should provide coherent explanations of such matters, provided that a sufficient number of key players can be induced to accept them. In truth, the Emperor had no new clothes, but this did not matter in Hans Christian Anderson's tale until the child cried out. Yet there may be (and it is the theme of this chapter that there are) powerful reasons why constitutional doctrines of doubtful validity and provenance should be revisited, not necessarily in order to discredit them for all purposes or to test their limits philosophically but, rather, to answer the question 'How do we move forward?' as opposed to the question 'Can we provide a reason for our current constitutional settlement that the great and the good will accept?'

The thesis I present here is that none of our current doctrines contains scope for delivering any mechanism for principled constitutional change. If such mechanisms are ever to be developed, we need either a codified constitution with express provision for amendment or, to say the least, a new and flexible set of constitutional doctrines enabling several layers of political power to be coordinated (most notably, a partnership or dialogue between the three relevant organs of State – the executive, Parliament and the senior judiciary) in a way that allows for regulating principles for constitutional change to be established and implemented. How the latter might be achieved is (currently) anybody's guess, though it would probably be a good start not to make the assumption that everything can be solved by primary legislation. What, emphatically, will not solve the conundrum is an outdated doctrine of parliamentary sovereignty (in substance executive control), or one of common law constitutionalism (in substance, rule by an unelected judiciary).

---

[5] See HLA Hart, *The Concept of Law*, 2nd edn (Oxford, Clarendon Press, 1997) esp ch 5.

At first sight the problem does not seem so very great. Constitutional change does occur; haphazard it may sometimes be, but this is surely due as much to the need for slow and incremental change endorsed by legitimate consensus in a democratically-elected Parliament as it is to the absence of a principled doctrine prescribing how our constitutional arrangements should be ameliorated.

To subscribe to this position (what might be regarded as the constitutional equivalent of palliative care) is, though, to ignore the symptoms and regard the situation as tolerable only because the patient is still breathing. Anyone familiar with how constitutional change occurs knows that there are two fundamental problems. These are that: (i) there are no criteria for identifying constitutional laws, and (ii) in consequence there are no procedures in place for developing our constitutional arrangements.

These problems are interrelated. Arriving at a principled method for identifying constitutional laws involves consideration of process as well as of definition. Indeed, the first is logically prior to the second, for it is obviously necessary to work out by what process constitutional laws are to be defined before one can, sensibly, apply the definition. It also seems likely that the process itself is integral to the definition.

If we take for a moment, as exclusive paradigms, the constitutional-change processes that would be required if a parliamentary sovereignty model or a common law constitutional model prevailed for this purpose, the above point becomes even more clear.

In the sovereignty model, as articulated by Dicey, Parliament is free to make and unmake its laws at will. The title of the David Bowie track 'Here today, gone tomorrow' reflects the essence of this model. Its constitutional resonance is, in the present context, that no principled legislative framework can be developed for mounting constitutional change precisely because such a framework would be no more binding on successive Parliaments than would be any other law of a qualitatively different nature.

Let us suppose, though, that this threshold obstacle were capable of being overcome. How might Parliament (and in practice the executive) go about (if it could ever be persuaded to think about it) the problem of defining a constitutional law? The issues surrounding definition are complex and are not addressed here. But Parliament, in a sovereignty model, could go about its task in only one (or both) of two self-appointed ways. It could seek to legislate for a definition; further, or alternatively, it could adopt a special process and (like the proverbial 'rabbit out of the hat') define legislation that it had subjected to such process as – by definition – 'constitutional'.

These options are, of course, not truly separate. For there would appear to be little point in seeking to define in legislation that which was entailed in a constitutional law in the absence of some special process attaching to that law. Conversely, it would seem a slightly barren exercise to go through a specific Parliamentary process focusing on constitutional laws, without identifying something in advance that required such a process.

So process and definition are, inevitably, entwined in the sovereignty model. Yet what emerges from either legislative definition or a parliamentary process-orientated approach (taken in isolation) comes, I suggest, nowhere near creating a principled framework for constitutional change.

We can, *in abstracto*, envisage the task of seeking to create a legislative framework for constitutional change. In theory at least the framework might resemble those articles of a codified constitution providing for amendment of certain parts of the constitution. We even have a quasi-precedent for such legislation in section 2 of the Fixed Term Parliaments Act 2011, which legislated for a 'super-majority' for early Parliamentary elections (that is, prior to the otherwise fixed term) in certain carefully defined circumstances.

But whilst it is one thing to legislate for the specific case, it is quite another to legislate for a comprehensive statutory code for identifying constitutional laws and what happens to such laws. A much more nuanced model is needed, it might be thought, than that afforded by parliamentary sovereignty.

Leaving aside the point that the more comprehensive the code, the more analogous the end result would be to a codified constitution, there would seem to be only two possible modes of defining a constitutional law. Parliament might choose to provide merely a set of general criteria, or it might decide to legislate more comprehensively. Each option contains its own pitfalls under a sovereignty model.

If Parliament were to opt for a set of general criteria, a number of difficulties arise. For an Act of Parliament to have the status of a constitutional law, there would have to be some practical consequences attached to that status at least in terms of entrenchment (requiring a super parliamentary majority to amend it) and/or in terms of the enhanced parliamentary scrutiny to which it might be subject. There is also likely, in respect of such laws, to be a need for special principles of judicial interpretation or remedies obtainable in the courts.

Yet both the statute that prescribed the criteria for identifying a constitutional statute and the various statutes to which the enabling statute accorded constitutional status would seem likely to fall to be interpreted in the courts where disputes arose. The more general the criteria in the enabling statute, the more scope there would be for the courts developing principles to decide whether or not a particular Act of Parliament was or was not truly 'constitutional'.

If, as seems likely, the courts became involved in construing statutes in order to determine whether they possessed constitutional status by reference to a series of general criteria contained in the enabling statute, a serious constitutional position could ensue. On the footing that constitutional status merited a particular form of parliamentary scrutiny, the courts' retrospective judgment that a statute that had not undergone the requisite scrutiny was, nonetheless, a constitutional statute would place the courts in a position where they were indirectly adjudicating on proceedings in Parliament – a course of action precluded by Article 9 of the Bill of Rights. Yet if the courts were to refrain from such adjudication, other consequences of constitutional status (such as special principles of interpretation or appropriate judicial remedies) would seem to be unobtainable even though expressly legislated for.

Providing general legislative definitional criteria for constitutional laws condemns the legislature to very uncertain terrain. If the courts can adjudicate on whether the statutory definition is satisfied, it places Parliamentary process at the mercy of the judges. Yet if the courts are prevented from adjudicating on the constitutionality of statutes in such circumstances, that will, no doubt, leave the principle of Parliamentary sovereignty intact, but it will also risk collapsing definition into process. If Parliament adopts a scrutiny process in order to determine whether a particular statute is constitutional in nature it matters not whether or not Parliament provides a clear definition because the 'consitutional' status of the statute will ultimately be decided by the outcome of the scrutiny process.

Similar problems would be likely to surface if Parliament were to choose a different legislative route (comparable, perhaps, to its approach in respect of human rights legislation), namely, to subject legislation to some form of parliamentary certification of constitutional status (or lack of such status) every time that an Act of Parliament is given Royal Assent. Here, the approach might – by contrast to the general criteria approach – be statute-specific and might (by reference either to prescribed constitutional criteria or to individual considerations perhaps to be outlined in the certificate) accord constitutional status with prescribed constitutional effects to the statute in question.

The courts are used to so-called conclusive evidence clauses, and it is unlikely that the record of a simple parliamentary opinion (however comprehensive Parliament's consideration of the issue) that the statute in question was constitutional would protect the Act from being subject to judicial review (with the same potential for constitutional clashes as identified earlier). If, however, the courts were prevented by parliamentary sovereignty from adjudicating on the constitutionality of the particular statute, this would make the 'comprehensive definition' approach as susceptible to principled objection as the 'general criteria' option. It would mean that in substance, definition was giving way to process, so that Parliament had only to operate a self-fulfilling prophecy in order to make solely that which it was prepared to admit as 'constitutional' legally constitutional.

Common law constitutionalism, as a model for principled constitutional change, is equally flawed as an effective doctrine. It has to be conceded, though, that it possesses rather more potential for destabilisation than parliamentary sovereignty pure and simple. The notion that parliamentary sovereignty is but a construct of the common law was voiced (expressly or implicitly) by as many four Law Lords in the challenge to the Parliament Act case.[6] Lord Steyn went so far as to suggest (at [102]):

> The classic account given by Dicey of the doctrine of the supremacy of Parliament, pure and absolute as it was, can now be seen to be out of place in the modern United

---

[6] *R (Jackson) v Attorney-General* [2005] UKHL 56. See, apart from Lord Hope and Lord Steyn cited here, Baroness Hale at [159] and Lord Carswell at [168].

Kingdom. Nevertheless, the supremacy of Parliament is still the general principle of our constitution. It is a construct of the common law. The judges created this principle. If that is so, it is not unthinkable that circumstances could arise where the courts may have to qualify a principle established on a different hypothesis of constitutionalism. In exceptional circumstances involving an attempt to abolish judicial review or the ordinary role of the courts, the Appellate Committee of the House of Lords or a new Supreme Court may have to consider whether this is [a] constitutional fundamental which even a sovereign Parliament acting at the behest of a complaisant House of Commons cannot abolish.

These words, coming from an eminent, albeit well-known liberal Law Lord are surprising enough. But they were echoed by another Law Lord in the same case who is generally renowned for his conservative instincts. Lord Hope observed (at [126]) that the principle of parliamentary sovereignty was 'created by the common law'.

Few have thought through with more clarity the dangers of the counter-majoritarian dilemma than Lord Bingham. In his justly celebrated *The Rule of Law*[7] he makes it clear that he fundamentally disagrees with the above-mentioned observations of Lord Steyn and Lord Hope (with whom he sat on the same case). After citing with implicit approval Richard Elkin's critique of the idea that the judges created parliamentary sovereignty as 'unargued and unsound', 'historically false' and 'jurisprudentially absurd',[8] Lord Bingham points to the fact that common law constitutionalism would lead to unelected judges claiming enormous political power for themselves, and endorses Professor Jeffrey Goldsworthy's comments that

> it would be a transfer of power initiated by the judges, to protect rights chosen by them, rather than one brought about democratically by parliamentary enactment or popular referendum. It is no wonder that the elected branches of government regard that prospect with apprehension.

What is illuminating, however, is that Lord Bingham does not suggest that the doctrine of parliamentary sovereignty has any statutory provenance or any other clearly-established historical legitimacy. It is legitimate solely because 'it has for centuries been accepted as [fundamental] by judges and others officially concerned in the operation of our constitutional system'.[9]

Thus, if the judges were to claim a power of the kind to which common law constitutionalism would point, there would be a massive injection of instability into our constitutional arrangements. Such instability would be the unilateral product of a decision by the judiciary to abandon the necessary fiction of parliamentary sovereignty propagated by Dicey, to the effect that Parliament can make and unmake any law it wishes. On that hypothesis Parliament would no longer be free to 'unmake' the 'law' that placed the common law at the apex of our constitu-

---

[7]   T Bingham, *The Rule of Law* (London, Allen Lane, 2010)
[8]   See 'Acts of Parliament and the Parliament Acts' (2007) 123 *LQR* 91, 103.
[9]   Bingham, above n 7, at 167.

tional power pyramid. Claims of this kind, therefore, would be to erode parliamentary sovereignty as a constitutional doctrine to vanishing point, and to replace it with an ultimate source of power vested in unelected judges as opposed to a democratically-elected legislature. The problem of defining constitutional laws might be ameliorated by a common law model of constitutionalism, but it would be substituted by (paraphrasing Lord Hailsham in his Dimbleby lecture) a non-elective dictatorship.[10]

If we step back for a moment and recognise the subtle power balance that lies at the heart of our post-Glorious Revolution constitutional settlement, it can readily be seen that real power resides neither in an all-sovereign Parliament nor in a judiciary imposing a supposedly normative but necessarily subjective value system on the organs of government. As Sir Stephen Sedley has convincingly argued:

> Parliamentary sovereignty itself is not a given but is part of a historic compromise by which the counterpart of the common law's deference to Parliament as the single legislative power has been Parliament's recognition of the courts as the single adjudicative power. I have argued – unoriginally – in the past that the legislative and judicial arms of the state are each sovereign in their proper spheres, whereas the executive is answerable politically to Parliament and legally to the courts. This is why, for example, the courts may not call Parliamentary proceedings in question, and why Parliament will not call judicial decisions in question. It is also why, while Parliament may authoritatively decide what law the courts are to apply and how they are to go about applying it, its authority may intelligibly be said to be conditional on the courts' continued performance of their constitutional role of determining and enforcing legality. Laws without courts are as mischievous as courts without laws.[11]

It is not the existence of this 'historic compromise' that is, or should be, in contest but the fact that it is camouflaged in fictional narrative to give a monolithic picture of parliamentary sovereignty for the purpose of analytic coherence. The problem is that, as far as the scope for principled constitutional change is concerned, the fiction operates to prevent any permanent mechanism for change from being created. One example may suffice. In its Fifteenth Report of 2010–12 on 'The Process of Constitutional Change', the House of Lords Constitution Committee, in considering whether it was possible to identify constitutional legislation, recorded that:

> Having limited our field of inquiry to specific, decisive acts of constitutional change, we recognise that the majority of change proposals will require legislation. The doctrine of parliamentary sovereignty means, as David Howarth told us, that: 'there is no uncontroversial method of distinguishing constitutional legislation from other legislation. In form, all primary legislation is the same'.[12]

---

[10] See 'Elective Dictatorship', *Listener*, 21 October 1976, 496–500.
[11] S Sedley, 'Everything or Nothing' (2004) *London Review of Books* vol 26 no 19.
[12] House of Lords Constitution Committee Fifteenth Report of 2010–12 on 'The Process of Constitutional Change' (18 July 2011) at para 9, p.9.

Although this did not stop the Constitution Committee from concluding that there was a species of constitutional legislation that was 'qualitatively different from other forms of legislation and that the process of leading to its introduction should recognise this difference,'[13] it was the very reason why the Government rejected the Committee's modest recommendations for improved legislative scrutiny of 'constitutional' legislation.

In its response to the Committee's report[14] the Government (without recognising any irony) observed that:

> It is intrinsic in the United Kingdom's constitutional arrangements that we do not have special procedures for dealing with constitutional reform. Comparing processes in the United Kingdom with those in other countries which do have written constitutions and special procedures for the reform of those constitutions is therefore of limited value. The first stumbling block, as the Committee has itself noted, is the problem of the definition of what should be subject to special treatment. It is for this reason that the Government continues to believe that special procedures are inappropriate.[15]

A response of this kind, of course, erecting the impasse of problems of definition of constitutional legislation as 'the first stumbling block', made it unnecessary to consider any other stumbling blocks, none of which was identified. Yet the reason for the impasse was that which lay unstated as the reason for its being intrinsic to our constitutional settlement that we have no special procedures for addressing constitutional reform – the doctrine of parliamentary sovereignty.

Whatever else may be less than perfect about our current obeisance to parliamentary sovereignty, its real practical deficiency is that it has a chilling effect on constitutional change. We have a 'Constitution' which has been said to consist merely of 'what happens'.[16] In this, Parliament, at times, resembles other British cultural institutions such as the BBC. Those who follow what can be passed off as constitutional change at Westminster will recognise this graphic description of similar processes at the BBC:

> It's one of the rituals of British cultural life; new controllers of Radio 4 announce that they want to shake up the schedules. The Radio 4 audience goes bananas, and *The Archers* is shifted from 1.45 pm to 2 pm. Everyone's outrage is both sufficiently exercised and appeased, and everyone goes home happy.[17]

In stark contrast to this, at other times the lack of any principled mechanism for constitutional change can produce disturbing and untoward results. One of the most significant constitutional reforms of the last decade was the creation of a new Supreme Court. Yet it was not the subject of prior Parliamentary debate; it was simply announced on 12 June 2003 as one of a package of 'far-reaching

---

[13] *Ibid*, at para 9.
[14] The Government Response to the House of Lords Constitution Committee Report 'The Process of Constitutional Change' Cm 8181.
[15] *Ibid*, at para 27.
[16] JAG Griffith, 'The Political Constitution' (1979) 42 *MLR* 1, 19.
[17] 'Is Radio 4 just too gloomy?', *Observer New Review*, 20 January 2013, 4.

reforms' as part of a Cabinet reshuffle. These executive-led proposed reforms included abolition of the ancient office of Lord Chancellor,[18] the creation of a new Department of Constitutional Affairs, a new independent Judicial Appointments Commission, reform of the Speakership of the House of Lords and, last but not least, the creation of a Supreme Court. Professor Andrew le Sueur, writing an editorial comment in *Public Law* at the time, said:

> The abolition of the office of Lord Chancellor, the creation of a new Supreme Court and an independent Judicial Appointments Commission are goals that are to be welcomed. These are not, however, 'sensitive matters' to be decided by a cabal of ministers outside the Cabinet – or, indeed, by the Government alone. The Government's aims are laudable, but the process by which it set in motion these important reforms does not inspire confidence . . . It is worrying that the minister in charge of the constitution seems not to recognise that the process of constitutional change is as important as the end result.[19]

The fact that major constitutional reform of this kind can be viewed solely as a matter of executive policy is, perhaps, even more worrying than whether or not a particular minister recognises the importance of the process of constitutional change. But of course, the shift in practice from parliamentary sovereignty to executive sovereignty (Lord Hailsham's real 'elective dictatorship') means that constitutional change is, necessarily, a creature of the executive and no more or less independent from government control than any other aspect of policy.

It is, perhaps, unnecessary to take sides as between the deficiencies of parliamentary sovereignty or common law constitutionalism in evaluating how improved mechanisms for constitutional change might be created. One possible mechanism is obviously that of a codified constitution. In that model, though, the constitution would be supreme, and both Parliament and the judges would be subject to its provisions. A formal constitution of this kind would contain its own provisions for amendment and for principled reform. To plead for such a construct at the present time is, surely, a bridge too far. If our prevailing constitutional doctrine is that of parliamentary sovereignty, and if, as Bogdanor emphasises, this kind of sovereignty is incompatible with codification precisely because codification in whatever form could simply be repealed by a later statute, the only way that codification could ever take place is with abandonment of the sovereignty principle. Most countries (with the notable exceptions of the United Kingdom, Israel and New Zealand) seem to get on quite well with a codified constitution and without Diceyan sovereignty, but that is hardly the point. It is fanciful to suppose that those with a vested interest in retaining omnipotent sovereignty (being the same as those with the only power to retain or ditch it) would do anything other than let sleeping dogs lie.

---

[18] In the event, this proved rather more difficult than had been imagined, and only the judicial functions were removed in the Constitutional Reform Act 2005.

[19] A le Sueur, 'New Labour's Next (surprisingly quick) Steps in Constitutional Reform' [2003] *Public Law* 368, 376–77.

Failing a codified constitution, the most effective way of implanting the seeds of principled constitutional reform – beyond improved legislative scrutiny generally – would seem to be, first, to recognise that, at their heart, our constitutional arrangements rest on a pragmatic compromise and, secondly, to turn that recognition into something more formal. The first part of the exhortation (recognition of a pragmatic compromise as being central to our constitutional settlement) is, perhaps, easy enough, and certainly easier than the second (elevating that tacit acceptance into something more formal). Professor Dawn Oliver fulfils the first part when she detects the rationale of parliamentary sovereignty as being 'comity between institutions and workability'. But it is possible that she then gives the game away by accepting that this is merely a suggestion, and by observing that 'the dominant *though unarticulated* reason why courts in the UK accept parliamentary sovereignty is that it represents a way of avoiding a conflict between the courts and the executive which the courts could not win'[20] (emphasis added).

If the reason why parliamentary sovereignty is accepted as a constitutional rule of recognition rests on pragmatic compromise rather than on any legitimate or democratic claim of Parliament to be the omnipotent source of power, this needs to be articulated. It is surely illogical (being incompatible with what is supposed to be a mere compromise) to cede to Parliament game, set and match by according it not merely hierarchical priority but also a sovereignty unmatched (and unclaimed) by almost any other Parliament.

Thus, the courts might – short of a codified constitution – have to concede the trump card to Parliament (who else is left at the table?); but it does not at all follow that the shifting and uncertain nature of the power balance between the courts and Parliament must lead to legitimising a constitutional doctrine (sovereignty) that for the reasons already stated obliterates the likelihood of effective mechanisms for constitutional change.

From a practical perspective, setting out the rules of the game in some sort of formal concordat might be a good first step. And such a rule book would of necessity (consistent with recognition of the pragmatic compromise that we have) be one in which Parliament and judiciary were seen to be equal rule-makers. But this would require dialogue on a scale that has never happened (or been supposed capable of happening) before. A constitutional concordat between judges and Parliament took place in 2004, when the judiciary felt itself to be threatened as rarely before by the plethora of 'constitutional' reforms coming from the Government discussed earlier. But a concordat of the kind that I have in mind would be less self-interested. It would be focused on devising constitutional mechanisms for change that looked not to constitutional positioning or power-play but, rather, to the reality of our constitutional arrangements as a compromise with differently vested sources of power; to the fact that Parliament and not merely the executive should be responsible for introducing constitutional laws,

---

[20] UK Constitutional Law Group Blog, 3 May 2012, available at http://www.ukconstitutionallaw.org/blog.

and to the fact that the judiciary should also play a part in ensuring that the process of defining constitutional legislation falls within a general framework of reference that does not depart from the rule of law.

The idea of a concordat involving our key constitutional players is, of course, by no means the only possible mechanism for achieving principled change. What is crucial, though, in my view is to ensure that imprecise (even outdated) constitutional concepts do not prevent progressive constitutional development from taking place.

To suggest this is to advocate neither radical change nor the substitution of one constitutional principle for another. It is simply to recognise that the legitimacy we currently accord to parliamentary sovereignty should not leave our constitutional development in the hands of a policy-driven and politically-minded executive in the name of a principle, when our wider constitutional settlement is based on an historic compromise between the executive, the legislature and the judiciary.

10

Queen Elizabeth II and the Evolution of the Monarchy

ROBERT BLACKBURN

OR THE GREAT majority of the population, Queen Elizabeth II is the only monarch on the throne they have ever known. She became Queen on 6 February 1952, with her coronation taking place the following year on 2 June 1953. Throughout 2012, her Diamond Jubilee year, national celebrations took place, with glowing tributes expressed by all for her dedicated service to the UK and Commonwealth.[1] This extraordinary achievement, a 60-year tenure of public office as the UK Head of State, exceeded only by Queen Victoria, has been of great importance to how the monarchy as an institution is now perceived in public opinion, and indeed within the thinking of the political elite. For the personality and character of the monarch, and how he or she interprets and self-defines his or her role in the areas of public and constitutional life in which he or she has a part to play, are pivotal to the working and evolution of the institution itself.

The Queen has stood above politics, and faultlessly has maintained an impartiality and discretion on sensitive matters in her dealings with the 12 Prime Ministers who have served during her reign. In terms of popular support for the monarchy, Queen Elizabeth's reign has been remarkably successful. Polling taken around the time of the Diamond Jubilee weekend in June 2012 showed endorsement for the UK remaining a monarchy, rather than becoming a republic, at 80 per cent. An even higher proportion, 90 per cent, express approval for Queen Elizabeth personally. The reigns of Edward VII (1901–10), George V (1910–36), and George VI (1936–52) are also regarded as having been popular, though this could not be verified and measured in the same way as the professional public opinion polling used today. This level of public support has been a considerable achievement of the House of Windsor when one reflects upon attitudes towards the monarchy in the late nineteenth century, when republican

[1] For Addresses to the Queen made in both Houses of Parliament, see *Hansard*, HC 7 March 2012, cols 849–78, and HL15 March 2012, cols 377–84; and for details of the Jubilee celebrations and events, see <http://www.thediamondjubilee.org>.

sentiments were high and William Gladstone doubted the monarchy would survive much longer.[2]

However, a deeper analysis of public opinion discloses a different and more shallow type of support for royalty compared with that of 60 years ago. In the midst of the post-War national spirit of unity and pride in one's country, the monarchy was a central and profound part of British culture. A poll taken shortly after the Queen's accession disclosed that as many as 35 per cent of the population even believed that Elizabeth had been personally chosen by God to serve as monarch.[3] Such quasi-religious attitudes towards the monarchy have certainly been transformed since then; and so too has the pervasive deference to social hierarchy in Britain as the class structure has gone into decline, which is perhaps the most striking sociological change over the past 60 years. In 2008 the British Social Attitudes poll and its regular trend question, asking 'How important or unimportant do you think it is for Britain to continue to have a monarchy?' showed that that only 32.7 per cent of people thought the monarchy very important and 29.6 per cent quite important,[4] with perceived importance being distinctly lower among younger age groups. Polling research of Ipsos-Mori in 2012 points in the same direction, showing, for example, that the royal family comes only fourth as a source of national pride, behind the armed forces and the National Health Service,[5] and that more than half those polled think the royal family should get less money.[6] The early 1990s were a low point of public support for the monarchy and royal family, due to the matrimonial difficulties of the Queen's children and a series of embarrassing books and critical press accounts of their personal lives.[7] It is significant that the pre-existing virtual taboo on public criticism of the monarchy began to evaporate from that time onwards, and recently there have been a number of politicians, journalists and sections of the media who have even openly advocated abolition of the monarchy or radical reform of the royal prerogative.[8]

Two significant features emerge. First, the Queen as a person attracts almost universal affection and support for the way in which she personally has conducted herself and performed her royal duties. Secondly, the monarchy as an institution is now more fragile than is commonly supposed, and is less embedded in the national psyche and collective sense of national identity. It is therefore all the

---

[2] Letter to Earl Granville, 3 December 1870, extracted in HJ Hanham, *The Nineteenth Century Constitution* (Cambridge, Cambridge University Press, 1969) 33–34; and see V Bogdanor, *Monarchy and the Constitution* (Oxford, Oxford University Press, 1995) 28–30.

[3] V Bogdanor, *Power and the People* (London, Victor Golancz, 1997) 172.

[4] <http://www.natcen.ac.uk/media/329262/bsa%2026th%20questionnaire.pdf>.

[5] <http://www.ipsos-mori.com/researchpublications/researcharchive/2939/Britons-are-more-proud-of-their-history-NHS-and-army-than-the-Royal-Family.aspx>.

[6] <http://www.ipsos-mori.com/researchpublications/researcharchive/3080/Almost-all-Britons-satisfied-with-the-Queen-as-Monarch-but-Prince-William-is-the-most-popular-Royal.aspx>.

[7] Among them, A Morton, *Diana: Her True Story* (New York, Pocket, 1992).

[8] Among them, Tony Benn ('the Crown is a totally insupportable basis for a constitution': see *Hansard*, HC 17 May 1991, cols 549–56); J Freedland, *Bring Home the Revolution: The Case for a British Republic* (London, Fourth Estate, 1998); and the *Guardian* newspaper in a series of articles since 2000.

more important that the monarchy continues to evolve and adapt itself to new conditions, as indeed it has done throughout the Queen's reign.

This chapter considers some topical issues in UK constitutional law and politics that illustrate the ways in which the monarchy has evolved during the reign of Queen Elizabeth, the successful manner in which she has adapted her customary roles to promote the political neutrality essential to the survival of a modern monarchy, and the difficulties and challenges involved in achieving reform today, particularly with respect to the Government's current changes to the rules on royal succession.

*   *   *

The legal context within which the monarch reigns but does not rule remains a mystery to most people. Operating in an unwritten and uncodified system of government, even the very concept of the Crown as a legal entity is open to uncertainty and ambiguity.[9] The UK's executive administration is conducted in the name of the Crown as Her Majesty's Government, but is led by a Head of Government, the Prime Minister, whose existence and mode of appointment is not derived from or regulated by law.[10] The Crown as executive and Crown as monarch are distinguishable concepts in law for certain purposes, but the common law theory of the Crown prerogative powers remains ultimately vested in the person of the monarch, subject to their exercise in most cases by ministers on the Queen's behalf, and subject always to modification or repeal by an Act of the Queen-in-Parliament.[11]

So too the principles governing royal conduct remain uncodified, and rely on the good judgement of the monarch and her private secretary as to the conventions that apply in any given situation. The basic tenets of our constitutional monarchy, as they have remained during the Queen's 60 years in office, are that ministers are responsible for the government of the country, not the monarch; the monarch exercises her prerogative powers and duties in accordance with the advice of her ministers; the monarch will not make public speeches or utterances on matters of a politically controversial or party nature independent of ministerial advice; the monarch should not be personally criticised in Parliament for her Acts of State, and if she is, she will not reply; and it is for ministers to answer questions and criticisms of the public acts of the monarch.[12]

---

[9] Generally see M Sunkin and S Payne (eds), *The Nature of the Crown* (Oxford, Oxford University Press, 1999).

[10] For discussion, see the evidence given to an inquiry into the role and powers of the Prime Minister currently taking place of the House of Commons Political and Constitutional Reform Committee, 2012-13; also Graham Allen, *The Last Prime Minister* (London, G Allen, 2001).

[11] For the legal situation, see R Blackburn, *Halsbury's Laws of England: The Crown and Royal Family*, 4th edn (London, Butterworths, 1998) vol 12(1), 3–5; and for commentary, R Blackburn and R Plant, 'Monarchy and the Royal Prerogative' in Blackburn and Plant (eds), *Constitutional Reform* (London, Longmans, 1999).

[12] For a constitutional analysis of political criticisms made of the Queen's televised Christmas broadcast in 1984, see R Blackburn, 'The Queen and Ministerial Responsibility' [1985] *Public Law* 361. For

An issue that has been the subject of academic debate among professors of constitutional law has been whether the monarch possessed any residual discretionary powers, where moments of constitutional crisis or political difficulties have arisen with respect to the passage of legislation (royal assent), the timing of a general election (royal power of dissolution of Parliament) and prime ministerial appointment (where a single party fails to obtain an overall majority at an election, or a Prime Minister leaves office mid-term).[13] The better view is that any such personal involvement has now become obsolete, and that continued theorising about the existence and circumstances in which such powers might be utilised poses considerable dangers to the monarchy.[14] For as I have written elsewhere,[15] if the monarchy were ever to intervene and block prime ministerial advice, the institution would run the serious risk of meeting hostility from the political party then in government. Such royal intervention would necessarily embroil the monarch in party political controversy and throw the continued existence of the monarchy into doubt.

To her great credit, Queen Elizabeth and her private secretaries have understood this political truism, certainly in practice if not always in the flummery of royal communications.[16] For example, when doubts were expressed over Harold Wilson's request for the Queen to dissolve Parliament and hold a fresh general election in 1966 (two years after the previous election) and again in October 1974 (following another election earlier the same year), simply to try to achieve more Labour seats in both cases, there was no attempt to block prime ministerial advice on the matter or seek alternative advice.[17] A welcome and important development, under the 2010 Coalition Government, has been that any possibility of the monarchy now being drawn into controversy over general election timing has been terminated once and for all by the Fixed-term Parliament Act 2011, abolishing the prerogative of dissolution altogether and replacing it with a framework of five-yearly elections, subject to earlier election in specified statutory circumstances.[18]

So too, the Queen has not sought to involve herself in questions of prime ministerial appointment, leaving resolution to the parties themselves and the convention that the majority party leader will be Prime Minister; or in hung Parliament

---

an historical perspective on the principles and practice of constitutional monarchy generally, see Bogdanor, above n 2, esp ch 3.

[13] See especially I Jennings, *Cabinet Government* (Cambridge, Cambridge University Press, 1936) ch 13; R Brazier, *Constitutional Practice* (Oxford, Oxford University Press, 1988) ch 8; R Blackburn, 'Monarchy and the Personal Prerogatives' [2004] *Public Law* 546; R Brazier, 'Monarchy and the Personal Prerogatives: A Personal Response to Professor Blackburn' [2005] *Public Law* 45; and R Blackburn, *King and Country* (London, Politico's, 2006) ch 3.

[14] See Blackburn, *King and Country*, above n 13, ch 3, esp at 101–02; also Lord Hailsham, *The Dilemma of Democracy* (London, Collins, 1978) 193.

[15] R Blackburn, *The Electoral System in Britain* (London, Macmillan, 1995) 58.

[16] Thus modern etiquette requires a Prime Minister to entreaty, not demand or recommend, an exercise of the prerogative: see B Pimlott, *The Queen: A Biography of Elizabeth II* (London, HarperCollins, 1996) 341.

[17] See *ibid*, 419–22.

[18] The constitutional advantages of a fixed-term Parliament are set out in Blackburn, above n 15, ch 2.

situations that the incumbent Prime Minister has first claim on attempting to form an administration, but if he fails to do so or is defeated on a confidence motion in the House of Commons at the start of the new Parliament, the leader of the next largest party will be invited to take office. The issue of royal involvement was more problematic with respect to the resignation of a Conservative Prime Minister until the party adopted party leadership rules of its own in 1965.[19] There are still debates to be had about the wisdom and neutrality of the retiring Prime Minister Harold Macmillan's advice to the Queen in 1963 to appoint Sir Alec Douglas-Home as his successor in preference to RA Butler,[20] but in the constitutional vacuum created by the Conservatives lacking any standing leadership rules, the Queen's only sure path of royal non-involvement was to follow her Prime Minister's advice.

The five days of uncertainty following the inconclusive general election of 2010 was another test for the Queen's constitutional role in prime ministerial appointment.[21] Once again, she showed restraint in the heat and excitement of disputed claims and confusion about what the outcome would be, with the convention for resolution of such situations not widely or fully appreciated. With the Conservatives gaining 306 seats to Labour's 258, it was easy for commentators and the public to view the situation as being that David Cameron as Conservative leader had 'won' the election and should immediately take office. However strong such a moral claim, and it was one that the Liberal Democrat leader Nick Clegg took into account in his negotiation with both parties, the constitutional convention clearly permitted the incumbent Prime Minister, Gordon Brown, to remain in office to see if he could form an administration as a minority government, or in a parliamentary pact or formal coalition with other parties. Others had earlier suggested that the Queen might be the mechanism for determining the outcome.[22] Largely to head off such speculation, the Cabinet Office had produced a draft chapter on government formation for a manual it was preparing, setting out its understanding of the laws, conventions and rules on the operation of government; and in this document it set out the convention as stated above, adding that 'the Monarch would not expect to become involved' in the inter-party discussions, 'although the parties and the Cabinet Secretary would have a role in ensuring that the Palace is informed of progress'.[23]

---

[19] On party leadership rules and elections, see R Blackburn and A Kennon, *Griffith & Ryle's Parliament: Functions, Practice and Procedures*, 2nd edn (London, Sweet & Maxwell, 2003) 155–60.

[20] For a narrative, see Pimlott, above n 16, 256–61. The situation was different from that in 1955 when an earlier Conservative Prime Minister (Winston Churchill) resigned from office mid-term, as the person whom he advised to be his successor (Sir Anthony Eden) had been universally regarded as Conservative Party leader-in-waiting for many years.

[21] See R Blackburn, 'The 2010 General Election Outcome and Formation of the Conservative–Liberal Democrat Coalition Government' [2011] *Public Law* 30.

[22] See in *The Times*, eg, D Finkelstein, 'How to stop the Queen picking the next Prime Minister', 24 November 2009; and Mark Owen MP, 'We must head off the possible constitutional crisis if the result of the next election is close', 27 November 2009.

[23] February 2010 draft, 'Chapter 6: Elections and Government Formation', para 16; current version, *The Cabinet Manual* (Cabinet Office, October 2011) 2.13. The nature and purpose of the *Cabinet*

The consolidation of this convention of royal non-involvement over prime ministerial appointment in 2010, combined with the enactment of the Fixed-term Parliament Act the following year, represents an important stage in the evolution of the monarchy under Queen Elizabeth. In historical terms, it has halted any continuation of the constitutional theorising of Sir Ivor Jennings and others about 'personal' prerogatives and 'reserve' powers of the monarch. It has also, it is hoped, removed any suggestions that the monarchy might have a 'mediation' and 'conciliation' role in times of political crisis. Prince Charles, our future monarch, has let it be known, through his biographer and friend Jonathan Dimbleby, that he might be prepared to use his 'convening power' in times of national difficulty or public policy controversy, to try to seek general agreement around the issue in dispute.[24] Some clarification about such a role is important. There are historical precedents in the early part of the twentieth century for a monarch hosting inter-party conferences, such as the Buckingham Palace conference on the Home Rule Bill in 1914, but this had been proposed by the Prime Minister, Herbert Asquith, as a means of facilitating discussion, not to provide a platform for the monarch to play a proactive role in determining the outcome.[25] As Asquith had rightly stated to the King earlier in January 1910 during the storm over the Parliament Bill and future of the House of Lords, 'it is not the function of a Constitutional Sovereign to act as arbiter or mediator between rival parties and policies; still less, to take advice from the leaders of both sides, with a view to forming a conclusion of his own'.[26]

Nonetheless, it remains the case that in theory and practice, the monarch, as enunciated by Walter Bagehot in 1867, 'has, under a constitutional monarchy as ours, three rights – the right to be consulted, the right to encourage, and the right to warn,' adding, 'and a king of great sense and sagacity would want no others'.[27] We have glimpses of the Queen's use of these rights in very general terms from the memoirs or utterances of her Prime Ministers[28] and a few leaks, including of her disagreement with Margaret Thatcher's style of diplomacy in Commonwealth relations in 1986.[29] A full account, however, must await access to her papers and diaries by the author of her future official biography, such as that of George V by Harold Nicolson and of George VI by John Wheeler-Bennett,[30] supplemented by

Manual is multi-faceted: ostensibly an internal booklet of guidance for officials, it also represents an agreed statement between the Cabinet Office and Secretary, and Buckingham Palace and Queen's Private Secretary, intended for the media and public consumption.

[24] J Dimbleby, 'Prince Charles: Ready for Active Service', *The Sunday Times*, 16 November 2008.

[25] See H Nicolson, *King George V: His Life and Reign* (London, Constable, 1952) 242–43.

[26] Quoted in R Jenkins, *Mr Balfour's Poodle* (London, Heinemann, 1954) 133.

[27] W Bagehot, *The English Constitution* (1867; London, Fontana edn, 1963) 111.

[28] See, eg, J Major, *Autobiography* (London, HarperCollins, 1999) 509, where he refers to the Queen's 'encyclopaedic knowledge' on Commonwealth matters, and that he found her advice 'invaluable on many occasions'; and Tony Blair, at his speech at her golden wedding anniversary banquet on 20 November 1997, saying, 'she is an extraordinarily shrewd and perceptive observer of the world. Hers is advice worth having.'

[29] *The Sunday Times*, 8 June and 20 July 1986; on which see Pimlott, above n 16, 504–15.

[30] J Wheeler-Bennett, *King George VI: His Life and Reign* (London, Macmillan, 1958).

any diaries or memoirs of her private secretaries, such as those of Sir Alan Lascelles who served under the three monarchs immediately preceding the Queen.[31] There is considerable evidence of our future monarch, Prince Charles, giving numerous and passionate representations and views to ministers, but the quantity and force of these encouragements or warnings may be tempered once he becomes King.[32]

Meanwhile, the Queen's role as Head of the Church of England has in a de facto way mutated into one of being defender of religious freedom and faith generally across British society. Her first Jubilee engagement of 2012 was at a multi-faith reception held at Lambeth Palace, where she said her role and duty, and that of the Anglican Church generally, 'is not to defend Anglicanism to the exclusion of all other religions' but 'to protect the free practice of all faiths in this country'. In recent times, senior members of the Church have sought to emphasise this broader role as a means of promoting the relevance of the Anglican Church to the whole of society. Thus Richard Chartres, Bishop of London, told the BBC that 'minimal Anglican establishment is a way of serving the whole constituency and keeping the voice of faith in the public square'.[33] Prince Charles has long been in the vanguard of this development, in terms of promoting inter-faith dialogue and cooperation. His publicly-stated preference for being regarded as 'Defender of Faith' rather than 'Defender of The Faith',[34] when he becomes King, was greeted with controversy 20 years ago but is now almost universally supported.

The Queen performs a host of complex interrelated roles. These are derived not only from her position as UK Head of State, but from her position as Head of State of 15 other countries, as well as being Head of the Commonwealth of 54 independent States. There were just eight members of the Commonwealth at the time of her accession in 1952, and her personal dedication, social diplomacy and ability to foster goodwill across its growing membership has been incalculable to maintaining its unity and permanence. As the Prime Minister said in his Diamond Jubilee tribute in the House of Commons, the Queen has done more to promote this unique family of nations, comprising all the main religions and nearly a third of the world's population, than any other person alive.[35]

* * *

If much of the legal and administrative structure in which the monarchy operates has remained inert for most of the Queen's reign, recent years have witnessed a progressive modernisation in several important areas. Substitution of the royal power of dissolution by fixed-term Parliaments has already been mentioned. Royal finances have been placed on a more intelligible footing, avoiding the need

---

[31] *King's Counsellor, Abdication and War: The Diaries of Sir Alan Lascelles*, ed D Hart-Davis (London, Weidenfeld & Nicolson, 2006).

[32] See J Dimbleby, *The Prince of Wales: A Biography* (London, Little, Brown, 1994); Blackburn, *King and Country*, above n 13.

[33] BBC, *The Andrew Marr Show*, 3 June 2012.

[34] BBC, 'Charles: The Private Man, the Public Role', interview with Jonathan Dimbleby, 29 June 1994.

[35] *Hansard*, HC 7 March 2012, col 850.

for recurrent embarrassing debates in Parliament and the media about the Civil List, through the Sovereign Grant Act 2011. This new provision is not reign-specific and is designed to be more permanent, linking the Queen's income to that of the Crown estates.[36] The honours system, which operates on the basis of the royal prerogative, the Queen being regarded as 'the fountain of honours', has been the subject of several reviews and been made more transparent and rational, even if it still has its critics, with nominations encouraged from members of the public.[37] There has been codification of a number of royal prerogatives exercised by the Government, notably, treaty making and Civil Service regulation through the Constitutional Reform and Governance Act 2010.

The most topical legal change taking place around the time of the Jubilee reflected the evolution of human rights values in British society, as in other countries in the West, over the course of the last 60 years. This concerned the royal succession rules, which the Coalition announced it would amend by legislation in 2013 to remove the male preference in line to the throne and the disqualification applicable to a monarch or person in line to the throne if he or she marries a Roman Catholic. The rule of male primogeniture is a product of ancient common law; and the anti-Catholic provisions are set down in the 1688 Bill of Rights and 1701 Act of Settlement, designed after the Glorious Revolution to secure the Protestant succession against the claims of the Catholic Jacobites.[38]

This reform, which some imagined was straightforward, proved in fact complex both politically and legally, and illustrates the difficulties that can arise in modernising an ancient institution. Because the Queen is not only monarch of the UK, but also monarch of 15 other countries, each with its own constitution, the change in succession law needed to be implemented by way of legislation introduced in each State, simultaneously taking effect so as to avoid any possibility of divergent succession rules amongst all the States involved. This, then, required prior international diplomacy to reach agreement on the reform, which took a considerable time to negotiate, culminating in a joint statement of all the Prime Ministers of the Commonwealth realms on Friday, 28 October 2011, announcing their common intention to make the changes and work within their respective administrations to bring forward the necessary measures. Such common agreement is doubly necessary because, so far as UK legislation is concerned, any alteration in the law touching the succession to the throne also requires the assent of the Parliaments of the Commonwealth realms, under a binding convention set out in the preamble to the Statute of Westminster 1931.

In popular and political opinion, the existence and effects of the Human Rights Act 1998 and Equality Act 2010 had made the existing provisions on royal succes-

---

[36] See the Lord Chancellor's statement and debate on the Civil List prior to First Reading of the Bill: HC Deb 30 June 2011, cols 1144–78.

[37] Cabinet Office, *Review of the Honours System* (2004); *Three Years of Operation of the Reformed Honours System* (2008), *Second Report on the Operation of the Reformed Honours System* (2011). For criticisms, see House of Commons Public Administration Committee, *Propriety and Peerages* (2007–08) HC 153, and *Propriety and Honours* (2007–08) HC 1119.

[38] Generally see Bogdanor, above n 2, ch 2.

sion look particularly anomalous. Most of the other European monarchies had already amended their constitutional law to implement gender equality in their royal succession, including Sweden in 1980, The Netherlands in 1983, Norway in 1990, Belgium in 1991 and Denmark in 2006 after a referendum on the matter.[39] In the UK Parliament, there had been several Private Member's Bills and debates building up pressure for reform, such as those by Lord Dubs[40] and Keith Vaz.[41] Of special interest is that on one such occasion, where a Bill on the matter was being debated, the minister responding on behalf of the Government, Lord Williams, made it know that the Queen had personally approved of the reform. He told the House,[42]

> I should make it clear straight away that before reaching a view the government of course consulted the Queen. Her Majesty had no objection to the government's view that in determining the line of succession to the throne daughters and sons should be treated in the same way. There can be no real reason for not giving equal treatment to men and women in this respect.

When challenged by a peer that it was constitutionally improper for the views of the monarch to be made public on legislation before the House, Lord William replied that the text of his speech 'has been specifically cleared with those to whom reference has been made'.

Opinion and pressure for change to the anti-Catholic provisions regarding the royal succession had developed steadily in recent decades. Many leading politicians remarked on the offensiveness of the discrimination, such as on the Conservative side Michael Howard ('it is an anachronism that Catholicism should be singled out') and Michael Forsyth ('the British constitution's grubby secret and nobody wants to tackle it'); and on the Labour side Tony Blair (who converted to Roman Catholicism shortly after resigning as Prime Minister in 2007) and John Reid ('as a Roman Catholic myself, I am only too well aware of the very deep feelings and passions which surround this issue'). Some attempted Private Members' Bills have been presented to Parliament to repeal the anti-Catholic provisions as a whole, including their application to the monarch, such as Kevin McNamara's Treason Felony, Act of Settlement and Parliamentary Oath Bill in 2001.[43] The Scottish Parliament has passed resolutions calling for such complete repeal, for example in 1999, resolving that it

> believes that the discrimination contained in the Act of Settlement has no place in our modern society, expresses its wish that those discriminatory aspects of the Act be repealed, and affirms its view that Scottish society must not disbar participation in any aspect of our national life on the grounds of religion . . .[44]

---

[39] Similar reform for the Spanish monarchy has the support in principle of the main political parties but awaits implementation.

[40] Succession to the Crown Bill, 2004–05, HL11.

[41] Succession to the Crown Bill, 2010–12, HC133.

[42] HL Deb 27 February 1998, cols 916–17.

[43] HC Deb 19 December 2001, col 377.

[44] *Journal of the Scottish Parliament*, No 41, 16 December 1999.

In response to the Commonwealth statement on reform in October 2011, the Scottish First Minister Alex Salmond welcomed the news, but added it was 'deeply disappointing' that Catholics were still barred from the throne. He said:

> It surely would have been possible to find a mechanism which would have protected the status of the Church of England without keeping in place an unjustifiable barrier on the grounds of religion in terms of the monarchy . . . It is a missed opportunity not to ensure equality of all faiths when it comes to the issue of who can be Head of State.[45]

Naturally, senior members of the Catholic Church in the UK have often protested publicly on the subject too.[46]

However, there are complexities in this reform that explain the Government limiting its repeal of the anti-Catholic provisions to the spouse of the monarch only, and not to the monarch himself or herself. The reason for not undertaking a complete repeal of the anti-Catholic provisions is the Established Church of England and the formal role of the monarch as its Head and Supreme Governor. Under a tranche of other historic statutes, including the Bill of Rights 1689, Act of Settlement 1701 and Coronation Oath Act 1689, the monarch on or shortly after his or her accession makes a royal declaration of Protestant faith, is under a duty to participate and be in communion with the Church of England, and must swear an oath to uphold the established English and Scottish Churches. The Queen is a devoted Anglican, and clearly views the oaths she took on her accession with a deep commitment. Evolutionary change has been, and is, taking place in the links of Establishment, with the Prime Minister no longer personally involved in the selection of Bishops and Archbishops,[47] and the position of the Lords Spiritual in the House of Lords under threat,[48] but the prospect of a Roman Catholic acting as Head of the Church of England would pose grave difficulties for the future of establishment.

There is a high correlation between those who advocate full repeal of the anti-Catholic provisions in the Bill of Rights and Act of Settlement, and those who favour disestablishment of the Church of England. Some political quarters have openly advocated disestablishment, and this has been a Liberal Democrat general election manifesto commitment for some time.[49] At present, the Government has expressly emphasised its commitment to the Established Church[50] with the Sovereign as its Supreme Governor, as did the Labour administration immedi-

---

[45] BBC, 28 October 2011.

[46] These are discussed in Blackburn, *King and Country*, above n 13, 121–22.

[47] Since 2007 the agreed convention has been that the Prime Minister will automatically forward the recommendations of the Crown Nomination Commission to the Queen for formal appointment.

[48] On House of Lords reform proposals see C Ballinger, *The House of Lords 1911–2011: A Century of Non-Reform* (Oxford, Hart Publishing, 2012), together the latest government proposals albeit withdrawn in the House of Lords Reform Bill, HC 52 and House of Lords Draft Bill, Cm 8077, 2011.

[49] Their 2001 manifesto said that under their proposals, 'the Head of State will be able to be a member of any faith or none'. For arguments about disestablishing the Church of England see Blackburn, *King and Country*, above n 13, 129–36.

[50] Government Response, House of Commons Political and Constitutional Reform Committee, Rules of Royal Succession, 2012–13, HC 586.

ately before it.[51] The depth of this commitment, however, is unclear, and the value-driven claims for religious freedom and non-discrimination on grounds of faith in British society today are strong, particularly now that the proportion of practising Anglicans in comparison with other faith groups is in decline.[52]

It is foreseeable that the current Government's limited reform of the anti-Catholic provisions in the Act of Settlement will only serve to add further pressure behind claims for full equality of treatment and repeal of the anti-Catholic disqualifications on the statute book altogether. After all, it is only Roman Catholics who are singled out in this way, not other faiths including Muslims and Buddhists. Furthermore, removing references to persons who 'profess the popish religion' in the succession laws will essentially change nothing. Such a reform would neither address nor reconcile the fundamental issue, being the combination of the monarch's secular and religious roles and the possible future problem of a monarch being unable on grounds of faith or conscience to join in communion with the Church of England and swear to maintain the Churches of England and Scotland.

For two generations at least no such conflict will arise, for both prospective monarchs, Prince Charles and Prince William, are Anglican. If and when a future situation should arise, however, where the heir apparent belonged to a non-Anglican faith, the government of the day will be forced to choose between establishment and monarch. In other words, either the monarch's role of Head of the Church would need to be removed prior to or on accession, or the individual concerned would be deemed unfit to fulfil the role of monarch and required to abdicate in favour of the person next in line of succession who was Anglican.

* * *

The regulation of royal marriages is another example of the UK's idiosyncratic mix of past and present, law and convention, and evolution in response to social change. The UK Government announced, shortly after the Perth Statement in October 2010, that at the same time as changing the royal succession laws it would also amend the Royal Marriages Act 1772. This statute strengthened and provided a procedure for the pre-existing common law rights of the Crown to determine the upbringing and domestic affairs of the royal family, and required all descendants of King George II to obtain the formal consent of the monarch before they might legally be married.[53] This included the heirs to the throne, and both Prince Charles and Prince William went through the process of obtaining the Queen's permissions to their marriages in this way. The veto of a monarch is not absolute under the 1772 Act, and persons aged 25 years or more may appeal from

---

[51] *The Governance of Britain*, Cm 7170 (2007), para 57.

[52] *See Citizenship Survey* (2011), showing a 10% fall since 2005.

[53] For a detailed account of the Act's provisions and effects, see Robert Blackburn, written evidence, House of Commons Political and Constitutional Reform Committee, *Rules of Royal Succession*, 2010–12, HC 1615, Ev 16–17. The 1772 Act was prompted by George III's outrage at the choice of wives of two of his brothers.

a monarch's refusal by way of giving notice to the Privy Council then, after 12 months have elapsed, proceed to a wedding ceremony, unless both Houses of Parliament pass a motion expressing their disapproval of the marriage. Under the Government's Bill, the list of persons requiring the monarch's consent to marry will be limited to the first six in the line of succession, and the effect of non-compliance will no longer be to invalidate the marriage but to lose place in the line of succession.

Over the period since the 1772 Act, the number of persons covered by the Act's provisions had become a veritable multitude, and the situation was generally regarded as having become ridiculous.[54] It also laid itself open to legal challenge under the Human Rights Act 1998, for being a disproportionate restriction upon the right to marry, as protected by Article 12 of the European Convention on Human Rights. However, it is a mistake to think that this Act rankled with the great majority of royal descendants of George II. On the contrary, the whole process of correspondence with Buckingham Palace and Privy Council had usually been a source of great excitement, culminating in a grand and beautiful certificate issued to the happy couple, signed by the Queen herself, adding glamour and enjoyment to proceedings. In terms of statutory causation, if it was the marriage of Prince William and Kate Middleton in 2011 and prospect of the new Duchess's pregnancy that provided the catalyst for government action on removing the male primogeniture rule in royal succession, and if removing the Catholic disqualification applicable to a monarch's spouse was to help assuage Catholic resentment in the corridors of power and end any unjustifiable speculation about the implications of the Duchess of Cornwall having been formerly married to a Roman Catholic,[55] the main and rather more mundane reasoning behind reform of the Royal Marriages Act 1772 was to remove the cost and time in processing so many applications from George II's royal descendants.

There was nothing in the Royal Marriages Act 1772 to regulate the marriage of the monarch himself or herself. This is a quite separate matter, and the controversy over Edward VIII's choice of Wallis Simpson as his wife, a twice-divorced American, and his resulting abdication in 1936, was an enormous ruction in the history of the modern monarchy, casting its shadow over royal marital affairs ever since.[56] The romantic quality and conspiratorial politics of this episode remain topical in the popular imagination today, as evidenced just recently by a new Hollywood film being made on the subject,[57] and yet another biography of Wallis Simpson entering the best-seller booklist.[58]

The idea that there should be some form of political control over who becomes the spouse of the monarch might seem an unjustifiable personal intrusion today,

---

[54] See Bogdanor, above n 2, 44–46, 55–60.

[55] See Robert Blackburn, written evidence, House of Commons Political and Constitutional Reform Committee, *Rules of Royal Succession*, 2010-12, HC 1615, Ev 15-16.

[56] See P Ziegler, *King Edward VIII: The Official Biography* (London, Collins, 1990).

[57] *W.E.* (2011, directed by Madonna).

[58] A Sebba, *That Woman: The Life of Wallis Simpson, Duchess of Windsor* (London, George Weidenfeld & Nicholson, 2011).

but is clearly still a prevalent one in terms of popular and political acceptance of who is our monarch. The partnership of the individual who is Head of State is a matter of public interest to the well-being of the Government and the country. The monarch's consort is inter-woven into this public interest, for he or she will be supporting the monarch and be expected to participate in ceremonial and social diplomatic functions of the monarch. The constitutional laws of some other European countries have formal procedures governing the monarch's choice of spouse, such as in Spain and Sweden, where individuals must vacate the throne if they proceed with a royal marriage that is not approved by the government.

Political and religious objections drove Edward VIII from the throne and into exile in 1936, and it effectively prohibited Princess Margaret from marrying the divorcé Captain Peter Townsend in the mid-1950s. More recently, the same notion was the underlying assumption driving the extensive public debate and controversy over whether Prince Charles should marry Camilla Parker Bowles, now Duchess of Cornwall, which was eventually resolved with support from the Prime Minister and Archbishop of Canterbury, enabling the Queen to give her consent under the Royal Marriages Act. What has evolved over the last 60 years is not the constitutional machinery for controlling the marital actions of the monarch: this remains the non-legal principle that ultimately the monarch must accept the advice of the Cabinet, and if needs be, abdicate, as in 1936. What have evolved are the criteria and social values upon which the Cabinet will make up its mind on the matter. Divorce is commonplace today, whereas at the start of the Queen's reign it was still a source of social stigma. While the Government was unwilling to condone a monarch or future monarch marrying a divorcée in the past, by the time that Prince Charles expressed his desire to marry Mrs Parker Bowles in 2005, it no longer viewed divorce as an obstacle.[59]

* * *

Monarchy is the most enigmatic of our political institutions, and many of the rules governing its processes are nebulous in nature, poised between law and politics, myth and reality. Queen Elizabeth has brought great stability to the institution by masterfully working within this complex constitutional structure, blending traditions that chime with the present and echo those parts of British history and ceremony most people enjoy, with practical changes in her role, and supporting changes in the law and convention where shifting social values and morals have required evolutionary modernisation and reform. The Queen has set the gold standard for how a royal Head of State should perform his or her role in modern times. As the Prime Minister said in his tribute in the debate on the House of Commons' Address to the Queen on her Diamond Jubilee, 'it has been said that the art of progress is to preserve order amid change and change amid order, and in this the Queen is unparalleled'.

---

[59] See Blackburn, *King and Country*, above n 13, ch 2.

11

Constitutional Justice and Constitutional Politics in France

Policy Arguments in the Case Law of the Constitutional Council

DENIS BARANGER

I. INTRODUCTION*

S OME CONTEMPORARY DEVELOPMENTS in British law – notably, but not only, with the advent of the Human Rights Act – have shown that British courts could be dealing with the constitution despite the absence of a formal mechanism of constitutional review. France has long been in a rather similar situation, in the sense that the Constitutional Court (*Conseil constitutionnel*) was not created before 1958. Before that date, there was no culture of constitutional review in France. Yet there was a culture of dealing with constitutional politics in a judicial context. This culture has permeated the French approach to judicial review up to this day. It might go some way towards explaining some otherwise surprising features of the case law of the French *Conseil constitutionnel*. Amongst these is the rather impressive scarcity – or even, some might say, utter absence – of reason giving, as well as the very strange approach to politics which is apparent in the *Conseil constitutionnel*'s case law. This chapter is devoted to both of these phenomena.

* During the time I spent in Oxford, Vernon Bogdanor was one of the most welcoming as well as intellectually stimulating academics I have had the privilege to meet. I have been fortunate to work with him, and I remain immensely grateful for his human and intellectual generosity. He is also a notorious Francophile, and I hope he will accept this piece on French constitutional law as a token of my gratitude. A longer version of this contribution has appeared in French at <www.juspoliticum. com>. I am grateful to my fellow editors for allowing me to offer a (partial) translation in this volume.

A. The Framework of Constitutional Justice in France

From its creation in 1958 up until 2008, the Constitutional Council (*Conseil consti-tutionnel* (CC)) had stood apart from most other comparable constitutional courts in the west, in that it reviewed Acts of Parliament only *before* they entered into force. This model of a priori abstract review was (and still is) embodied in two main con-stitutional provisions. Under article 61(2) of the 1958 Constitution (hereafter 'C')[1]:

> Acts of Parliament may be referred to the Constitutional Council, before their promul-gation, by the President of the Republic, the Prime Minister, the President of the National Assembly, the President of the Senate, sixty Members of the National Assembly or sixty Senators. . . .[2]

Article 54 C creates another procedural vehicle for constitutional review. It has a separate purpose, namely, to allow for a check on the compatibility between trea-ties and the Constitution before those treaties are ratified:

> If the Constitutional Council, on a referral from the President of the Republic, from the Prime Minister, from the President of one or the other Houses, or from sixty Members of the National Assembly or sixty Senators, has held that an international undertaking contains a clause contrary to the Constitution, authorization to ratify or approve the international undertaking involved may be given only after amending the Constitution.

Since the constitutional reform of 2008, a new mechanism permits individuals to challenge statutes already in force that infringe their constitutional rights:

> If, during proceedings in progress before a court of law, it is claimed that a statutory provision infringes the rights and freedoms, guaranteed by the Constitution, the matter may be referred by the *Conseil d'Etat* or by the *Cour de cassation* to the constitutional council, within a determined period.

This new procedure of preliminary reference,[3] known as *Question prioritaire de constitutionnalité* (QPC), has not, however, induced the Constitutional Council significantly to alter the way in which its decisions are drafted. The CC's 'style' has remained essentially the same.

B. The Constitutional Council's Judicial Style

The CC has developed case law that is widely seen as having improved the rule of law and the protection of civil liberties. It has, it is often said, given France the bill

---

[1] Art 61(1) C creates a procedure of mandatory review for organic laws, referendary bills and the standing orders of the Houses of Parliament.

[2] All the translations of the 1958 Constitution used in this chapter are from the *Légifrance* website, at <www.conseil-constitutionnel.fr/conseil-constitutionnel/francais/la-constitution/la-constitution-du-4-octobre-1958/la-constitution-du-4-octobre-1958.5071.html>.

[3] I use the translation suggested by Gerald Neuman in his illuminating article: 'Anti-Ashwander: constitutional litigation as a first resort in France' (2010) 43 *New York University Journal of International Law and Politics* 15, 17.

of rights that was missing in the 1958 Constitution. Few members of the general public bother to read the Council's decisions. But the general point of view among legal academics is that the Council's judicial style is satisfactory. While the early cases were very short and did not seem to give adequate reasons, this has changed: 'Today, while not reaching the size of foreign constitutional courts, the decisions are lengthy, carefully justified and look like lessons in constitutional, parliamentary, criminal or financial law.'[4] Yet this positive assessment is not unanimous. A minority of observers point to the insufficient reasons given in some specific cases. Words such as 'elliptical', 'obscure', 'incoherent' have been used in doctrinal literature. Mostly, there is a sense that the CC's reason giving is insufficient. Certainly, there is no absolute standard. Long decisions can lack adequate justification, while *brevitas* has been commended, in some contexts, as a judicial virtue. This is particularly the case in French law, where courts generally prefer clarity – which is equated to brevity – to lengthy opinions. Yet legal commentators have sometimes been struck by the remarkable brevity of some of the CC's decisions. What should we say, for instance, of the reasons given for the 2008 decision by which the CC 'reviewed' an amendment to the standing orders of the '*Congrès*' (a body which is empowered to alter the Constitution according to article 89 C): 'The (relevant) provisions have been enacted in keeping with article 18 of the constitution and do not violate any other constitutional rule.'[5]

This is the most basic level of reason giving imaginable. This judicial style has been replicated in responses to the preliminary referrals brought under article 61-1. If anything, most 'QPC' decisions are even shorter than the 'DC' ones (those delivered under articles 61(1), 61(2) and 54 C). In fact, one commentator deplored the utter 'lack of reason giving'[6] of the important 'QPC' decision of August 2010 regarding the statute reforming the university system.[7]

i. Hyperformalism

In order to move beyond the impression that the CC's decisions are 'too short' or provide inadequate reason giving, I suggest to making use of what American legal theory has had to say about 'formalism'. Formalism has been defined as 'the theory that all questions of law can be resolved by deduction, that is without recourse to policy, except for questions arising from rules that explicitly require policy argument'.[8] Formalism consists in supposing that the solution to legal problems involved deducing particular conclusions from more general or more abstract premises. The formalist judge 'applies the rule by establishing that the wording of the rule fits the facts of the case'.[9]

---

[4] D Rousseau, *Droit du contentieux constitutionnel*, 7th edn (Paris, Montchrestien, 2006) 155.
[5] Décision no 2009-583 DC, 22 June 2009, 'Résolution modifiant le règlement du Congrès'.
[6] O Beaud, *Les libertés universitaires à l'abandon?* (Paris, Dalloz, 2011) 288.
[7] Décision no 2010-20/21 QPC, 6 August 2010.
[8] D Kennedy, *A Critique of Adjudication (fin de siècle)*, (Cambridge, MA, Harvard University Press, 1997) 101–02.
[9] *Ibid.*

In the case law of the CC, formalism is not simply one of several methods that are used in the course of constitutional adjudication: it is the exclusive method. I would therefore submit that the 'style' of adjudication of the CC is 'hyperformalist'. In fact, recourse to the deductive mode is self-evident and is never questioned. French courts have never been, it seems, impressed by Oliver Wendell Holmes's famous remark that 'general propositions do not decide concrete cases'. Hyperformalism is visible in several features of the Council's process of decision making: the principle that judicial deliberations ought to remain secret; the principle of unanimity, ie that there are no dissenting opinions; the order in which decisions are drafted, by way of a 'judicial syllogism'.

It is as if constitutional 'norms' made their appearance in a moment of judicial epiphany. They appear as self-evident truths, the content of which, applicability to the case and implications for the reviewing process do not stand in need of justification. Consequences unfold themselves mechanically, in an impersonal fashion, without appearing to require any explanation or demonstration along the way:

(a) The Council's choice of a certain set of applicable constitutional norms – generally called 'norms of reference' – is never justified. The syllogistic reasoning increases the 'oracular' quality of the CC's work. An example of this is the 1971 case in which the CC famously decided that the content of the Constitution's 1958 Preamble was legally enforceable, as well as – by reference in the 1958 Preamble – that of the 1946 Preamble and the 1789 Declaration of the Rights of Man and the Citizen. From 1958 to 1971 it was held that the Preamble did not have legal force. Yet when the CC reversed this position, it did so in a very 'minimalist' way, simply by stating:

> Having regard to the constitution, *and especially its preamble*. . . . Among the fundamental principles acknowledged by the laws of the Republic and solemnly reaffirmed by the preamble of the constitution, it is appropriate to [*il y a lieu de*] include the principle of freedom of association. This principle is the foundation of . . . the statute of 1 July 1901.[10]

Why should the 1958 Preamble be considered from then on as legally enforceable? Why is it 'appropriate' to count freedom of association as one of the principles to which the 1946 Preamble is pointing (although it is not expressly referred to in its text)? No answers were provided in the 1971 case. It was only in 1988 that the CC provided some explanations as to the criteria according to which a certain principle should count as a 'fundamental principle acknowledged by the laws of the Republic'.[11]

(b) Secondly, this apparent automaticity also applies to the consequences that should be drawn from a comparison between the 'major' premise (the constitutional norm) and the 'minor' premise (the legislative provision). The

---

[10] Décision no 71–44 DC, 16 July 1971, 'Loi complétant les dispositions des articles 5 et 7 de la loi du 1er juillet 1901 relative au contrat d'association' (emphasis added).

[11] Décision n° 88-244, 20 July 1988, 'Loi portant amnistie'.

deduction process, and its possible justifications or alternatives, is entirely opaque. Let me take the example of a decision of November 1986,[12] rendered during the first of those chaotic periods of French politics known as *cohabitations*. Some opposition parliamentarians had referred a controversial electoral reapportionment bill to the Council. The CC first spelled out the reference norms applying to the case:

- the principle of equality before the law, drawn from article 2 C;
- article 3 C, in so far as it states that 'National sovereignty shall vest in the people, who shall exercise it through their representatives and by means of referendum . . . Suffrage . . . shall always be universal, equal and secret';
- article 24 C, which states that 'Members of the National Assembly . . . shall be elected by direct suffrage';
- article 6 of the Declaration of 1789, which states that the law 'must be the same for all'.

The CC went on to state that:

As a result [*il résulte de ces dispositions*] the National assembly, appointed by direct universal suffrage, should be elected according to bases that are essentially demographic [*sur des bases essentiellement démographiques*].

As far as substantive law is concerned, such a 'deduction' is hardly open to reproach. It was, it seems, perfectly justifiable to translate the democratic principles expressed in the Constitution into the 'fundamental rule' (*règle fondamentale*) of '*bases essentiellement démographiques*' of the reapportionment exercises. This was certainly *justifiable*, yet the case makes no attempt to justify it. Formalism takes the shape of a minimalist approach to judicial reason giving. No explanation is given as to why this set of constitutional norms should apply to the case. And nothing is said about why and how the 'fundamental rule' should be deduced from these constitutional norms.

This minimalist style is not restricted to the CC's control of parliamentary legislation. It also extends to its competence, under article 54 C, to control the compatibility between treaties and the Constitution, so as to make their ratification possible. The CC refers to certain elements of the act or treaty which is submitted to its control without commenting on them. Then, in a separate paragraph, it draws the apparent conclusion that the provision in question is (or not) compatible with the Constitution. In commenting on one of the high-profile cases regarding the compatibility of the Maastricht Treaty with the Constitution, one of the best experts on the CC's case law, while approving the decision's substance, regretted this minimalist approach. He spoke of a 'pedagogical disappointment' and a 'lack of explanation':

---

[12] Décision n° 86-218 DC, 18 November 1986, 'Loi relative à la délimitation des circonscriptions pour l'élection des députés'.

The [CC] does not say *in what way* the Treaty's provisions (have the effect of) jeopardizing the 'essential conditions of exercise of national sovereignty'. It contents itself with expounding at length the three phases of the creation of the *monnaie unique*, by quoting the relevant articles of the Treaty. It is as if the very fact of mentioning these modalities would suffice in themselves to prove, self-evidently as it were, that they have an adverse effect on these 'essential conditions'.[13]

ii. Justifications

However surprising this approach to judicial review might seem, especially to non-French eyes, it does not lack justification. At least three justifications should be mentioned:

(a) *The rationality argument.* The CC 'has' reasons, but does not 'give' them, at least not in full. An implicit premise of the mainstream doctrinal approach is that judicial review is inherently rational. It is the business of academic commentary to make this rationality come to light by reconstructing it. Certainly, the CC does not enunciate a large number of reasons in its judicial decisions, but reasons are there, as is evidenced by the recourse to the 'judicial syllogism'. Hyperformalism, in other terms, is only a radical variety of rationalism. That the CC should be rational is also made abundantly clear by the methods it uses to decide cases. It requires the legislator to legislate rationally. An important aspect of this requirement of rationality is the proportionality principle. The CC itself also shows its concern for rationality by treating like cases alike. In other terms, it is very keen to create a body of precedents and stick to it.[14]

(b) *The 'if it ain't broke, why fix it?' argument.* The argument runs like this. Despite its shortcomings, the CC's method has proved its worth. Its case law has had beneficial effects on the rule of law and civil liberties, and this is what should matter. The advantages largely outweigh the possible inconveniences. Since 1958, and especially since 1971, the CC has quashed many bills that violated important constitutional principles, especially in the field of civil liberties. It has created a body of case law that sets guidelines for lawmakers as well as for other public authorities. It matters little that the way its members are appointed is somehow questionable. The way in which they decide cases is also of little importance. George Vedel, a famous law professor as well as a member of the CC's panel from 1980–89 put it this way: '[I]ts irrationality, its rusticity, its empiricism have been some of the ingredients, and not the least of these ones, for its success'.[15] Undoubtedly there is something to this argument. An 'irrational' process brings about a rational outcome. The trick has

---

[13] D Rousseau, *Droit du contentieux constitutionnel* (Paris, Montchrestien, 2006) 349–50.

[14] See the remarks of a former member of the judicial panel: D Schnapper, *Une sociologue au Conseil constitutionnel* (Paris, Gallimard, 2010) 289 ff.

[15] G Vedel, 'Preface' in Rousseau, above n 13.

been seen before. However, how do we know that the outcome is rational? In other words, how can we be so sure that the CC's style, the brevity of its decisions and the opacity of its functioning are in fact conducive to greater freedom or better protection for the rule of law? Should one have so much faith in the cunning of reason? Does not western legal culture emphasise the importance of means as opposed to ends? Law is very much concerned with the intrinsic, non-instrumental, value of forms. Reason giving is a formal requirement, yet one on which depends the very existence and manifestation of legal substance.

(c) *The deference argument.* Only hyperformalism is consistent with the Council's office. This may be expressed in different ways:

(i) Courts should not meddle with politics. The Council's hyperformalism is a way for it to refrain from setting foot in the political arena. To quote John Bell, 'the distinction between judging and politics remains embedded in the common understanding of a legal system'.[16] This comment has not aged, and France is no exception. If anything, the distinction is enforced more strictly south of the Channel.

(ii) The Council is not an advisory body. In an early case, the CC had stated that it had no competence to deliver 'advices' except in the cases provided for by the Constitution (as in article 16 C, which deals with executive emergency powers).[17]

(iii) The CC is a court and not an academic commentator or a kind of 'philosopher judge' in the way Plato spoke of 'philosopher kings'. This is a variety of the 'separation of powers' argument. It obviously makes a lot of sense. Yet this argument is weakened by several facts. First, the CC has developed a practice of issuing home-made 'commentaries' on its own cases, as well as press releases. They appear on its website as well as in other journals. Secondly, the 'advising' or 'guiding' role of the CC is in fact emphasised by its (numerous) supporters as one of its main roles. It is commonplace for legal commentators and the media to call the Council 'the wise' (*les sages*). Like other constitutional courts, the CC regularly issues 'reserves of interpretation' (*réserves d'interprétation*) by which it interprets statutory provisions in such a way as to render them compatible with the Constitution. This removes the sting from the relevant provisions and makes it possible to judge them compatible with the Constitution, should they be interpreted according to these guidelines.

---

[16] J Bell, *Policy Arguments in Judicial Decisions* (Oxford, Clarendon Press, 1983) 1.
[17] Décision no 61-1 AUTR, 14 September 1961, 'Demande d'avis'; (1961) *Recueil des décisions du Conseil constitutionnel* 55.

iii. Constitutional Politics in France: the Constitutional Council and Political Reasons

To sum up: the French Constitutional Council decides cases in a 'hyperformal' way in which reason giving is reduced to a minimum. This practice is justifiable, as we saw. It is in keeping with French legal culture. In any event, it does not violate the Constitution. The CC is supposed to give reasons for its decisions,[18] and it does so, however sparingly. Yet hyperformalism goes against the tide of contemporary law, in France as well as in most western countries. The duty to give reasons has been constantly reinforced in most courts of law, as well as for other public authorities. Contemporary political philosophy (John Rawls, Jurgen Habermas), which thinks universally and normatively, has insisted on the paramount importance of this duty.

My purpose here is by no means to advocate a change in the manner and form of constitutional adjudication in France. It seems more interesting to show that it is related to a very specific approach to politics which permeates French public law. In the French language, only one word – '*politique*' – is used to refer to 'party politics' as well as to 'policy'. French lawyers, as well as the general public, are keen to understand '*politique*' as something which essentially differs from 'law' (*droit*). The office of judges, it is thought, is to say what the law is, not to meddle with '*politique*'. Yet there is more to politics than this narrow approach. It is quite obvious that the Constitution itself is a political reality. It purports to provide a framework for political life in a given political community. It is based on a certain understanding of society, a certain set of values. It is meant to constrain the action of political authorities. A French lawyer has garnered some fame by saying that, thanks to the CC, the law had 'seized politics' (*la politique saisie par le droit*).[19] He meant that, during the first *cohabitation* of a left-wing president and a right wing parliamentary majority in 1986–88, the CC acted as a moderator of political strife. The Constitution, as stated by the CC, forced the ministry and the majority to moderation in implementing their political agendas. Yet it is somewhat difficult to understand how exactly 'the law' has 'seized' politics and purified it. Constitutional litigation is inherently political, just as it is inherently legal. It is commonplace to speak of 'policy-making' on the part of constitutional courts, or of 'judicialised legislative politics'.[20] Some constitutional cases are the basis of, or significantly inform, the conduct of whole areas of public policy. If this is the case, it seems hardly plausible that constitutional courts can indeed steer clear of political activity. It seems more apposite to set aside the unhelpful myth of 'politics seized by the law' – or at least to treat it as an element of ideological justification,

---

[18] See the *ordonnance organique* of 7 November 1958 which provides for such a requirement for all the respective competences of the CC. The 'advisory opinions' of art 16 C fall under a similar requirement.

[19] L Favoreu, *La politique saisie par le droit: alternances, cohabitation et Conseil constitutionnel* (Paris, Economica, 1988).

[20] See, eg, A Stone Sweet, *Governing with Judges: Constitutional Politics in Europe* (Oxford, Oxford University Press, 2000) ch 3 (*in fine*), available at <www.oxfordscholarship.com/view/10.1093/019829 7718.001.0001/acprof-9780198297710-chapter-3>.

not of scientific description – and to ask oneself in what way constitutional courts take political reasons into consideration without ceasing to act judicially.

The notion that judges legislate has been commonplace in English-speaking countries since Dicey's 'judicial legislation' and Holmes's 'interstitial legislation'. French legal theory, thanks to Michel Troper, is now familiar with the notion that the CC is a 'co-legislator'. If these words are to be taken seriously, this should induce us to look behind the usual explanations of the office of courts in terms of separation of powers. French doctrinal discussion about adjudication and the normative power of courts, however, has not enjoyed the level of sophistication reached in English-speaking countries. The usual account remains that the legislation/adjudication divide involves another cleavage between politics (the business of legislators) and law (the role of courts). It would seem that the distinction carries a lot of ideological force in the French context, especially when it comes to providing justifications for the rule-making power of the CC. Yet it has little practical value, and this is the more apparent when this rule-making exercise is performed in the field of constitutional law. It is next to impossible to distinguish the law of the Constitution, of which courts would be the guardians, from political arguments, of which they would respectfully stay clear.

As far as the CC is concerned, it obviously handles political arguments *lato sensu*. To take only one fairly straightforward example, equality before the law (one of the constitutional principles most frequently referred to in French constitutional litigation) cannot be anything but political. It reflects a political understanding of life in society: that of democracy and democratic values. In France, this principle is central to the idea of a republican State. The CC has done a great deal to shape it through a long line of cases. The same obtains of such principles as national sovereignty. What are they if not political? Constitutional principles are rarely anything else than reconfigured politics. This is of course not the same kind of politics as that that takes place in and between parties; it is politics at the level of society as a whole, expressed in legal form. Constitutional courts have become the place where contradicting views of the common good – the categorical imperative of political activity – are confronting each other, with the aim of becoming the expression of political unity. Constitutional politics is not expressed in the same way as the politics of electoral platforms, party strife and the other forms of day-to-day political controversy in media or houses of parliament. It might be that some arguments of 'pure law' intervene in constitutional adjudication. But I find it hard to see what 'pure law' could mean in this context. All the possible arguments that come up in constitutional litigation – from the courts' jurisdiction to substantive issues – have a political aspect. Every particle of constitutional litigation is politically charged. When the CC denied its jurisdiction with regard to constitutional amendments, it quite plausibly did so for reasons that had to do with politics.[21] To become 'constitutional politics' – an expression that was

---

[21] I take the liberty to refer to: D Baranger, 'The Language of Eternity: Judicial Review of the Amending Power in France (or the absence thereof)', (2011) 44 *Israel Law Review*, 408–410.

frequent in the nineteenth century and has since lost currency – political arguments must be such that they can be expressed in a court of law. The most important 'test' in this regard is not so much one of neutrality as one of universality[22]: in a given community, a political reason that is not acceptable by all has to be cast aside from constitutional adjudication. It cannot be expressed in constitutional form. Be that as it may, the law, especially the law of the Constitution, is inherently political in so far as it deals with issues of life in society. Were it not political, it would be irrelevant.

II. THE CONSTITUTIONAL COUNCIL AND POLICY ARGUMENTS

In the American and British theory of adjudication, a policy argument comes up as a substantive justification to which judges appeal 'when the standards and rules of the legal system do not provide a clear resolution of a dispute'.[23] The 'policy argument' mode is an alternative to the 'deductive mode'. In France, if the concept of 'policy argument' is to be in any way helpful, it should be accepted that policy arguments come up in the course of what appears to be a fully deductive exercise. The mode of reasoning which is characteristic of French constitutional adjudication is, as was said earlier, one of extreme formalism. The CC, as well as most other French courts, adheres to the notion that legal problems can be solved exclusively through deduction. Duncan Kennedy has summarised the attitude of American lawyers to judicial reasoning as being one that relies upon an implicit distinction between a 'deductive mode' and the mode of 'policy arguments'.[24] In the deductive mode, the judge always reasons from the more abstract and/or the more general towards the more concrete and/or particular. In the 'policy argument' mode, to the contrary, the premise is that:

(a) the issue of law is not solved by resorting to a valid rule; and
(b) the valid norm requires that the judge should take into account some 'non-deductive' reasons in order to choose an inferior rule.

In the case of American law, such policy arguments may encompass: social utility, morality, rights (such as free speech) or other 'legal values' (Kennedy), such as preference for a rule as opposed to an equitable principle.

It will not do simply to look the other way and deny that there is a political aspect to constitutional adjudication. What is needed is the methodology to point out what exactly is political in it, and what legal form it takes. One of the virtues of reasoning in terms of policy arguments – a term of art almost entirely unknown in

---

[22] In other words, the test can to some degree be compared to Kant's test of universalisability. This is the more so in countries such as liberal democracies of the west where morality is very much understood as consisting mostly of universal, rather than local, cultural or historical, principles.

[23] Bell, above n 16, 23.

[24] D Kennedy, *A Critique of Adjudication (fin de siècle)* (Cambridge, MA, Harvard University Press, 1997).

French legal theory and legal language – is that it helps identify the political dimension in the process of adjudication. I would submit that the CC has recourse to such policy arguments, although this is acknowledged neither in case law nor in doctrinal literature, and is most probably unconscious. The strength of the 'politics seized by law' argument is such that any claim that there is a political element to judicial reasoning is treated as heresy. The deductive mode seems to be all there is to judicial methodology. In decisions that are so concise, so neutral, so beautifully juridical, what place would there be for policy arguments? Yet even in these remarkably brief cases, there appear to pop up some expressions that seem strikingly close to policy arguments: 'public order' (*ordre public*), 'good administration of justice' (*bonne administration de la justice*), 'requirements of public services' (*exigences du service public*) and so on. In fact, authorities that refer bills or statutes to the CC, as well as individuals who bring a referral process by way of a 'QPC', are keen to use such arguments in their statements of claim.

In the US or in Britain, courts convert arguments drawn from extra-judicial discussion into policy arguments, ie arguments of general interest that will be incorporated into judicial reasoning, through, for instance, a test of proportionality or a test of reasonableness. Thus, political reasons are 'universalised' so as to leave the sphere of party politics or sectarian interests, and may be such as to be accepted by all. A reason one gives aims at persuading a certain person or a group. Otherwise, it does not count as a reason. In this way, the legal understanding of reason has moved imperceptibly from an Aristotelian 'right reason', or the absolute 'Reason' of classical metaphysics, to the 'reasons' of contemporary moral deliberation. In the case of courts, especially constitutional ones, reasons must be such as count for all. They aim at the public good. They are political without being partisan. In France, the CC's hyperformalism indicates how these political reasons should be expressed in a form that is different from that of public debate or parliamentary deliberation; otherwise, they do not pass the test of universalisation and cannot be 'constitutionalised'. The danger is obviously that the more these norms fit the (implicit) test of universalisation, the more shallow or 'empty' they are, thus leaving some room for arbitrariness on the part of the court as well as the public authorities that will implement statutory law in the future.

In French doctrinal literature, the general approach to these principles, rules, fundamental rights, etc is a normative one. All the component parts of a judicial decision are 'norms' belonging to different normative categories. These categories are generally created by the CC itself. Divergences from their precise categorisation are the bread-and-butter of the constitutional lawyer. An instance of this is the ongoing discussion about the status of the rights contained in the 2004 Charter of the Environment. The Charter is a part of the Constitution, thanks to the reference made to it since 2005 in the Constitution's Preamble. Article 1 of the Charter creates a 'right for everyone to live in an environment that is balanced and respectful of good health' ['*droit . . . à vivre dans un environnement équilibré et respectueux de la santé*]. Some constitutional experts have expressed the view that this 'right' was in fact an objective of constitutional value (*objectif de valeur constitutionnelle*:

OVC). These objectives are not expressed directly in the Constitution, they are creatures of the CC's case law. An OVC is a kind of judge-made constitutional sub-principle that binds the legislative power. It will bind the legislator in so far as it is seen as necessary as regards respect for a constitutional principle. For instance, freedom of opinion is a constitutional principle, expressed in article 11 of the 1789 Declaration of the Rights of Man and the Citizen. The 'pluralist expression of the social and cultural trends', however, is an OVC created by the CC and which is ancillary to freedom of opinion. The legislator has to fulfil this objective when it regulates the media.[25] Another example is the objective of 'intelligibility and accessibility' of legislation.[26]

What we see at play here is a process in which bits of judicial reasoning that operate like policy arguments are squeezed into pre-existing normative categories – some drawn from the Constitution or its (enforceable) Preamble, such as the 'fundamental principles recognised by the laws of the republic'; others created by the CC or by doctrinal writing, such as the objectives of constitutional value or other *sui generis* categories such as 'principles of constitutional value' (for instance, the 'constitutional principle of the protection of public health',[27] which is also called, in the same decision, an 'imperative'). In other cases, the CC has used a broad categorisation, such as that of 'goal of general interest' or 'protection of general interests'. This was the terminology used in 1985 to define some broad objectives of environmental law, such as a duty to respect the 'natural character of spaces', the 'quality of landscapes' or the 'ecological equilibrium'.[28] But beyond these broad normative appellations, how should one label the 'necessity to defend public health', or to 'protect natural spaces' or to ensure a certain degree of pluralism in the medias, if not as policy arguments? More often than not, in fact, these policy arguments appear without any reference to a normative category. This was the case as regards the 'goal of political or social appeasement' which justified an act of amnesty in 1988.[29] More recently, the CC has mentioned 'the legal complexity of the law regarding the enforcement of punishments'. This complexity, it said, was an obstacle to the participation of ordinary citizens in certain judicial panels.[30]

The fact that the analysis in terms of policy argument has not been imported from English or American academic writing is itself of significance. Considerations of policy are frequently translated into norms by the CC in order to fit into deductive ('syllogistic') judicial reasoning. The academic discipline of 'constitutional

---

[25] Décision no 82–141 DC, 27 July 1982.
[26] Décision no 2005-512 DC, 21 avril 2005, 'Loi d'orientation et de programme pour l'avenir de l'école'.
[27] Décision no 90-283 DC, 8 January 1991, 'Loi relative à la lutte contre le tabagisme et l'alcoolisme'.
[28] Décision no 85–189 DC, 17 July 1985, 'Loi relative à la définition et à la mise en oeuvre de principes d'aménagement'.
[29] Décision no 88–244 DC, 20 July 1988, 'Loi portant amnistie'.
[30] The *tribunal de l'application des peines* or the *chambre de l'application des peines*. Décision no 2011–635 DC, 4 August 2011, 'Loi sur la participation des citoyens au fonctionnement de la justice pénale et le jugement des mineurs'.

litigation' (*contentieux constitutionnel*, a blooming branch of constitutional law) treats these policy arguments as 'norms of reference', or in other words as sources of the CC's review. It is certainly correct to do so. Nothing should bear on judicial reasoning that is not normative. Yet this is at the same time entirely tautological. As soon as something enters the field of judicial reasoning (by being mentioned in a case), it becomes normative *per se*. This is also somewhat sterilising, in so far as it conceals the heterogeneous nature of judicial reasoning. An imperative of public policy does not have the same nature as a fundamental right. The 'preservation of public interest' or the 'requirements of public order' do not have the same legal status as civil liberties. In fact, they are often used to counterbalance such rights or liberties in the course of a test of proportionality. This is especially the function of the argument regarding 'the safeguarding of public order'. The CC customarily refers to 'the necessary conciliation between the respect of liberties and the safeguard of the public order without which these liberties could not be exercised'.[31]

III. CONCLUSION

The purpose of this chapter has been to defend the view that the case law of the Constitutional Council could be analysed in terms of policy arguments. To analyse the meaning and precise scope of this phenomenon is a task for the future. However, a few concluding remarks might be in order. By having recourse to policy arguments, the CC acts as the guardian of collective interest. At the end of the day, most policy arguments in the CC's case law fall within a single, all-encompassing one, the mother of all policy arguments *à la française*: general interest. Thus they might be called 'public policy imperatives' or, to use a label created by the CC itself, 'imperatives of general interest'.[32] This technique shows that the CC is more than just the bulwark of individual liberty that is often depicted in specialist literature. It defends other values that are central to French public law, first amongst which is a fairly traditional understanding of public intervention as based on *intérêt général*. In other words, policy arguments are a means by which the Constitutional Council brings to life the coldest of the cold monsters of French public law: the State.

---

[31] Décision no 85-187 DC, 25 January 1985, 'Loi relative à l'état d'urgence en Nouvelle-Calédonie'.
[32] Décision no 86-218 DC, 18 November 1986.

Epilogue

S O WHERE DOES this leave the British Constitution: has it changed or not? It is no longer the same, but we have not experienced a radical break. It was perhaps for this reason that Queen Elizabeth II struck an almost philosophical tone when she summed up the changes to both chambers of Parliament on the occasion of her Silver Jubilee in 2002. It is fitting to let Her Majesty have the last word:

> We in these islands have the benefit of a long and proud history. This not only gives us a trusted framework of stability and continuity to ease the process of change, but it also tells us what is of lasting value. Only the passage of time can filter out the ephemeral from the enduring. And what endure are the characteristics that mark our identity as a nation and the timeless values that guide us. These values find expression in our national institutions – including the Monarchy and Parliament – institutions which in turn must continue to evolve if they are to provide effective beacons of trust and unity to succeeding generations. I believe that many of the traditional values etched across our history equip us well for this age of change. We are a moderate, pragmatic people, more comfortable with practice than theory.[1]

---

[1] The Queen's Address to Parliament 2002 may be found at <http://www.royal.gov.uk/ LatestNewsandDiary/Speechesandarticles/2002/TheQueenrepliestoLoyalAddressesfromParliament 30Apr.aspx>.

Index

Page numbers in **bold** indicate reference to a table.

accountability:
  constitutional conventions, 121
  holders of public office, 74
  political accountability, 121, 136
Ackerman, Bruce, 2
adjudication (theory of):
  France, 188–90
  UK, 188–9, 190–1
  United States, 188–9, 190–1
adversarial politics, 57
American Constitution, 3, 7
  see also United States
anti-Catholic provisions:
  Act of Settlement, 174
  Bill of Rights, 174
  royal succession, 172–3
anti-terror legislation:
  Anti-terrorism, Crime and Security Act, 64
  freedom of speech, 32
  right to jury trial, 32
Anti-terrorism, Crime and Security Act 2001:
  declarations of incompatibility, 64
  European Convention on Human Rights, 64
apolitical organisations, 2
  QUANGOs, 2, 72–3
  tribunals, 2, 76–7
  see also arms-length bodies
arms-length bodies, 71–7
  Bank of England, 75
  Commissioner for Public Appointments, 74–5
  Committee on Standards in Public Life, 73–4
  Monetary Policy Committee, 75
  non-departmental public bodies, 72–3
  Office for Budget Responsibility, 76
  Office for National Statistics, 75–6
  QUANGOs, 2
  tribunals, 2, 76–7
  UK Statistics Authority, 75–6

'bad politics', 71, 77, 82, 84, 89, 91
Bagehot, Walter, 3, 8, 94, 170
  primacy of the Cabinet, 15
Balfour, Arthur, 57
Ballinger, Chris, 52
  House of Lords reform, 174
Bank of England, 75

Beer, Samuel H, 57
Belfast Assembly:
  electoral system, 3
Bill of Rights, 8, 30–3, 40, 45–9, 66
  Bill of Rights 1689, 132, 156, 172–4
  United States, 30
Birkinshaw, Patrick, 101
Blackstone, William, 8
Blair, Tony, 21, 29, 33, 170n28, 173
  constitutional conventions, 102, 130
  constitutional reform programme, 57–50
  devolution, 23–7, 47–8
  freedom of information, 53
  hereditary peers, 48
  House of Lords reform, 48
Blair government:
  British Constitution, 22–9
    devolution, 23–7, 47–8
    House of Lords reform, 27–9
  constitutional reform, 43
  public service reform, 50
  Scottish devolution, 48
  Welsh devolution, 48–9
Blom-Cooper, Louis, 30
Bogdanor, Vernon, 7, 8, 39–40
  devolution, 23–4, 142–3, 146, 152
  dissolution of parliament, 130
  federalism, 152
  historic constitution, 17
  Human Rights Act, 32–3, 61
  ministerial responsibility, 135
  new British constitution, 19, 32, 35, 53
  parliamentary sovereignty, 153, 161
  public participation, 51
  redistribution of power, 33
  resignation of the government, 133
  prime ministerial appointment, 125
  traditional constitution, 56
Brazier, Rodney, 30–1
British Constitution:
  Acts of Parliament, 11–12
  Blair government, 22–9
    devolution, 23–7
    House of Lords reform, 27–9
  centralisation, 9, 15
  devolution, 3
  electoral reform, 3

British Constitution (*cont*):
European Union, 3
framework for government, 7
historical context, 17–21
House of Lords, 3, 27–9, 33
Human Rights Act 1998, 2–3, 29–32, 33
legal constitution:
  courts, 62–3
  declarations of incompatibility, 63–6
  Human Rights Act, 61–6
  incompatibility, 63–6
  judiciary, 60–1
  legislative activism, 62–3
  Lord Chancellor's role, 58–60
  Northern Ireland, 58
  purposive interpretation, 63
  Scotland, 58
Lijphart, Arend, 7
majoritarian constitution, 7, 57
media debate, 39
'new British constitution', 32
parliamentary sovereignty, 4, 10, 16, 57
political constitution, 56–8, 69–71
political parties, 10, 16
public debate, 39
reforms, 2, 22–9
  devolution, 23–7
  House of Commons reform, 35–7
  House of Lords reform, 27–9
  human rights, 33–4
  political parties, 22–3
  politics, 22–3
regulation of behaviour, 7
responsibility:
  collective, 10, 16
  individual, 9–10, 15
separation of powers, 4, 8, 15
statutory impacts:
  Acts of Parliament, 11–12
sovereign Parliament, 4, 10, 16, 57
Supreme Court, 3, 33, 160
texts in support:
  Acts of Union, 40
  Bill of Rights, 40
  Great Reform Acts, 40
  Magna Carta, 40
  Petition of Right, 40
traditional constitution, 56
unwritten constitution, 8, 15, 39–40
Westminster Model, 7
see also constitutional conventions;
  constitutional reforms; constitutions
British Empire, 14
British society, 51–2
indicators of change, **13–14,** 15–16
Brown, Gordon:
constitutional reform, 33
POWER Inquiry, 51

Budget Responsibility and National Audit Act
  2011, 135
Butler, David, 41–2

Cabinet, 9, 15
Cabinet Manual, 84, 100–1
collective cabinet responsibility, 16, 107–8,
  109
ministerial responsibility, 110
Cameron, David:
constitutional reform, 33, 37
Campaign for Freedom of Information, 49
Canada:
human rights legislation, 66
central government:
local government (relations between), 39
centralisation, 9, 15
administrative devolution to provinces, 9, 146
Westminster, 9, 144, 146
Whitehall, 9
Charter 88, 42, 46, 49
impact, 46–7
proportional representation, 42
Chartism, 20
Civil Service Code, 73, 80, 100–1
Civil Service Reform Plan, 81
Clegg, Nick, 18, 33
alternative vote, 18
constitutional reform, 33, 37
Codes of Conduct:
Civil Service Code, 73, 80, 100–1
Ministerial Code, 73, 84
Colley, Linda, 40–1
Commissioner for Public Appointments, 74–5,
  81
Code of Practice, 75
Committee on Standards in Public Life, 73–4
common law:
constitutional conventions, 122–3
constitutionalism, 105
Common Market, 41, 44
Commonwealth:
freedom of information legislation, 49
conduct:
backbenchers, 82
Codes of Conduct
  Civil Service Code, 73, 80, 100-1
  Ministerial Code, 73, 84
Committee on Standards in Public Life, 73–4
Select Committees, 81–2
constitutional conventions, 2, 56–7
Budget Responsibility and National Audit
  Act, 135
budgets, 131–2, 135
common law systems, 122–3
consensus, 99–112
constitutional laws distinguished, 99, 112,
  114–19

constitutional principles distinguished, 97
continuity and change, 121–39
definition, 118
Dicey, AV:
  convention and law, 112–13
disagreement, 104–5, 107, 109–12
dissolution dates, 128–30
examples of Conventions:
  Budget Responsibility and National Audit
    Act, 135
  budgets, 131–2, 135
  dissolution dates, 128–30
  Finance Acts, 131–2
  Fixed-term Parliaments Act, 128–30
  loss of office, 132
  loss of revenue, 132
  Parliament Act 1911, 133
  Prime Minister as member of the House,
    138–9, 124–8
  raising of revenue, 130–2, 139
  taxation, 131, 133
Finance Acts, 131–2
Fixed-term Parliaments Act, 128–30
functions, 95, 97, 118–19, 122
generally, 93–9
institutions, 94, 106
laws:
  conventions distinguished, 112
  Dicey, AV, 112, 113–14
  royal prerogative, 112–13
  US Constitution, 113
legal norms, 96
  United States, 114
loss of office, 132
loss of revenue, 132
majoritarianism, 57
Ministerial Code, 117–18
modification, 135–8
Morton, Peter, 95–9
non-legal constitutional norms, 95–9, 112,
    117, 118–19
  Cabinet Manual, 100–1
  Codes, 100, 101–2
  Ministerial Code, 96
Parliament Act, 133
political accountability, 121
political theory, 93
precedents, 122
Prime Minister, 138–9
  as member of the House, 124–8
raising of revenue, 130–2, 139
regulating conduct, 94
role, 121
royal prerogative, 112–13, 121
Salisbury Convention, 56, 122
Sewel Convention, 122
taxation, 131, 133
transformation, 135–8

types, 94–5, 97, 118–19, 121
uncertainty, 100–5
West Lothian question, 123–4
constitutional models:
  common law constitutionalism, 155
  constitutional change processes, 153–63
  parliamentary sovereignty, 153–63
constitutional priorities:
  Cook-Maclennan agreement, 46
constitutional reform, 17–18
  coherency, 35–6
  Conservative-Liberal Democrat coalition, 18
    fixed term parliaments, 18–19
    House of Lords Reform, 18
    voting system for Westminster, 18
  Dickens, Charles, 55
  devolution, 2, 14–15
    Additional Member System, 24
    historical context, 22–9
    Northern Ireland, 27
    Scotland, 22–7
    Scottish National Party, 24
    Sewel Convention, 26–7, 122
    subsidiarity, 24
  executive policy, 161
  House of Commons reform, 35–7
  House of Lords reform, 27–9, 52
    Supreme Court, 3, 33, 160
  Labour Governments (1997–2010), 18,
    47–51
    devolution, 19
    Freedom of Information Act, 49
    House of Lords reform, 27–9
    Human Rights Act, 19
    reform programme, 47
    role of Lord Chancellor, 19
    Supreme Court, 19
  'new British constitution', 32
    distribution of power, 32
  prime ministerial power, 36–7
    Blair, Tony, 36
    Brown, Gordon, 36–7
    Cameron, David, 37
    Clegg, Nick, 37
    'constitutional premiership', 36
    personal system of government, 36
  rights:
    Human Rights Act, 29–32
    European Convention on Human Rights,
      30–1, 49
    Thatcher administration, 45–6
    West Lothian question, 19, 19n11, 123–4
Constitutional Reform Act 2005, 3, 8, 66
  Lord Chancellor, 59
  separation of powers, 4
Constitutional Reform and Governance Act
    2010, 80, 84
Constitutional Reform Centre, 46

Constitutionalism:
   common law, 105, 155–60
constitutions:
   Commonwealth, 40
   definition, 7
      Lijphart, Arend, 7
      Marshall, Geoffrey, 7–8
   self-governing dominions, 40
   see also American constitution; British
      constitution; constitutional conventions;
      constitutional reform; France
Cook, Robin, 25, 29
   devolution, 45
   House of Commons reform, 34
courts, 1–2
   legislative activism, 62–3
   policy preferences, 87–8
   political influence, 88–9
   political parties, role of, 85–7
Cowling, Maurice, 20–1, 29
Crick, Bernard, 43, 69–70, 90–1
Crossman, Richard, 43, 114, 116

de Tocqueville, Alexis, 2
declarations of incompatibility:
   Belmarsh case, 64
   case law, **64–5**
   Human Rights Act, 64
development of the Constitution, 1
devolution, 2, 14–15
   Additional Member System, 24
   constitutional reform:
      historical context, 22–9
   media interest, 43
   nationalism, 33
   Northern Ireland, 27, 53
   public interest, 43
   Scotland, 22–7, 53
      funding of public services, 33
   Scottish National Party, 24
   Sewel Convention, 26–7
   subsidiarity, 24
   Wales, 53
   West Lothian question, 19, 19n11, 123–4
Dewar, Donald, 25
Dicey, AV, 3, 36, 133
   constitutional conventions, 93–4, 124
   judicial legislation, 187
   parliamentary sovereignty, 10, 30, 112–14,
      153–4, 155, 158
   traditional constitution, 56
Dickens, Charles:
   constitutional reform, 55

educational reform, 14
elected mayors, 53
elective dictatorship, 45, 57, 161
Electoral Commission, 49

electoral reform:
   Additional Members Systems, 3, 11
   Alternative Vote system, 35, 37, 52
   Belfast Assembly, 3, 11
   European elections, 3, 11
   List Proportional Representation, 3
   London Assembly, 3, 11
   Northern Ireland, 11
   Scottish elections, 3, 11
   Single Transferable Vote, 3, 11
   Supplementary Vote in London, 3
   Welsh Assembly, 11
   see also electoral systems
electoral systems:
   first-past-the-post, 11, 16
   proportional representation, 3, 11, 23–8,
      42
English question, *see* West Lothian question
Equality Act 2010:
   royal succession, 172–3
European Convention on Human Rights, 40
   incorporation into UK law, 45, 49, 66
   votes for prisoners, 66
European elections, 3, 11
European Union, 39
   integration, 53
executive:
   bad politics, 71, 77, 82, 84, 89, 91
   balance with legislative, 39
   codes of conduct:
      Cabinet Manual, 79–81
      Ministerial Code, 78–9
   collective government responsibility, 108
   restrictions on politicking, 78
   separation of powers, 8–9

Factortame, 4
fixed-term parliaments, 53
Fixed-term Parliaments Act 2011, 106, 109
France:
   constitutional politics, 186–8
   see also French Constitutional Council
Freedom of Information Act, 49, 53, 137
French Constitutional Council, 2, 179, 191
   constitutional politics, 186–8
   judicial style, 180–8
      hyperformalism, 181
      justifications, 184
   justifications:
      deference argument, 185
      'if it ain't broke, why fix it' argument, 184–5
      rationality argument, 184
   policy arguments, 188–91
   role, 180

globalisation, 8
Goldsworthy, Jeffrey, 153–4, 158
Government of Wales Act 1998, 8, 100

Great Reform Acts, 8
  Great Reform Act 1832, 20
Griffith, John, 45, 69–71, 78, 82–4, 90–2

Hague, William, 28
  criticism of constitutional reform, 55
Hannan, Daniel, 55
Hart, Herbert Lionel Adolphus, 96, 154
hereditary peers, 48
  accountability, 19
Hill, Christopher, 34–5
Hogg, Quintin (Lord Hailsham), 59–60
  elective dictatorship, 45, 57, 161
holders of public office:
  Committee on Standards in Public Life, 73–4
Holme, Richard, 46
Holmes, Oliver Wendell, 182, 187
House of Commons reform, 35–7
  committee system, 35
    weakness, 35
  lack of, 34–5
House of Lords reform, 52
  admission of women as members, 41
  creation of life peerages, 41, 53
  Judicial Appointments Commission, 50
  Supreme Court, 3, 9, 30, 33, 160
Hughes, Simon, 29
human rights:
  freedom of expression, 66
  right to respect to private life, 66
  royal succession, 172–3
  votes for prisoners, 66
  see also European Convention for Human
    Rights; Human Rights Act 1995
Human Rights Act 1998, 2–3, 4, 8, 53, 67
  constitution, as a, 61–66, 67
    courts, 62–3
    legislative activism, 62–3
  declarations of incompatibility, 63–6
    Anti-terrorism, Crime and Security Act, 64
    terrorism, 64
  interpretation, 63
  freedom of speech, 32
  independent judiciary, 31–2
  purposive interpretation, 63
  right to jury trial, 32
  royal succession, 172–3
  terrorism, 31
hung parliaments, 10, 16

independence, 44
  Scottish referendum, 44
    constitutional change, 150–1
    direct democracy, 150
    Edinburgh Agreement, 150–1
    federalism, 151–2
    generally, 141–3
    historical context, 143–6

Independent Parliamentary Standards Authority,
  83
Irvine, Derry, 22, 25, 49

Jenkins, Roy, 22
Jenkins Report, 11, 48
Jennings, Ivor, 126, 170
  constitutional conventions, 97–8, 99–100
    three-part inquiry, 122–3
  courts, 56, 67
  parliamentary sovereignty, 10
Johnson, Boris, 35
judicial activism, 9, 39
Judicial Appointments Commission, 50
judicial review:
  absence, 56
  increasing, 33
judiciary, 8
  activism of judges, 9, 39
  declarations of incompatibility, 64
  assertiveness, 31, 33, 67
  declarations of incompatibility, 64
  influence, 9, 67
  political role, 67
  role of Lord Chancellor, 9
  semi-federal system, 60–1
  separation of powers, 9, 30
  Supreme Court (establishment), 9, 30, 160

Kaiser, Wolfram, 40
  decline of radicalism, 40
Kavanagh, Dennis, 41–2
Kennedy, Charles, 28
Kennedy, Duncan, 188
Kennedy, Helena, 51
Keynes, John Maynard, 35, 131
Kinnock, Neil, 42, 45

Labour Party:
  hostility to reform, 46
  incorporation of ECHR into UK law, 47
  see also New Labour
legislative:
  activism, 62–3
  balance with executive, 39
  ministerial responsibility, 110–12
  non-partisan requirements:
    backbenchers, 82–4
    Select Committees, 81–2
  separation of powers, 8–9
Legislative and Regulatory Reform Act 2006,
  4
Liberal Party:
  devolution, 46
  incorporation of the ECHR, 46
  proportional representation, 46
life peers, 41, 53
  cash-for-honours, 19

Lijphart, Arend:
    majoritarianism, 7, 57
    traditional constitution, 56
Livingstone, Ken, 35
local government:
    central government (relations between),
        39
'logic of appropriateness':
    constitutional conventions, 57
London Assembly:
    electoral system, 3
Lord Chancellor, 3
    Constitutional Reform Act, 59

Macaulay, Thomas Babington, 20
McGuinness, Martin, 27
McHarg, Aileen, 103
McIlwain, Charles Howard, 104
Magna Carta, 8
Major, John, 42
    Open Government initiative, 49
majoritarian constitution, 7, 57, 90
Mandelson, Peter, 21
March, James, 57
Marshall, Geoffrey, 7–8, 98, 103–4, 107,
    129
Marxist theories, 20
media influence, 14
Ministerial Code, 73
ministerial responsibility, 110
monarchy, 2
    'defender of faith', 171
    discretion, 165
    evolution, 165–77
    impartiality, 165
    prerogative of dissolution, 168, 171
    prime ministerial appointment, 169–71
    public support for, 165–7
    regulation of royal marriages, 175–7
    role, 2
    royal conduct, 167
    royal succession, 172–5
        anti-Catholic provisions, 172
        primogeniture, 172
    stability, 177
Monetary Policy Committee, 75
Montesquieu, 3–4, 8, 58–60
Morton, Peter:
    constitutional norms, 95–99, 103–4
    'footpath conventions', 100, 102, 107
    institutions, 109

nationalism, 40
    Scottish nationalism, 14–15, 33
    Welsh nationalism, 14–15
New Labour:
    constitutional reform, 43
    see also Blair government

Northern Ireland:
    devolution, 27
    electoral systems, 11
    importance of constitutional issues, 41
Northern Ireland Act 1998, 100
Norton, Philip, 19, 52

Office for Budget Responsibility, 76
Office for National Statistics, 75–6
Official Secrets Act 1911, 49
Olsen, Johan P, 57
Open Government, 49

Parliament Act 1911, 136
parliamentary reform, *see* constitutional reform:
        House of Commons reform; House of
        Lords reform
parliamentary sovereignty, 2, 4, 10, 16, 57,
        153–63
    common law constitutionalism distinguished,
        154, 157
    constitutional change, 153–63
        executive policy, 161
    courts, 156–7
    Dicey, AV, 10, 30, 112–14, 153–4, 155, 158
    doctrine, 2, 3, 4, 160
    domestic legislation, 4
    Goldworthy, Jeffrey, 153–4
planning policy, 87–8
Plant, Raymond, 42
political parties, 10, 90
    bad politics, 71, 77, 82, 84, 89, 91
    courts (influence on), 85–7
    donations to, 51
    POWER Report, 51
    voters, 88–9
Political Parties, Elections and Referendums Act
        2000, 3, 142
politicians:
    bad politics, 71, 77, 82, 84, 89, 91
    conflict resolution, 70–1
    executive:
        Cabinet Manual, 79–81
        Ministerial Code, 78–9
    parliamentarians:
        backbenchers, 82–4
        Select Committees, 81–2
    regulation of activities
        arms-length bodies, 72–7
        self-regulation, 77–8
    see also executive; legislative
POWER Inquiry, 51
    citizen participation, 51
    donations to political parties, 51
    local councils, 51
    parliament, 51
    party whips, 51
    voting age, 51

Prevention of Terrorism Act 2005:
  declarations of incompatibility, 64
prime ministerial power, 36–7
  Blair, Tony, 36
  Brown, Gordon, 36–7
  Cameron, David, 37
  Clegg, Nick, 37
  'constitutional premiership', 36
  personal system of government, 36
privatisation, 71–2
proportional representation, 3, 11, 23–8, 42
public service reform, 50

QUANGOs, 2
  see also arms-length bodies

referendums:
  benefits, 150–1
  Scottish independence, 44
    constitutional change, 150–1
    direct democracy, 150
    Edinburgh Agreement, 150–1
    federalism, 151–2
    generally, 141–3
    historical context, 143–6
Reform Act 1867, 20–1
regulation of utilities, 71
relationship between the state and the individual, 21
Rentoul, John, 3, 29n65
responsibility:
  collective, 10, 16
  individual, 9–10, 15–16
Rhodes, Rod, 37
Robinson, Peter, 27
Royal Commission on the Constitution, 44
Royal Marriages Act 1772, 175–7

Salmond, Alex, 25, 33, 174
Scotland, 37
  devolution, 22–7, 42, 53
    funding of public services, 33
    historical context, 22–9
    media interest, 43
    nationalism, 33
    public interest, 43
    Scottish National Party, 24
    Sewel Convention, 26–7
  elections, 3
  electoral systems, 11
  extension of powers, 147–8
  federalism, 151–2
  fiscal powers, 148
  home rule, 44
  importance of constitutional issues, 41
  independence, 44
  independence referendum, 44
    constitutional change, 150–1

direct democracy, 150
Edinburgh Agreement, 150–1
federalism, 151–2
generally, 141–3
historical context, 143–6
West Lothian question, 19, 19n11, 44–5, 123–4, 152
see also devolution, independence, referendums
Scotland Act 1998, 8, 100, 142
Scotland Act 2012, 142, 148
Scottish Parliament:
  legislative competence, 123
Select Committees:
  Crossman, Richard, 43
  reform, 43
separation of powers, 3, 8
  Lord Chancellor, 3–4
social control, 20
Social Democratic Party (SDP):
  creation, 46
society:
  indicators of change, **13–14**, 15–16
sovereign Parliament, *see* parliamentary sovereignty
standards:
  Committee on Standards in Public Life, 73–4
  Independent Parliamentary Standards Authority, 83
state:
  relationship to individual, 21
Straw, Jack, 47
Supreme Court, 3, 9, 30, 33, 160
Supreme Court Act 1981, 138

taxation, 131, 133
terrorism:
  human rights, 31
Thatcher Government:
  constitutional reform, 45
Thompson, Edward Palmer, 20
Tomkins, Adam, 98
Treaty of Rome, 8, 10, 15
tribunals, 2, 76–7
Trimble, David, 27
Turpin, Colin, 98

UK Statistics Authority, 75–6
United States:
  election procedures, 113
  formalism, 182
  freedom of information legislation, 49
  law v reality, 113–14
  theory of adjudication, 188–9

Wahrman, Dror, 20
Wales:
  electoral systems, 11

Wales (*cont*):
    executive devolution, 48–9
    Government of Wales Act, 8, 100
    home rule, 44
    importance of constitutional issues, 41
    independence, 44
Warren, Earl, 59
West Lothian question, 19, 19n11, 44–5, 123–4, 152
Westminster Model, 7

traditional constitution, 56
Wheare, Kenneth, 98, 99–102
Women:
    admission as members of House of Lords, 41
    suffrage, 3
Wright, Tony, 46, 82

Youth, Justice and Criminal Evidence Act 1999, 63

Lightning Source UK Ltd.
Milton Keynes UK
UKOW04f0942100716

278013UK00005B/94/P